Musings *of an*

Improbable

Existence

ROGER L. DIXON

NEWMAN SPRINGS PUBLISHING
320 Broad Street
Red Bank, NJ 07701

First originally published by Newman Springs Publishing 2021

ISBN 978-1-63881-540-2 (Hardcover)
ISBN 978-1-63881-541-9 (Digital)

Printed in the United States of America

For my exceptional daughter, Kelly

Orientation

I began writing this book to document my rather unusual life for my daughter, Kelly. It begins with the curious details of my accidental existence beginning with a secret, illegitimate birth in Pecos, New Mexico, and subsequently following a most unlikely path eventually culminating in a Distinguished Scientist position at Fermi National Accelerator Laboratory (Fermilab) in Batavia, Illinois. The route followed was most improbable. However, the entire universe also seems improbable. If one looks at the sky on a dark night, it is easy to be overwhelmed by the magnitude of the improbability.

As I wrote, I felt compelled to add another aspect to the book. I decided to introduce each chapter with a paragraph containing snippets of science. Through no conscious intent, these chapter introductions eventually turned into a somewhat scientific and occasionally humorous quest to explore the rather mysterious and profound nature of existence, paying special attention to its most perplexing attribute: time and its passage. Whoa! I realize this sounds like it could be a tortuous ordeal just waiting to ensnare you. It is not. The book is nothing more than the simple-yet-unusual story of my life told alongside some short and sometimes-humorous notions related to science.

The book can easily be appreciated by those who do not want to be bothered by scientific detail but enjoy laughing at the amusing details of life, the universe, and existence. Nature's most profound and obscure concept, *Nothing*, is explored in exhaustive detail in these pages. In addition, the book tells the simple story of science and a user-friendly scientist. It also attempts to cross the boundary between hard science and speculation to explore the nether regions of existence while extending our understanding into the twilight regions of our being. Whoa! Really? Well, maybe…

For those who want to embark on such a journey but are afraid to cross the boundary into the darkness, try drinking half a glass of good scotch whiskey before you begin reading. And please be reassured that I have chosen to go only so far as the light of reason provides some illumination even though I am not afraid of the dark—or so I say. However, as I write these words, I am not certain where this journey will take us. Should the book end abruptly, make certain the door is open and then run like hell!

CHAPTER 1

A Big Bang and a Small, Mysterious Whimper

NOTHING... POSSIBILITY; CREATION; SOMETHING! SPACE; TIME; MATTER; UNIVERSE; ACTION: EXPANSION; LIGHT; SOUND; EXISTENCE! STARS, PLANETS; CHEMISTRY; BIOLOGY; EVOLUTION; CURIOSITY: HOW? WHY? CAUSE? WHAT IS NOTHING?

*****

M y own life also began with a bang. It was not as large as the "Big One". Nevertheless, it seems more complicated and difficult to reconstruct. In fact, I am still attempting to understand it by putting facts and various accounts together in random ways to see if any of them make sense. If I eventually conclude that none make sense, I will probably disappear in a puff of blue smoke—well, maybe not. I like drama.

I was born in Pecos, New Mexico, downstream of the headwaters of the Pecos River near the south end of the Truchas Wilderness area in northern New Mexico. It was a very special place in the culture of the Southwest long before I became an insignificant part of its history. In fact, Pecos was inhabited long before my European ancestors discovered the continent where I was born. The Pecos area is known to have been occupied by native people from around 800 AD, and the Pecos Pueblo dates to around 1450 AD. Coronado visited the Pueblo in 1541. At one time, it was the largest Pueblo in the Southwest. Legend has it that Montezuma was born at Pecos. However, the beautiful native people are very adept at creating legends for the invasive species to chase about. According to the Montezuma legend, he migrated south where he became the leader of the Aztecs and established a civilization at the current location of Mexico City. Similar legends are common among many of the Pueblo People of New Mexico. Perhaps they were all born to confuse and deceive the intruders from Europe. Or maybe it was just poor record-keeping. After all, they had no pencils, no paper, no television, and no laptops. They must have been doing something right to find themselves in this bemused state of being.

The Pecos Pueblo was abandoned in 1838, but the legends persist to the present. My version of one legend relates that in order to keep the Pueblo alive, the Pueblo dwellers were told by the spirits that they had to keep a fire burning in a cave that contained a serpent. They were also instructed to keep the serpent alive. Eventually, some inattentive Pueblo maidens tending the fire let it go out. After this event, the last of the Pecos people moved out of the Pueblo and into the Jemez Pueblo, where most of them had already gone. This event prepared the way for my entrance many years later…or maybe not.

I was born in the Reuter Hotel in Pecos. This probably had little to do with the beautiful people who once inhabited the Pueblo and much to do with the location of my great-grandfather's homestead and an uncle's ranch. My uncle's ranch was located up Dalton Canyon not far from Pecos, while Great-grandfather's homestead was on the other side of Boreas Peak from Pecos. The homestead was central to Mother's family.

I don't know much about the Reuter Hotel. I can't even say for certain where it was located even though it was pointed out to me more than once. I can't seem to remember any clear details of this most important place in my life. I do know from the legends of my birth that the Reuter Hotel consisted of a couple of small cabins that Mrs. Reuter rented out to temporary visitors. Okay, you caught me exaggerating. There are no legends concerning my birth in Pecos even though it was a secret affair as I will explain.

It is not a surprise that I don't remember anything about that very eventful day in my life, but it is a disappointment. Or does it hurt to be born? Maybe I am fine with not remembering this event. Nevertheless, I have put together the story of my first birthday that is at least consistent with some facts well-known in the family even though this narrative has some important details missing. The story relies on several sources including Mother, Grandmother, my birth certificate, some New York City tabloid articles, and a *Millie the Model* comic book, in addition to the highly reliable family lore. Well, maybe the last item is just plain family exaggerations.

I am told that my birth event occurred on August 14, 1947. I have no reason to doubt this fact even though life began for me somewhat earlier in a more mysterious event. It is not mysterious because no one bothered to tell me the facts of life. Rather, it is mysterious because the biological rules and regulations that apply to assembling a regulation human being are rather strict. The initial creation is much like the Big Bang, at least in name if not in magnitude. It can be mysterious, and it can happen for no good reason. However, there are certain physical laws that must be obeyed. For example, there are rough minimum and maximum lengths of time required to successfully assemble a brand-spanking-new human being able to survive in the world with assistance from a mother, a father, some doctors, nurses, and most important, lawyers. These requirements are much more stringent than those for horses, cows, and pigs.

On two occasions, Mother attempted to explain to me how my own birth satisfied these important requirements, thinking this would provide me with enough information to enable my certification as a genuine human being. She failed each time. Nevertheless, I appear to be human, admittedly with some deficiencies that I will probably admit to later if I can't get out of it.

So what are the facts of my birth that I shall hereby submit to support my admittedly weak case for legitimacy in the human race? They come from the aforementioned sources. Mother never attempted to accommodate the facts contained in the comic book or the tabloid articles because she didn't know I had them. These items were given to me by my grandmother when I was in college. She did not tell me where she got them, but family lore has it that a mysterious stranger appeared in some cloudy past and gave the tabloids to her along with the *Millie the Model* comic book. A more mundane version indicates that she got them from Mother. I am voting for the more intriguing version involving a mysterious stranger. Nevertheless, I should begin at the beginning and tell the story as I now understand it.

Mother was born Millicent Laura Shearer in Las Vegas, New Mexico. She was the sixth of eight children that my grandparents had. They were each on their second marriage. Mother was Grandmother's fifth and Grandfather's second child. She was the oldest of three that they had together. Las Vegas was near a ranch that Mother's grandfather had homesteaded. Her parents were salt of the earth, and she was a true-blue county girl.

Mother's version of my story was simple. I first heard it when I was eight or nine years old after it came to my attention that the name on my birth certificate was not the name that I was attending school under. Mother explained to me that Dad was not my real dad. I did not know what this meant since I had not yet experienced the pleasure of becoming a "dad" myself although I had dealt with some naughty urges that I did not understand. Mother told me that my father was Morton Alpren, that she had been married to him, and that they had lived in New York City. This revelation was incredibly exciting to me. I was someone special because I had a secret. Of course, I could not keep the secret. I probably told my friends at school about it right away with enhancements even though I was not certain what these newly acquired facts really meant.

I do not remember which details I was given during this first discussion with Mom. Nevertheless, I did learn additional details over time. According to Mom, she and Morton lived in New York City, where he was attending Columbia University. The tabloids indicate that he was working for his father in the textile industry.

Maybe both accounts are correct. What I mostly heard in that first conversation with Mom was that she had attended many baseball games at Yankee Stadium and had become a serious baseball fan. I was apparently paying less attention when I was told that she and Morton had divorced. I probably did not understand such things. Also I did not wonder why my New York father never came to see me, and I don't remember learning anything about how they met and married; but she may have supplied some of these details. I was curious, but I don't remember whether I asked any questions during the question-and-answer session at the end of her talk or if there even was a question-and-answer session. In any case, I was too young to formulate a good question.

Our discussion was brief and in private. Nevertheless, I am certain I shared Mom's revelation with my younger brother and perhaps others since it made me feel different and special. The story kept me happy for a while. It was not long before I was embellishing the story in my head, and I may have been telling an enhanced version to others. I did not keep a secret very well. Rest assured, I am not, and will not be, enhancing the story in these pages. Trust me. I am a respected scientist who only deals in well-established facts.

As I indicated, the most interesting part of Mother's New York story for me was the baseball. She had apparently become a Yankee fan in New York and had learned much about the game. It was not long before she had me following World Series games through the box scores that she would keep for the games while I was at school. Baseball was more interesting than the father business. I soon understood the significance of Micky Mantle hitting home runs. Meanwhile, I put the father business aside because I didn't understand what it meant. Besides, it was not as interesting as Micky Mantle and his teammates. Well, one of them had the nickname *Moose*. How could I ignore that?

Over the years, I have been able to add details to my origin's tale much as scientists have gathered information about the beginning of the universe. Similarly, I have attempted to make a consistent story of my creation. Instead of cosmic microwave background detectors and other scientific instruments, my instruments have been my ears and eyes. My sources of information include my grandparents, other members of my family, and plain, old family lore. In addition, I used the newspaper stories and my birth certificate to complete the picture. I have not figured out what the *Millie the Model* comic book means. It is still a puzzle.

As indicated, I received the newspaper articles and the comic book from my grandmother. I seem to remember that I was in college at the time. The newspapers appear to be what are called tabloids these days. Grandmother never told me where she got these items, and she did not offer any explanation when she gave them to me. She simply said, "You should have these." I don't really know when Grandmother received the newspapers. I do know that Mother never knew that I had them.

When I attempted to put all the information together to make a consistent story of my origins, I succeeded at a superficial level, but I failed to uncover a most important detail of my creation, namely who the missing perpetrator of my existence was. My first attempt at this came when I was in college. Here are the details I have:

The year was 1943. Mother had discovered in high school that she had a talent for singing. After she graduated, she began singing at a USO club at Camp Luna, a military base that was located near her hometown, Las Vegas, New Mexico. World War II was progressing well for the Allies. Nevertheless, new recruits for the Army Air Corps were still being trained at Camp Luna. Mother's talent must have been considerable. I would not learn of it until I was a teenager and she sang at a cousin's wedding. What a surprise! She blew me away.

There is a story in the family lore about one event, a talent contest that occurred on New Year's eve 1943 at the movie theatre in Las Vegas. The show was for the Camp Luna troops, and they voted to determine the winner of the contest. Mother won hands down and was given the title "Sweetheart of Camp Luna." According to the lore, it was this event that attracted the attention of one Army Air Corp soldier by the name of Morton Alpren. It was not long before they were involved in a serious relationship.

It is not clear from the stories whether my grandparents were happy with the relationship. Nevertheless, Morton and Mother quickly began planning a wedding. Morton was from a wealthy family in New York. Sometime after marriage entered the picture, Morton's father came to New Mexico from New York to meet Mother and her family. Wedding plans were discussed.

The visit went well at first. However, something did not feel right to Grandfather. It may have been the rapid progression of the wedding plans or a dislike of the people involved. He became angry during the discussion, and he tossed Morton and his father out of the house. This tactic provided but a temporary solution to his problem. Nevertheless, only the strong force that holds the quarks together to make a proton is more powerful than the physical attraction between a young male and female smitten by the urge to become one—or maybe one and half. Like the quarks in a proton, the farther apart the interacting entities become, the stronger the attractive force. Mother and Morton were inexorably drawn to Blythe, Arkansas, where they were married. The war was winding down at the time, and it was over before Morton could be given the opportunity to go overseas to subdue unfriendly people.

With the arrival of the end of the war, the newlyweds were reunited in Morton's home in New York City, where he worked in his father's business and probably attended Columbia University. His father was a very successful businessman in New York who had immigrated from Poland. He made his money in the textile industry. Morton's mother was from Austria.

Even though his family was wealthy, Morton insisted that he and Mom live in a modest apartment in a modest manner according to the tabloids. This arrangement apparently did not satisfy Mother. It was a rather plain existence, and she knew that they could be living much more extravagantly. She was disappointed and bored. The tabloids indicate that they lived in the Adler Hotel. Was this modest? I don't know.

It was Mother's boredom that led her to baseball and the New York Yankees. She may have gotten acquainted with some of the players. Well, this is the little boy in me speculating. Mother told me some of these facts when she was teaching me about baseball. She was creating a Yankee fan, something many people would find distasteful. To tell the truth, I only learned about the Yankees and the Dodgers. The other teams were all in the minor leagues, or so I thought. When I taught the other kids at school what I knew about baseball, they went off into the world believing me because I have always been way too credible for the public good.

The marriage was not working. It soon ended in divorce. I never knew Morton because Mother was back in New Mexico before I was born. Why didn't he come to see me? This was not a question I ever asked myself. Apparently, no one in Mother's family in New Mexico knew the details of the breakup.

After the birth certificate discussion that I had with Mom when I was very young, I did not have another discussion with her on the subject until right before she passed away. At the time of the original discussion, I had learned that Orval Dixon, the man I called *Dad*, was not really my dad. Practically, this meant nothing to me. However, it gave me my secret. I continued to call Orval *Dad*. Nothing changed until much later when he and Mom separated and divorced. Of course, I eventually became aware of what it took to construct a regulation human being, and a "dad" was part of the recipe.

I don't remember talking with Mom again about Morton Alpren until the discussion shortly before her death. She attempted to level with me. We had the discussion sitting on her kitchen floor, backs up against the refrigerator. She told me her version of how I had become. She was crying very hard as she seemed to be trying her best to tell me the truth. She couldn't. She told me that she had gotten pregnant, and when she informed Morton of this fact, he had insisted that she get an abortion. She had refused, and this was the reason I existed.

Even in this heartfelt moment, I knew that she was not telling me the real story because I had long since received the tabloids from Grandmother. I still did not tell her that I had them. I concluded that the tears were because she could not tell me the truth even then. Nevertheless, I hoped she felt like she had cleared things up with me. I don't know if this helped. Maybe she didn't know the truth anymore.

After our conversation, I understood that it was left to me to determine how I had come about. In principle, the problem should be simple. All I have to do is figure out the identity of one of the two technical people who collaborated to create a human embryo that became me. I am clearly human… Or so I think.

I was somewhat unfair to Mother during our last conversation because I didn't tell her about the additional information I had that came from the items Grandmother had given to me. These items made Mother's abortion story unlikely.

The first of the mysterious items is a *Millie the Model* comic book. It sheds little light on the mystery. The remaining items are three New York newspapers, or tabloids, that contain articles with spicy details of Mother's divorce from Morton. It should not be a surprise to anyone that comic books and tabloids are not the most reliable sources of information. As it turns out, they are the only clues I have for understanding my origins. Even so, they don't provide answers to my most pertinent questions: namely, the identity of the missing perpetrator of my existence. Nevertheless, the information content in these items is not zero. I still do not know who I am, but I know who I am not. For example, I might not believe the rather spicy details of my mother's sex life detailed in the tabloids, but I think I can believe dates, names, photos, and perhaps shoe sizes. I filtered much of the rest of the information contained in the articles for my own sanity.

Allow me to begin with the cover of the comic book since the clue it holds is not obvious to me. It shows Millie and a man sitting on a sofa. Millie is on the phone, saying, "Sorry, Joe, I can't go out with you tonight! Doctor's orders!" The man on the sofa is giving an okay sign with his thumb and forefinger as he listens, and there is a doctor's bag on the floor in front of the sofa. The doctor's bag is inscribed with "s. o. ROGER, M.D." The comic book also has a month, "AUG." followed by "NO. 13."

The first detail of note is that *Millie the Model* is not spelled the same as Milly, my mother. The second detail is that my name, Roger, is on the doctor's bag. I don't have any idea what these not-so-obvious clues might mean or if they are even clues. It seems unlikely that the comic book does not contain a clue because of the circumstances under which I received it. Nevertheless, I don't seem to have enough information to figure out what the clues might be. Am I missing something? The fact that the comic book contains the names *Millie* and *Roger* on the cover should mean something, shouldn't it?

Two of the tabloid articles are front-page stories from the *New York Daily News* detailing the proceedings of Mother's divorce from Morton. The other is from the *Daily Mirror* with many of the same details. The *Daily News* articles are dated August 21, 1946 and September 6, 1946. The *Daily Mirror* article is also dated August 21, 1946. The first *Daily News* story is dated exactly fifty-one weeks before I was born, or one week short of twelve months. The second details a follow-up visit to the court by Mother in which she asked for additional support from Morton.

One of the articles includes a photo of Mother in a cheese-cake pose. The articles made Mother out as "hot," describing her as a "blue-eyed bombshell" from "Heavenly Haven Ranch" in New Mexico. The other two articles have headshots of Mom. She looks alluring in all the photos. The words indicate that she couldn't get enough sex from Morton and she was getting too much from other sources. There was talk of shoes found under the bed and Morton not having enough stamina or energy to satisfy her. As amusing as these articles might be for some, they are difficult for me to read. However, it would have been more difficult not to read them. Okay, I had read them more than once. I was looking for clues after all.

Going through Mom's papers recently, I found many notes and letters written to her after the articles appeared in the papers from men who wanted to try to satisfy her. They are disgusting. I have no idea why she kept them. Maybe I have yet to find out.

So what do these articles tell me? Normal babies arrive about nine months after the concept is created. Admittedly, I found an article indicating that the world-record pregnancy is 375 day, or 15 to 25 days longer than Mom's pregnancy might have gone had she and Morton not been able to do without each other during the divorce proceedings. Given the state of Mom's marriage at the time of the tabloid articles, it is more likely that I would be the world-record holder by a long shot. Instead, I will conclude that Mom was not pregnant at the time of the divorce. The recipe for me was stirred together later.

There was no Heavenly Haven Ranch, but Great-grandfather had a ranch that he had homesteaded in the mountains west of Las Vegas. My grandparents lived there part of the time. It was called The Old Homestead Ranch. Perhaps, Camp Blue Haven, a religious camp near the Ranch, inspired the reference to Heavenly Haven Ranch. This is particularly amusing, given the nature of Camp Blue Haven. Even though it was near the family ranch, there was no relationship between Mother's family and Camp Blue Haven.

The accuracy of the sensational stories is, well, not quite spot on. Nevertheless, Mother somehow got herself into a situation that invited the stories. She was an incredible, intelligent woman who apparently could not handle the attention that her looks brought her. The stories don't surprise me. Nevertheless, she was always very special to me. She continued to live on the edge throughout her life, finally falling off the cliff after being escorted to the brink by her third and final husband along with his two children. I will put off telling this part of the story until much later.

Perhaps the most reliable and important source of information relating to my mystery is my birth certificate. It not only proves that I was born, but it also indicates that I was alive, at least for a little while. Even this document contains a bit of questionable information as I will explain.

The birth certificate indicates that I came to light in the Reuter Hotel located in Pecos, New Mexico, on the afternoon of August 14, 1947. I have read between the lines of this little yellow document to dig out part of the story of my beginnings. The Reuter Hotel consisted of one or two small cabins that Mrs. Reuter rented out to temporary visitors to Pecos.

Besides Mother and Grandmother, a doctor was present in the cabin. I was the last to arrive. The doctor's name was Dr. Leslie H. Fitzgerald. Not included on the birth certificate was a fact that I later learned from Grandmother. She told me that my birth was slightly complicated because I was born with the umbilical cord wrapped around my neck. It was easily removed since it didn't have a complicated knot, such as a hangman's noose, tied in it. Nevertheless, I was a little blue at first, but all went reasonably well without further complication.

The birth certificate indicates that I was born alive at 1:42 p.m. I know this is probably true because I have a birthday every year on August 14. However, I don't get a tingle at 1:42 p.m. even though I tingle much of the time. It was a Thursday. It was the first of two Thursdays where my life took an important turn. This one was early afternoon. The second one, some fourteen years later, would be in the late afternoon. I remember this second one well. It was not a pleasant experience, but like many unpleasantries, it had a very positive outcome for me. To maintain chronological consistency, I will put off telling that story. I will come to it in due course unless I can figure out a way to get out of it. But let me get back to the messy process of being born and a few other details of my early life.

I would venture to bet that I was the only member of the human race born in the Reuter Hotel/cabins, but I could be wrong. For all I know, it could have been a baby factory masquerading as a "hotel" in the little town of Pecos. A better guess would be that the only other creatures born on the premises of the "hotel" were a large number of rodents and insects who found their existence in the nooks and crannies of the cabin.

My father's name is given on the birth certificate as Morton Sanford Alpren of the Bronx, New York. His occupation is listed as a textile manufacturer. I was only told by Mother that he was a student at Columbia University. It was his father who was the textile manufacturer. Like I know, but it was my birth after all. I get to question questionable facts, especially since my entire birth is questionable. Yet here I am, typing away.

Mother's name is shown in two ways on the certificate. The first is Millicent Laura Shearer. In another location on the birth certificate, her name is given as Mrs. Millicent Alpren. Her occupation is given as "housewife." My father's name is given as Morton Alpren, and my name is given as Roger Lee Alpren.

Grandmother's name is not given on the birth certificate even though she was probably the most important person present for my birth. She had seven children of her own, including Mother. Several of them were born at home without a doctor present. She could have explained the proper technique for delivering a baby to Dr. Fitzgerald.

Unfortunately, the tabloids that so eagerly reported Mom's adventures before my birth did not follow up on the outcome. No reporters came to Pecos to cover my birth.

In spite of the curiosity that was planted and grew in me after Mother's initial revelations, I never confronted her with the information in the tabloids that Grandmother gave to me. I wanted her to find peace for herself. She never did. Maybe I did not know what would be best for her.

All these questions have been a fascination for my entire family for years. "My entire family" includes my seven uncles and aunts and innumerable cousins. Well, I like to imagine that I am the big story, but early on, I learned that breaking bones was the best way to become "the big story." Otherwise, I was just another one of the snot-nosed country kids in the family. Nevertheless, there were speculations. Mine are the most informed, or so I say.

I figure that one of two things happened during the marriage. The first possibility is that Mom got pregnant and Morton insisted that she get an abortion, possibly because he was aware of her infidelity. In this scenario, Mother got the abortion and felt very guilty about it. After the marriage was said and done, she managed to get pregnant again by some means in order to replace the baby that had been aborted. Apparently, this would have been easy for her. She had plenty of volunteers among her male friends after all.

However, there is a second possibility in which Mom didn't get pregnant during the marriage and no abortion was necessary. Nevertheless, she continued to entertain men during her last few months in New York after the divorce case was settled. She may have wanted something to take home to go with her story. Or maybe she was just doing what she did best with no strategy. I am a "something," but I do not quite fit the story she told. Because the story did not hang together, speculations began. I am the only important speculator because I say so. No one knows the outcome of Mother's adventures in New York better than me.

Because I had other information, even if it was from some sleazy tabloids, I attempted to come up with alternate story that fit the facts I had. (Well, the tabloids claimed to be newspapers, but the stories about Mother look like tabloid articles to me.)

The first important fact to consider is the date of the stories in the papers, which was approximately one year before I was born. Newspapers don't fib about the dates they are put out, do they? The conclusion has to be that there is no reasonable scenario in which I am the son of one Morton Alpren. I don't have a clue who my biological father is or was or if I even had one—wait! Let's not go there. Furthermore, DNA evidence indicates that I am not related to the Alpren family, which had central European origins. I am mostly British Isles with no recent central European ancestors according to the evidence.

I probably don't have all the high-class genes of a possible aborted Roger, but I am good replacement for show if one doesn't look too closely. I did prove to be moderately trainable, if rather stubborn at times. Admittedly, my shirttail comes out of my blue jeans quite often.

Mother arrived back in New Mexico to stay in late December or early January of 1947. I don't know why she had stayed in New York so long after the divorce or if that is where she was. Anyway, whatever she did, I was an outcome. I have always rather liked being an outcome with a mysterious cause. It is not so bad. I know that half of my genes are really good ones, even if they have a somewhat subdued tendency (in me) toward the wild.

It was not long before I gained a father who helped raise me. His name was Orval Dixon. We did not have any biology in common, but I have never been a big fan of biology anyway. He was not into biology either. He was more of an auto mechanic and a small-time race-car driver who was frequently confused about whether he was driving on a race track or on a public street or highway. I loved the excitement that he brought to my life, not to mention a little brother who loved seeing and being in car crashes as much as I did. I should note here that true to form, Mom was probably pregnant with my brother when she and "Dad" got married. He was quite a bit older than her, and she had originally intended to marry his son—such complications! I also eventually got a little sister, certified legitimate. I owe much to the man that I called *Dad*.

I spent a lot of time during my early years staying with my grandparents while Mother attempted to get her adventurous life sorted out. The problem was that she was more of a shuffler than a sorter. There were some calm periods when the wild side was dormant, but the call of the wild was always just below the surface. Mom certainly gave me something to write about. She was very intelligent, and in spite of her untamed style, she was not a bad mother. I learned much from her, and she did well by all of her children even though there were many adventures along the way. I will deal with them in future chapters.

CHAPTER 2

My Salt-of-the-Earth Genes

DETAILS: IT WAS BRILLIANT! LOUD! SPACE; WAVES; LIGHT! TANGLES: MATTER! FORCES: ACTION! CHANGE: TIME; EXPANSION; POSSIBILITIES: UNIVERSE? WHERE? WHY? HOW? ... REALITY? INFINITY?

*****

As Mother attempted to get her life sorted out, I spent much of my first two years with my grandparents. They spent the warm months on the Old Homestead Ranch near Las Vegas, New Mexico. Winters were spent in the nearby town, Las Vegas, New Mexico. My great grandparents had homesteaded the Ranch in 1907. Both were still alive and living on the Ranch when I was very young. Surprisingly, I have good memories of them.

The Ranch was about eighteen miles west of Las Vegas, New Mexico. To get into town, one had to travel almost the entire eighteen miles on an unbelievably rough jeep road that connected to US Highway 85. The junction was a mile or so south of Las Vegas. Highway 85 followed the route of the Santa Fe Trail south from Vegas and then west to Pecos and onto Santa Fe, which is about nineteen miles west of Pecos. Pecos was the last stop on the Santa Fe Trail. It was my first stop. These days, I-25 has taken over the responsibility for following the Santa Fe Trail. The closest settlement to the Ranch is San Geronimo, and the nearest town is the original Las Vegas, which is also on I-25 some twenty miles from the Ranch.

My great-grandfather, Richard Arthur Shearer, was of Scottish descent with his ancestors arriving from Scotland in the 1830s or 40s. His father had made his way from Virginia to California during the gold rush. He was not looking for gold. He was a newspaperman, and he settled in San Francisco. According to family lore, he got into trouble for writing and printing one or more pro-Confederate editorials. As a result, his printing press found its way to the bottom of the bay with the help of some excitable Union soldiers.

Great-grandfather was born on August 28, 1862, in Monterey County, California. Abraham Lincoln was president at the time. For some reason, it fascinates me that I remember and loved Great-grandfather, a man who was a little bit alive when Lincoln was president as much as I was a little bit alive when Great-grandfather was alive. I probably should just feel old and not so fascinated.

Great-grandfather ran away from home when he was about twelve years old. He took his younger brother with him. They got a job in a sawmill, and very soon thereafter, his little brother got his arm cut off and bled to death. I was told that Great-grandfather never got over this event, but he seemed fine to me.

Great-grandmother, Mary Ollie Attwell Shearer, was born on July 4, 1868, in Franktown, Nevada. She was born into a Mormon family. She also ran away from home early in her life. I ran away a time or two in my life but never got very far. I was always back before a ghoul-infested darkness set in.

Great-grandmother's grandfather was Emanuel Penrod, one of the codiscoverers of the Comstock Lode in Nevada. He sold his interest in the mine before it was known what an incredible silver strike it was. He took the money from the sale and opened a general store. So it goes.

Great-grandfather was a merchant, and Great-grandmother was a midwife and a beautician. She and Great-grandfather lived in Elko, Nevada, when my grandfather, Charles Vivian Shearer, was born in

1889. He had one younger sister named Arolvi. She married but never had children.

When my great-grandparents arrived in Las Vegas, New Mexico, in about 1900, they opened a general store. In addition, Great-grandmother opened a beauty parlor next door to the store. She was also a midwife. My great grandparents lived and operated the store and beauty salon in town until about 1907 when they decided to close up shop and move a few miles to the Mineral Hill area, about fifteen miles outside of Las Vegas. Great-grandfather soon established a homestead a few miles west of Mineral Hill. The name he gave to the homestead was The Old Homestead Ranch, which I will simply call the Ranch.

It was not long before Great-grandfather entered the logging-and-lumber business while continuing to keep his mercantile business going. He established a rural store and post office on, or near, the homestead. In addition, he set up a small sawmill on his property. The sawmill still existed and was occasionally used when I was a small child. There was and still is a lot of timber on the mountains west of Las Vegas where the homestead was located in spite of several major forest fires in the area over the years.

My great-grandparents apparently did quite well after the move to the country. Great-grandfather built a rather large stone house that he still lived in when I was a small child. His most-prized possessions were a large library and an organ. I don't remember these items, but I heard much about them when I was older. In fact, I don't remember ever being in the stone house, but I surely was. I do remember that I learned very quickly that Great-grandfather always had a cookie for me. Whenever I saw him, I would run to him as fast as I could. He would pick me up, reach into his dirty jeans pocket, and pull out a cookie. When I was older, Mom told me that this really irked her. She did not want me eating dirt. She didn't seem to understand that dirt is good for kids. It makes them tough. Apparently, I should have eaten more dirty cookies.

Great-grandfather passed away on March 15, 1950, when I was about two and a half years old. Meanwhile, Great-grandmother died on January 1, 1952. I remember being at my aunt Audrey's in Las Vegas when my uncle Frank arrived to inform us of Great-grandmother's passing.

Great-grandfather's stone house burned when I was about two years old. Great-grandfather passed away soon thereafter. It was often said in the family that he died of a broken heart. Apparently, when he had attempted to save his books and his organ from the fire, the organ got stuck in the door, blocking the way out of the house. He ended up losing most everything of value in the house.

I have a memory of Grandfather holding me up to a window in one of the stone walls so that I could see the smoldering ruins inside. Those walls were still standing a few years ago when I visited the Ranch, which is no longer in the family. Over the years, the stone walls have been used to support the roofs of a number of storage buildings. When I was away in graduate school, the entire area burned in a huge forest fire. All was destroyed at the Ranch except for the stone walls of Great-grandfather's house. When I was invited to visit the Ranch a few years ago, I was very pleased to see those stone walls holding up the roof of another storage building in the middle of a healthy forest.

My grandmother, Mabel Waddell, was born near Cedar City, Nebraska, in 1891. Her father, Edward Albert Waddell, was born in Charleston, Illinois, on June 2, 1861. He was a farmer. Grandmother's mother was Alice Henrietta Applegarth, born April 13, 1870, in Atwater, Minnesota.

Great-grandmother left her husband, Edward, when she was pregnant with Grandmother. During this time, she ran around the West, hiding from Edward. I never knew either of Grandmother's parents even though Great-grandmother had come to New Mexico from Portland, Oregon, for my birth in May 1947. However, she gave up on me well before August, when I was born. She went back to Portland where she lived until her death. She never came back to see me.

I think there might have been a little fib someone told her concerning my expected arrival date. The real date did not meet the specifications for legitimacy required to accommodate the date of Mom's divorce. Mom may have hoped no one would notice. She must have known by this time that everyone was noticing her. Mom liked being the story, but the story she wanted for herself was mostly fantasy.

Grandmother grew up in Lincoln, Nebraska, where she graduated from high school and became a teacher. It was not long before she married a friend from Lincoln. His name was Laverne (Vern) Clifford Clements. He wanted to be a cowboy, and he thought that Nebraska was not a good place to realize his ambition. Consequently, he decided to move to New Mexico to live his dream. Family stories indicate New Mexico was more of a nightmare than a dream for him.

He and Grandmother settled near Avis, New Mexico. The cowboy business did not work out as planned. He had trouble earning a living. Furthermore, Grandmother was almost raped by several of the ranch hands where Vern was working. She proved to be too tough for them to succeed. Nevertheless, Vern had had enough. He and Grandmother moved back to Lincoln, where their oldest daughters Audrey and Opal were born.

After a while, Vern decided to try New Mexico a second time. He chose Taos as the location for his second attempt. He failed once more. Meanwhile, their third child, Edward, was born in Taos before they moved back to Nebraska. With two strikes against him, Vern finally succeeded on the third and final attempt when he and Grandmother settled near Las Vegas, New Mexico, where their youngest child, Betty, was born.

All the moving back and forth from Nebraska to New Mexico was very difficult for Grandmother as she and Vern were starting a family. Nevertheless, she did fairly well living in the Wild West with a husband who wasn't around much. She had been a schoolteacher in Nebraska and eventually became a schoolteacher in New Mexico. While she was married to Vern, much of the effort to provide for and take care of their four children fell to her.

When they lived near Taos, they had very little money. In order to feed her children, Grandmother had to rope range cattle and tie them off between two trees, front legs to one tree and back legs to the other tree, in order to milk them. She proved that not only was she a tough survivor but she was also an incredible mother. I will also note that early photographs of her indicate that she was also beautiful. She surely believed in cowboys to put up with all the hardship she endured. I know from experience that watching too much Roy Rogers and Gene Autry on television can do this to a person.

Grandmother's children born during the time she was married to Vern were Audrey, Opal, Edward, and Betty. Grandmother had decided early in life that she only wanted to have two children. I'm fairly certain she could count. She must have misplaced the plan or lost count during all the moving back and forth from Nebraska to New Mexico. By the time her fourth child, Betty, was born, she had become a committed New Mexican.

Since Grandmother had been a teacher in Nebraska before coming to New Mexico, she eventually got a teaching certificate in New Mexico by attending two summer sessions at New Mexico Normal University in Las Vegas. To be a certified teacher in New Mexico, she had to take a course in New Mexico history. New Mexico Normal University later became New Mexico Highlands University, my alma mater for my undergraduate studies.

Grandmother was teaching in the small community of Chapelle, New Mexico, when she first encountered Grandfather. Chapelle is approximately twenty-two miles south of Las Vegas. Grandfather was the station agent for the Santa Fe Railroad, which ran through Chapelle. Grandmother and Vern had begun to struggle with their marriage. Grandfather must have taken a fancy to her when he first ran into her in the small community. He noticed that she was having a difficult time taking care of her children and teaching. Also she and the children did not seem have enough to eat much of the time. He started bringing them small items that they needed. Well, you can figure out where this is going.

Anyway, Grandfather had already divorced his first wife for being unfaithful. The relationship with my Grandmother was meant to be, if I was meant to be. Grandmother had grown tired of following Vern around while he pretended to be a cowboy. He also seemed to be losing interest in her. (I am writing between the lines here. I am qualified to do this because Mother once took a writing class and she told me all about it, but she forgot to tell me the part about staying out of trouble while typing near the speed of light.) Okay, I am probably being unfair to Vern.

One thing is certain: My grandparents began a relationship in Chapelle that led to marriage. Mother was the first of three by-products of the marriage. She was born in Las Vegas, New Mexico, in a hospital. As we have already seen, Mother was probably more than my grandparents bargained for.

From the beginning of Mother's life, there were difficulties. Mother was born with a defective hip. Grandmother had to take her to San Francisco to see a specialist. He put her in a body cast, something which both Mother and I experienced in our lives. However, I had to earn my body cast since I was not born needing one. Mom had it easy; she required her cast out of the gate, or whatever it's called. I will come to my body-cast story in due time. Anyway, Mom's body cast completely fixed her problem, enabling her to live free from plaster and other constraining rules and regulations that go along with a defective hip. However, she had to return to the shop several times before being fully certified to embark on her adventurous life. These trips were financially possible because Grandfather worked for the railroad and could get passes for Grandmother and Mom to go to San Francisco as necessary.

I have not yet mentioned Mother's two younger and relatively boring siblings, Jessica and Frank. As it turned out, all seven of Grandmother's children considered one another as full and equal brothers and sisters. They were always very close, and Mother was even accepted as a full-fledged member of the family even after her New York adventures. I was the outcast. Well, maybe not. I was accepted too and didn't have to stand putting my nose into a corner too often. Obviously, there was something wrong with a family that didn't look the other way when Mom and I were present.

Grandfather's oldest daughter, Grace, from his first marriage never quite made the team. Mother thought this was wrong. However, her judgment concerning right and wrong was most likely quietly ignored. Okay, Grace did eventually make the team, but only after I was mostly grown. She began attending family reunions.

CHAPTER 3

Early Days with My Grandparents

No eyes and ears to bear witness. Virtual possibilities bring space into existence tugging at it, deforming it into realities: Space curves creating FORCES: strong, electromagnetic, weak, gravitational; and tangles drawing itself into knots: PARTICLES; MASS: electrons, protons; neutrons, mesons...stars, galaxies, clusters of galaxies...planets, flowers, beasts, humans, Clowns, laughter... Clowns?

*****

The first few years of my life were spent partly with Mom and partly with Grandmother and Grandfather. During the winters, my grandparents moved into town because it could be very difficult to get back and forth to the Ranch over the very rough roads after winter conditions set in.

A note of caution: For the early times with my grandparents and Mother, I will appear to remember things that will get me in trouble with the scientific memory experts. Of course, I know that memory experts would say that it is impossible for me to remember things from so early in my life. Since I have spent most of my life as a scientist, it makes sense for me to go along with the scientific point of view even though I seem to have these memories. Well, since I am retired, maybe I can cut myself a break and say that the scientists are full of it. This would allow me to remember whatever I want to remember from any time in my life, maybe even before it officially began in Pecos. On second thought, it is probably better to have a more scientific understanding of my stories. Try this: It is possible that I was told about these early events when I was somewhat older and they became memories from the telling, complete with pictures in my mind. Such stories were certainly told. However, there are memories included in these pages that only I could possibly know about. Are they false? They don't seem false to me, but I can't prove that they are real. Alas! Science can be so constraining. If we are willing to give up its power, we can believe anything we like.

Wait! Maybe there is a better way to fix it. How about an explanation that says I am the son of Mother and an alien father named Roznocker the Great from a planet far, far away where there are no such rules and regulations to constrain what I remember? Leave it to Mom to find this guy. This scenario might explain many other things about my life as well—or maybe not. I'll try to behave for the rest of this telling, but I am not making any strong promises.

Mother was trying to get her life straightened out during the first two years of my life. She worked as a bookkeeper in Pecos for part of the time, and I have very vague memories of being with her during this time. I surely spent more time at the Ranch with my grandparents where I have a few more memories since they moved into town during the winters and I have memories of staying with them during those times also.

Because I spent so much time with my grandparents during my first few years, I became very close to them. After Mom got a new husband, I began spending more time with her and my new dad. Even then, I continued to spend significant time with Grandmother and Grandfather. We had a bond that could not be broken. Furthermore, Mom did not want it broken. It lasted for the rest of my grandparents' lives.

I have early memories from both the Ranch and different places my grandparents lived in town. Their house on the Ranch was an adobe brick house lying perhaps a hundred yards east of my great-grandfather's stone house. There were three small cabins lying along the path from the stone house to the adobe house.

Most of my Ranch time was spent in the adobe house. It consisted of one large room with a kitchen and entrance on the west end and an open bedroom at the other end. In between was the living area. Grandmother and Grandfather slept in twin beds in the bedroom area. A tall set of cabinets rose to the ceiling between the two beds, effectively making two small bedrooms, each completely open to the rest of the house. Clutter and furniture filled the entire house from front to back. If one wanted to retrieve something that was not close to the narrow path through the clutter, one needed a grappling hook or time to move stuff out of the way.

The "living room" area was in the middle of the house, surrounding a fireplace located on the north wall. The fireplace was normally bricked, closed with adobe bricks in the winter, and the bricks were removed in the summer when fires were often burned. During the cool evenings, the fire sucked the warm air from the house up the chimney, drawing cooler air in from outside and effectively creating air conditioning. If this seems backward, it was. My family always had its own, better, way of doing things. Sometimes, it actually worked as in this case.

There was a wood cooking stove in the kitchen area that was also used for heat when necessary. There were no other sources of heat in the house even though there was electricity. Furthermore, there was no plumbing in any of the Ranch houses or cabins. Water was carried from a well that, I would guess, was an eighth to a quarter of a mile away. Restrooms? Head west past the row of cabins and then up the hill to the one and only outhouse. Swimming pool? Go jump in the small creek on the property.

Grandfather's cabin was a short distance from the adobe house along the path that continued west past two other small cabins and then to either the outhouse if one veered north, or to Great-grandfather's stone house, a little to the south, and across the entrance road from the Ranch housing complex. Complex? Calling it a complex would give my great-grandparents and grandparents a belly laugh. It was a ranch with two houses and some shacks scattered about.

For as long as Grandmother and Grandfather lived at the Ranch, Grandfather's cabin was a special place for me. It was where I spent time learning the secrets of the universe as perceived by Grandfather. He did not sleep in the cabin although there was a cot in it that I sometimes used for naps. Grandfather's ham radio equipment and most of his tools were located in his cabin. I spent a lot of time with him in that cabin right from the beginning. Those times created very special memories that seem to have lasted to the present day.

Great-grandmother slept and mostly lived in a small cabin that was next to Grandfather's cabin. Her cabin, like all the cabins, was a single room. Besides her bed, she had a desk and a chair—nothing more. Well, there was a slop jar for urgencies that occurred on a dark night. Great-grandmother was very frail. I don't recall her paying any attention to me at all. I don't even remember hearing her talk although I surely did. She would come to the adobe house for meals, which Grandmother prepared for all of us. I remember her walking along the path to the main house holding onto a special handrail with one hand and using a cane with the other. I would watch from a distance, totally mesmerized. There was very little danger that I would get in her way. I had been strongly warned by both Grandfather and Grandmother not to get close to her and cause her to fall.

Next to Great-grandmother's cabin, there was a small playhouse that was used for storage. I never saw what was in it. It was always locked; not that I went around trying doors, much less kicking them in. I was only a few years old after all.

Dominating the Ranch Complex (there I go again) was Great-grandfather's stone house. It was just south of the entrance road and west of the adobe house and cabins. The latter were located just north of the entrance road. Even after the stone house burned, the stone walls remained, continuing their domination of the scene.

As I indicated, there was no indoor plumbing in any of the houses at the Ranch. Everyone used the one outhouse unless one got lost on the path leading to it and was diverted into the oak brush. The latter only worked for the male population, especially on a very dark night with glowing eyes peering from the bushes along the path. Well, there were also slop jars available for use in the black of night for those afraid of heading up the path on a moonless night with the glowing eyes watching your every step. Well, this my version of the walk to the outhouse in the dark. I seldom made it all the way after the sun went down.

Water was hand-pumped and carried from a well. To get to the well, one continued west past the stone house and made a large radius turn to the south. The well was located at the southwest corner of the property in a garden plot where the main crop seemed to be rocks and weeds. Well, Grandmother did manage to grow some corn and other vegetables in the garden. Both well and garden were near a stream that seemed to be dry much of the year. It occasionally had water in it if there had been enough rain.

Even though the distance to the well was modest, it may as well have been half the distance to the moon when I was carrying my small bucket of water back to the house. It was especially far if one was carrying a full bucket or two buckets like my grandfather carried. With an empty bucket, the distance was almost manageable for me. I was given a small bucket to carry to and from the well to teach me that we all had to contribute to our survival or maybe just to make me feel useful. It didn't work; I did not feel useful. Sometimes, the water I started out with from the well arrived at the adobe house; sometimes, it didn't. In the latter case, I would arrive with freshly washed pants, wet socks, and muddy shoes.

In my early days at the Ranch, we had a phone. The phone system was an old-fashioned one similar to what is sometimes seen in old movies. There was a box on the wall with an input, or microphone sticking out of it, and a receiver or speaker part of the phone hanging on the side of the box. When anyone in the area got a call, everyone's phone would ring. It was possible to identify who the call was for you by listening to the sequence of short and long rings. If you lost count, or were conveniently uncertain, you could pick up the receiver and listen or say something into the phone to find out if you were being called. It was always possible to listen in on anyone's conversations. For some reason, this system went away when I was quite young, and it was not replaced by a modern system. People in the area simply did not have phones for a long time.

Grandmother had a dozen or more cats living in the attic of the adobe house. A ladder was permanently left in place just outside of the front door at the west end of the house to provide access to the attic for both cats and humans.

One evening, I remember Grandfather heading out in the dark to make use of the outhouse facilities. He had only been gone for about a minute before he returned reeking of eau de skunk. Grandmother did not appreciate the fragrance and did not want him in the house, but she had no choice. All the water stored for drinking and cooking along with all the available lemon juice, vinegar, and dirty socks were stirred together in an effort to create a potion that would neutralize Grandfather's unwanted fragrance. (Well, maybe not the dirty socks.) The effort was futile. The more he and Grandmother tried prescribed remedies, the happier the skunk became with her work. Nothing helped. The failure of the strong elixir convinced me that I was glad I had already spent a good amount of time with Grandfather because I didn't see how we could ever spend any more time together.

When asked how he had gotten crossways with the skunk, he told us he had seen something in the dark in front of him. He assumed it was one of the cats, and he gently booted it out of the way. Smelly mistake! The country kitty hightailed it out of the way, but only after sharing its incredibly strong fragrance with Grandpa. There is no way to get past a skunk encounter quickly enough, and there is no way to learn to enjoy the perfume they so willingly share. We were all forced to bear the fragrance for the rest of the evening and for several days afterward—or was it decades? It seemed like decades at the time.

Grandmother had her cats; Grandfather had a very crazy dog named Wags. Wags would see his hind legs behind him when he approached his food dish, causing him to attempt to chase them away, fearing that they belonged to another beast that was attempting to eat his food. Wags eventually became so crazy that my grandfather had to put him down with his .38 caliber pistol. He did not trust Wags around me or any of the grandchildren or people who visited the Ranch. After this event, I was always careful not to attempt to chase my legs away. I felt much safer many years later after I inherited the .38 caliber pistol that put Wags out of the leg-chasing business. I am allowed to have only one bullet. I lost it. How does one lose the only bullet one has? I surely need more than one bullet to cover my carelessness.

As I indicated, my grandparents did not spend much time during the winter at the Ranch. It was difficult to get to town in bad weather even in Grandfather's jeep. Furthermore, my uncle Frank was still in high school when I was very young. This was the most compelling reason for my grandparents to rent a house in or near town for the winter months.

One place that I remember was located in the countryside in the prairie southwest of Las Vegas. A favorite memory from this house was of Grandfather walking me down to the Santa Fe railroad tracks that ran behind the property to see the trains pass by. I remember hearing and feeling the very loud rumble that came with being so close to the trains. It frightened me. At the same time, it was thrilling.

It was in this house that I remember sleeping in a small bed in a bedroom that I shared with Grandmother and Grandfather. One morning, I opened my eyes, and the sun came up simultaneously. I quickly concluded that I had caused the sun to come up by opening my eyes. Unfortunately, I don't remember making any more observations to verify my conclusion. Apparently, I did not have the scientific method down yet. I was certain I was correct without further investigation. I finally got over such delusions of grandeur last month.

Other fond memories of living near town involve my uncle Frank. I remember waiting for the school bus to let him off at the gate to the property. I would run to the gate to meet him. When I got there, he would pick me up, and we would do something together. I remember two activities. One was that he would feed me Cheerios and we would pretend that I was eating little eyes. The other activity was going for a ride with him and some of his friends in a car. He had taught me to identify cars by make, model, and year. I am told I would get them all correct, which amazed his friends. This feat was much easier to accomplish in those days than it would be today. I certainly couldn't do it now even if my uncle Frank were still around to hold me up to the window.

I remained very attached to him over the years even though he always seemed to live far away. I did not see him as often as I would have liked. He became an Air Force fighter pilot who quickly graduated to training pilots in an altitude chamber. When asked why he had quit flying fighter jets so soon after entering the Air Force, he indicated that he had tired of chasing UFOs.

The small community of San Geronimo lay partway between the Ranch and Las Vegas. Many of the people who lived in San Geronimo used horses and wagons for transportation, and almost none of them spoke English. Grandfather spoke fluent Spanish, but Grandmother didn't speak any Spanish. Nevertheless, being a teacher, she spoke perfect English. Her perfection apparently did little to impress the local Spanish-speaking community. Nevertheless, she was not inclined to speak very loudly to get them to understand, a technique that apparently works for some. I know it worked for some of the dogs I have had.

I remember one morning when I was probably near my fourth birthday. My grandparents had to go into town for groceries and other supplies. I piled into the jeep with them, and we headed east toward Las Vegas on the very rough jeep road. Just outside of the small community of San Geronimo, the jeep decided, completely on its own volition, to make an unscheduled stop. Grandfather opened the engine compartment and determined the cause of the problem. Unfortunately, he needed a part in order to make the repair. Needing the part was fortunate as far as I was concerned because whenever the jeep broke down, Grandpa would fix it on the spot. This often took hours. I was not very patient during the repairs even though he always attempted to keep me busy by giving me little chores to do to help with the problem.

I remember one time when the carburetor quit working, Grandpa took it all apart. While he was figuring out what was wrong with it, he had me clean all the loose parts with gasoline. I did not enjoy being stranded and cleaning carburetor parts with no end in sight. I was very young, and I could not see the process converging even though I knew Grandfather had very significant mechanical and electrical skills. This is just the way one had to operate when living out in the country where it was not possible to call a tow truck. After something like three or four hours (seventeen weeks in small-child time), the carburetor was put back together, and the jeep started right up. I was very glad the ordeal was over. It was a good lesson in self-sufficiency: Don't be self-sufficient. Instead, call for emergency road assistance, and take a nap while waiting for them to arrive. You will be fine until you get the bill. This will be exciting also. Just for fun, see what happens if you don't pay it. You won't be bored.

On the particular morning that I began writing about before all the carburetor distractions, I felt fortunate when Grandfather announced that he couldn't fix the jeep without a part from town. We walked to the nearest house in San Geronimo and found out that a family was about to make the trip into town for groceries. It was to be by horse and wagon. This was the only means of transportation for many of the people in San Geronimo at the time. We hitched a ride with them. At first, the experience of riding in a wagon pulled by a team of horses was exciting, but the trip seemed to take for-ever according to my as-yet-uncalibrated sense of time. Sitting on the rough floor of the wagon was very uncomfortable as it bounced over the bumpy road. It was also a good way to get splinters in your keister. I quickly became very eager to hear the sweet song of a finely tuned combustion engine.

Grandpa got the parts he needed in town, and all of us, including the helpful neighbors, picked up groceries. Then it was back into the uncomfortable wagon to begin the long retreat to San Geronimo. I was not nearly so excited on the outbound trip as I had been when we began the inbound trip. The part must have fixed the jeep. I don't remember. I might have been in a boredom-induced coma by the time it was fixed.

Grandmother never learned to drive. The story was that every time Grandfather attempted to teach her, she would drive right off the road as soon as she attempted to shift gears. I was never present when this happened. They both gave up on her driving, and both seemed happy that she didn't drive.

Meanwhile, I was sitting on Grandfather's lap and steering the jeep well before I started to school. As soon as I could reach the gas pedal, clutch, and brake with my feet, I was driving over the rough road that led from the Ranch to town. I did not drive once we reached Highway 85, which took us the last mile or so into town. That is where the driving got easy. Grandfather could handle it from there without my help.

Of course, Grandmother was usually along on such trips. She just let it all happen without comment. It was the way of a world that would let her small grandchild drive just fine when she couldn't master it herself. Anyway, she knew she was so special that she didn't have to drive to show off. I did.

Grandfather was a ham radio operator. His ham radio setup was in his office cabin. He also had most of his tools and a cot in the cabin. He did not use the cot for sleeping; however, it was a good place for me to take a nap. I often nodded off while watching him go about his business. Besides his ham radio equipment and tools, his cabin was where his typewriter, books, and general clutter were located. I enjoyed spending time with him in his cabin, either listening to him talk on the radio when he wasn't using Morse code or just having him explain things to me. I was curious about everything in that office, and he was very patient with me. We really bonded during our office time.

When I first began listening to him talk on the radio, I thought the purpose of all the chatter was to talk about me since they were always saying "roger this" and "roger that" or "roger, roger. Over and out." My grandfather finally leveled with me concerning my importance to his ham radio buddies. I was okay with this because he told them about me, and they would say things explicitly to me. I loved being part of it.

Much of Grandfather's ham radio equipment was homemade. When he was building and testing equipment, I had the opportunity to learn about electricity, especially how it could bite. I learned to keep one hand behind my back while probing around in a piece of homemade electronics. This procedure provided some protection from electric shock. It helped in the case where your working hand

38

got into something "hot." If the other hand were behind one's back, there was no path for the current to flow across your chest, through your heart to the other hand, if it happened to be grounded somewhere else.

I never got into hot equipment to verify the validity of this safety procedure, but I did see my grandfather get bitten by the electric demons a number of times. It was never serious. Later in life, I discovered that I had not paid enough attention to this lesson. My lack of fear for electricity made executing my graduate-school research a rather noisy and entertaining affair—at least for my fellow graduate students.

The antenna system for the ham radio was a long wire strung between two poles that were fifty or one hundred feet apart. (I didn't really know what a foot that couldn't be put into a shoe was back then.) Each pole had a little metal half-moon on top of it that the antenna wire was attached to. The signal in the antenna wire came down to the cabin or went up to the antenna via two parallel wires that were held a constant distance apart by closely spaced ceramic insulators. This part of the system looked like a flexible ladder. It all seemed like magic to me, and it still does. The world is an incredibly mysterious place, especially if you don't allow yourself to begin overlooking the mystery because you get used to it.

When I was very young, I developed a habit of putting off understanding the great mysteries of ham radio, the stars, and flush toilets until after my next nap. Nevertheless, Grandfather's discussions with me beginning at a very early age kindled a real curiosity for the way the world worked in spite of the naps. He was very patient and treated me like I could understand anything. Nevertheless, radios never seemed mundane to me. When television came along, it was even more mysterious, this even after Mother built one from a kit.

It was not long before I wanted to understand everything, including how the flying saucers worked. At the time, many people in New Mexico seemed to be convinced that they existed and worked just fine. This was exciting and a little frightening. It is interesting that flying saucers were first reported near Roswell, New Mexico, during the summer I was born. Pecos is not all that far from Roswell! Coincidence? Where are the tabloids when you need them?

When I was a little older, I learned the facts of life in Grandfather's cabin. As it turned out, no one else was inclined to talk to me about such things. I think Mom arranged this discussion hoping that Grandfather would get too technical for me and I wouldn't understand it and would forget about the messy business. Okay, I don't really think this. Mother wanted it done right. I will note that I never benefitted from her extensive experience in such matters.

I admit that I had a little trouble believing the messy details of life. At the same time, I was eager to get on with them. If this was the way world worked, I wanted to be in the game. I liked learning about the special and different parts that men and women had and what they were for. I could hardly wait to try out the system, but I soon learned it was not that simple. Well, maybe Grandfather misled me a little about the simplicity of the sex business. He certainly did not get much into the complicated organisms known simply as "women." Such complexities are where Mother really excelled. It was probably good for me to observe her complexities. I concluded she was really something very special.

Anyway, I would soon have the normal teenage urge to be a simple male breeder. It did not take me long to figure out that humans, and most especially women, were apparently more complicated than me. As I matured, I strived to become a more complicated sexual animal, but my effort mostly ended up as a failed endeavor. I had to wait for experience along with maturity to set in. I am still waiting.

I thought Grandfather was brilliant, and he was. He had a number of patents including an early version of cruise control. He never made any money from any of them because he apparently had a learning disability when it came to business deals. He passed this gene on to many of us in the family.

Another thing he passed on to me was a very healthy curiosity and a respect for nature. I remember one night when I was very young, he explained the notion of the atom to me. He told me that everything was made of atoms and that it had been thought that the atom could not be split into smaller pieces. I was less than five years old when this seemingly important revelation was conferred on me. I had some trouble with the notion of the atom because this was before Legos. I did have Lincoln Logs and Tinkertoys. In any case, the principle of making everything out of small, similar objects with different arrangements slowly began to make sense to me.

Grandfather also revealed to me that scientists had figured out how to split the atom, and in doing so, they released a vast quantity of energy, allowing them to make a very powerful bomb. I did not understand energy, but I did understand bombs and explosions for some reason. The story fascinated me, and I imagined how an atom bomb might work. In my simple notion, the bomb was very, very heavy, and it had a very sharp point at one end. When it was dropped from an airplane, it would fall point down. The very sharp point would land precisely on one atom, splitting it and causing the huge explosion. I don't think I discussed this simple and totally incorrect notion with Grandfather nor with my physics professors later in life. I had more sense than that! As Grandmother would say, there are some things you just don't talk about. Well, my professors would have probably enjoyed hearing it. One of them might have even learned something from it.

As it turned out, Grandfather had some direct and indirect experience with the atomic bomb. He had worked at the boys' ranch that existed at the Los Alamos site well before it became the location where the first atomic bombs were assembled. He had worked there in the 1920s. He also had known the Oppenheimer family, according to family lore. Robert Oppenheimer and his family had been frequent visitors to New Mexico and to the Pecos area way before the bomb history began. Oppenheimer had also been a student at the boys' ranch at Los Alamos at about the time that Grandfather worked there. Years later, Robert Oppenheimer directed the effort at the Los Alamos Laboratory to assemble the first atomic bomb.

Family lore has it that Oppenheimer used Big Cross Trail to ride across the mountain range between Pecos, where he had a ranch, to visit Grandfather at the Shearer Ranch. I have no way of knowing if story has any validity to it. However, family lore is always dead on—

at least when it is convenient for me. In any case, the trail was built well before the bomb days began in New Mexico.

I discovered another atomic adventure that my grandfather had when I was looking through his diary sometime in the past few years. I found a note concerning a walk he had taken on the Ranch early one July morning near the end of World War II. During the walk, the sky lit up, and then the light decayed away. He took note of the time and kept walking. As he neared the ranch house, he heard, or felt, a rumble. Again, he noted the time. It had been about thirteen minutes since he saw the sky light up. He knew the speed of sound in air, so he calculated the distance to the source of the light, assuming the light and the sound were produced by a single event. He got approximately the correct distance of 155 miles as the crow flies from the Trinity site to the Ranch. Of course, he didn't know what the correct number was at the time, and he did not understand what he had seen and heard. New Mexico newspapers at the time reported that an ammunition dump had blown up. Mother told me that he had never believed the ammunition-dump story. Nevertheless, he had no idea what had just happened in southern New Mexico and the impact it would have on humanity. It would soon become apparent to everyone.

It is interesting that many years later when I was a postdoc at Cornell University, the head of the Laboratory of Nuclear Studies, Boyce McDaniel, told his own bomb story from a very different perspective. He had been a graduate student at Cornell during the time the bomb was being built and tested. As part of his graduate studies, he had worked on the bomb project and was at Trinity site on that fateful morning in July. After the bomb was detonated, he and some of his colleagues were headed back to Los Alamos. They stopped for breakfast at a small cafe along the way. While they were eating their breakfast, they overheard a couple of cowboys talking at the next table.

One of them said, "Ya know, Slim, I seen the strangest damn thing this mornin'."

The other said, "Whacha talkin' about, Tex?"

The first replied, "It didn't make no damn sense. The sun come up early and went right back down. I never seen nothin' like it." And they went on eating their breakfast in silence.

The dawn of the atomic age occurred a little more than two years before I was born. I have to admit that I was somewhat frightened by Grandfather's story of the atom when I first heard it. However, it would get worse. I dealt with it, but it was never comfortable for me when I was growing up. I would become very interested in the history of the bomb later in life when I was studying physics. I felt connected to it because it had happened so close to me in space, but a little off in the time dimension.

CHAPTER 4

Moving around Texas and New Mexico with Mom and Dad

SELECTION: EVOLUTION: COHERENCE: stars, planets, rocks, life, fish, flowers, ears, eyes, brains, hungry beasts; humans; tribes; clubs; warriors; clowns; emotions; beauty; ugliness; CURIOSITY: exhilaration; organization; language; books; ideas; more ideas; COMPETITION: rifles; bombs; destruction; wars; remorse; WHY?

*****

While Mom was still living in Pecos, she began a relationship with a man named Kenneth Dixon. He was a filling-station attendant in town. I don't know how much time I was spending with Mother in Pecos and how much time I was spending with my grandparents at the Ranch or in town. I have memories of all these situations during this period. Admittedly, the memories from Pecos are very vague and sketchy. Well, all the memories from this part for my life are incomplete visions through the fog.

I remember a log cabin. Was it the Reuter Hotel? I seem to remember that it had only one room with a large bed that Mom and I both slept in. I remember getting a toy fire engine for Christmas that I didn't know what to do with. I remember it being in my way in the bed. All these memories are in picture form. There are no corresponding words.

Ought oh! Here come the memory cops again. I thought I had dealt with them previously. I suppose they would be happy if I wrote that they are false memories that were injected into my system later by someone who told me the stories and they became memories with the pictures. In this case, the explanation does not make any sense. It is more likely that these memories were fabricated sometime later in my mind. This also seems unlikely, but I am trying to stay out of trouble. I can't help but ask, "Who would have told me about a fire engine that was in my way in bed?" It would have to be my own fabrication. Why would I make this up? In any case, if someone told me stories that became memories, they told me a lot of very personal stuff about me that I wish I didn't know.

It was not long before I was spending a significant time with my grandparents while Mother and Kenneth were becoming a serious item. They decided to get married, and for reasons known only to Rozknocker the Great, they decided to do it in California. Crazy stuff just happens in Mother's part of the universe, and it continued throughout her life. Knowing her was definitely worth the bother of being born.

Anyway, Mom, Kenneth, and Kenneth's father, Orval Dixon, headed to California with marriage plans. I don't have any idea why Kenneth's dad went along. Nothing is straightforward in Mom's life. When they returned from California, she was married to Kenneth's dad, not Kenneth. Go figure.

Much of this information came to me from Grandmother. More recently, brother Sam and I discovered some papers that indicated the trip to California began about four months before he was born. This was quite a revelation to us, and it is probably a clue as to why Mom came back married to Dad. The scenario we came up with was that Mom and Kenneth had a falling out on the trip. Until this discovery, we both always thought that Orval was my brother's father. I thought that Orval was my father until I was in the third or fourth grade when Mom leveled with me—almost. Well, she mostly confused me because I had no idea what it took to become a father, and she was not inclined to provide that part of the story. It almost sounded like I was free to go out and select a father for myself. She never leveled with Sam. In spite of all the father confusion, we both loved her dearly most of the time. Being her sons was quite an amusing adventure when one looks back on it from the far future.

Another early, and therefore illegal, memory from my early life was created when Mom picked me up from my grandparents to take me to Texas to live with her and "Dad" (Orval) in Anton. After returning from California married to Mom, Dad had taken a job in an auto repair shop in Anton. He was a first-rate mechanic. At the time, Mom was pregnant with my little brother, Sammy, and I was at the Ranch with my grandparents.

I remember being traumatized when she came to retrieve me to take me to Texas. My grandparents had effectively become my parents. I was two years old when this event occurred. I screamed and cried as she took me out to the car. She was apparently devastated by my behavior and didn't know what to do. She slapped me and put me in the back seat. I continued to whimper for a while.

It was dark when we left the Ranch to begin the trip to Texas. It was a long drive from Las Vegas to Anton. In those days, in that part of the country, women did not drive anywhere alone at night. Mom wore a man's hat so that it would not be obvious that she was a woman. It is very odd that I remember this detail. How would I know why she did it? For some reason, I think I do understand it. She probably explained my memory to me later.

I don't remember arriving in Anton, but I do remember being excited to be getting a little brother to play with. When he made his not-so-grand entrance onto the surface of our turbulent planet, he must not have been impressed. It was Texas after all. I remember him squalling most of the time. I also remember being very curious about him one day when he was in his basket on the dining table. I climbed up and grabbed the edge the basket, trying to see him. I succeeded in getting a good, close look at him when the basket tipped and my little brother and I tumbled to the floor with him landing squarely on top of me. This would not be the last time he ended up on top of me. Anyway, we both made a lot of noise. I was very impressed by the volume he achieved. Fortunately, neither of us was seriously hurt. My first impression: He was an ugly, noisy crybaby.

I also remember Mom and Dad taking him to a hospital to get a shot. I only understood shots from a gun. I have a memory that could not be correct. In the memory, it is dark. I am outside of the hospital waiting in the car when I see a silhouette in a window of Dad holding my brother up to the doctor who holds a pistol in his hand aimed at my squalling brother as he prepared to shoot him. A shooting did take place, but no one was seriously injured by the weaponized needle involved. One would not have come to this conclusion based on the loud squalling that my brother put up in protest. Did I hear the squalling? I feel like I did, but the story does not hold together. Nevertheless, it is in my memory.

After we moved back to New Mexico, Mother received a letter from a friend in Anton that included a newspaper clipping indicating that the doctor who delivered my brother had been arrested for being a veterinarian posing as a medical doctor. I never let my brother forget that he was delivered by a veterinarian. He always seemed kind of proud of it. Veterinarians have to know much more than plain old doctors, after all, in order to deal with many different physiologies that they are confronted with. I hope my brother's birth doctor got back to delivering multi-legged creatures after delivering my brother. He apparently did a reasonably good job for my brother except for the birthmark he left above Sammy's left eye.

Our stay in Anton was short, but memorable. Not only did I get a baby brother, but for the first time in my life, I saw an airplane up close. It had made an emergency landing in a field several hundred yards from our house. I could not see it from the house when Dad pointed it out to me, so he decided to take me to see the small plane up close. I was amazed at how big it was. It was a two-passenger single engine plane. I had only seen airplanes in the sky and had not imagined them large enough for people to fit into even though I think I had been told there were people in them. I may have thought that they were toy people. I did not believe a full-size person could fit into the tiny airplanes I had seen in the sky. I was fascinated. Besides learning something about airplanes, I got my first lesson in optics. I was beginning my physics studies. It was a simple thing, but it seemed important at the time. Dad tried to explain to me why airplanes looked so small in the sky, but his effort failed. Later, Mom tried. She also failed. At that age, I think I was supposed to get used to things that I didn't understand. I didn't like it.

Anton was also where I learned something about having a father who liked to drive fast and take chances. While we were living there, Dad talked Mom into selling the wedding ring from her New York marriage. It was apparently worth a good sum of money. They took the cash and bought a brand-new Mercury. Mom told me about selling the wedding ring to get the car when I was much older. Nevertheless, I have false memories of what happened next in the new car. On the very first night they had the Mercury, they went out driving. I was in the back seat. Dad was driving like he was behind the wheel of a race car "just to see what it could do." Mom was complaining. I think Dad found out more about what the car wouldn't do. He came up behind a large semi that was not going very fast. He badly mistimed applying the brakes. No problem? The front of the car fit neatly underneath the semi's trailer—almost. Unfortunately, the hood had to be removed to tuck it properly into this cool little hiding place.

It is interesting that most of what I remember about this incident has to do with seeing Mother's hair from behind. She had a thick braid that ringed the back of her head in the form of a crown that was tilted back. I thought it was pretty. I also remember being thrown against the rear of the front seat rather suddenly, probably when Dad got on the brakes hard. Apparently, no one was hurt because Dad reacted in time to get the car slowed enough to prevent serious injury. Almost no one had seat belts in those days. When they did become available, we did not get them on any of our cars because Dad was one of those guys who wanted to be "throwed clear." Anyway, they got the Mercury fixed, and Dad apparently took it easy for ten or fifteen minutes. Okay, he never really slowed down.

Our stay in Anton was just long enough for Sammy to be dropped off on the doorstep or wherever the stork deposits its deliveries. The stay was cut short by a tornado that passed too close to our house for Mother's comfort. It occurred late in the afternoon after Dad had come home from the shop. He was shaving as the storm approached. Mother was frantic. I could sense her fear. She was pleading with Dad to go to the storm cellar, which was entered by going outside of the house and down through an entrance near the foundation. Dad was telling her this happens all the time, that she shouldn't worry so much about it. However, he finally gave in, and we went to the cellar. I remember being scared, and I remember hearing a lot of loud banging. Later, I was told that we heard the tornado pass nearby, and it destroyed some houses in the neighborhood. Shortly after this event, we moved back to Las Vegas, New Mexico. Mother had made up her mind that she was not going to live in tornado country anymore. Mountain folk don't deal well with tornados. Dad accommodated her.

Dad was apparently a very good mechanic. After we moved back to Las Vegas, New Mexico, he either bought or built a race car. When I first saw it, I was very eager to take a ride because there was no engine cover. This fascinated me. I was certain I could figure out how the engine worked to move the car by sitting in the car right behind the engine when the car was moving. Dad was more than happy to give me a ride. He lifted me into the car and put me on his lap. We drove around a few blocks starting on Grand Avenue in Las Vegas, where his shop was located. I was sorely disappointed. The car made a lot of frightening noise, but I could not see anything moving in the open engine compartment. I don't think I could even see the radiator fan turning, but I had seen it from beside the car before I got in. I thought it must be important for making the car go. I was between two and three years old at the time. Whoa, I better move on. The memory cops just picked up their ticket pads.

A short time later, my parents got together with my uncle Edward Clements to build a dirt track for automobile racing near Las Vegas. My memory tells me that this race track was near Española, New Mexico, but my brother, Sam, convinced me that it was just outside of Las Vegas. He had learned this for certain a few years ago and convinced me that he was right. As it turned out, one of the drivers, Jim Nix, who I remembered because he won many of the races held at the track, lived just across the mountain from where my brother currently lives near Las Vegas. My brother's place is very near the Ranch. Anyway, the two of them had talked about the track, and Jim told him where the track had been located just outside of Las Vegas. Upon thinking about this location and comparing it to my false memories from that time, it all made sense.

Sam took me to see Jim one day, but Jim was very old and napped most of the time. He was napping when we arrived. I never got another chance to see him because he passed away soon thereafter.

I also have memories of being left in the hot car with my brother while Mom, Dad, and my uncle Edward worked on building the track. I remember being so thirsty and so hot that I would have given up the rest of my life for one sip of a cold Coke. It's a wonder that Sammy and I weren't brain-damaged. Oh, wait! Maybe Sammy was. Oh, gosh, maybe I was. Naw, that can't be, can it? However, if I were brain-damaged, it would explain a lot.

The races were interesting because they were not just races. There was always some gimmick. For example, some races started with the drivers having to swallow a raw egg and wash it down with a Coke before they jumped into their cars and took off. I remember a lot of yelling and excitement. I wish I had been able to talk to Jim about all this to compare my false memories with what he had probably forgotten.

Dad moved from job to job a lot in the early days of his and Mom's marriage. Besides Las Vegas, we lived in both Española and Santa Fe before I was old enough to go to school. I have illegal memories from all those places. Well, I think I am allowed some legal memories toward the end of the period, which was spent in Santa Fe.

We moved to Española after Las Vegas. We rented a house that was in an apple orchard outside of town. Sammy and I got our first dog, and we were really becoming great pals by then. We played constantly together, and yes, we learned how fun it was to get into trouble together. It was mostly Sammy who led the way to trouble. He was born with this instinct, or so I say.

The dog was a cocker spaniel named Lucky. Unfortunately, Lucky was not very lucky. He was allowed to run loose in the orchard, and someone poisoned him. Sammy and I were also poisoned, but we had our own version of how to get poisoned. We ate green apples off the apple trees. For a while, I was pretty well convinced that we were going the way of Lucky. Somehow, we survived, but it was a struggle.

There was an irrigation ditch that ran through the orchard and past our house. Water would sometimes come down the ditch without warning. We often played in the ditch. Looking back, it seems that playing in the ditch was a dangerous thing for two little boys to do. I guess we were really the ones who should have been named Lucky. *Lucky I* and *Lucky II* would have been appropriate.

We did not stay in Española long enough for our luck to run out. We moved to Santa Fe. Our first house in Santa Fe was in a residential section of town near the plaza. I am relying on a very unreliable memory to come up with this location. Anyway, Mom got a job at the La Fonda Hotel while we lived there. She worked nights and slept during the day, leaving Sammy and me to fend for ourselves while Dad was working. Fortunately, we had a good fenced in yard. We didn't get into too much trouble.

About the only memory I have from our first Santa Fe house was collecting juniper berries that fell from a juniper tree in our front yard. We filled our unused mailbox with them. Unfortunately for our juniper cache, some bigger boys found them and shot them all over the place with their sling shots, which were called something inappropriate in those days. Sammy and I watched from our bedroom window. It's a good thing we couldn't get outside. Sammy was already aggressive, and the two older boys would have probably left purple skid marks in their underwear for a day or two.

Santa Fe was where I learned that I did not like sugar very much. Mom and Dad would buy us Sugar Pops or some equivalent sweet cereal for our breakfast. I ate it without complaining, but one day, Dad gave me a bite of his fried eggs. I did not want sweet cereal anymore, and Mom accommodated me the best she could. I am still that way late in life. I tolerate sweets, but they are far from my favorite items to eat.

It was not long before we moved to another house in Santa Fe that was more out in the country. It soon became known as The Bug House. There were centipedes and spiders all over the place inside and outside of the house. By this time, Sammy and I were old enough to play outside with other kids. I remember trying to convince a young neighbor boy that there were people in the airplanes that flew over. He had not noticed the airplanes before, and he didn't believe that there were people in them when I pointed them out. I found it comforting that I was not the only one who had trouble believing this.

While we lived in The Bug House, I had a frightening interaction with a man who lived next door. I found an old piece of wire in our backyard. I picked it up and tossed it over the fence into his yard. I had not noticed that he was standing nearby. He picked up the piece of wire twisted into a loop and gave it back to me, saying, "If you do that again, I will wring your neck with it." I took this threat seriously. I was very frightened, but I don't remember telling Mom or Dad about it. I certainly did not toss anything else into his backyard. He's lucky I did not find a hundred-dollar bill in our backyard while we lived there...isn't he?

My little sister was born near the end of our stay in Santa Fe. Our next move came right after she was born. It was to Pot Creek, a logging-and-lumber camp near Taos, New Mexico. It was owned by Rounds and Porter of Wichita, Kansas. We would live at Pot Creek for about seven years. I had just turned six at the time of the move. However, before we moved, I remember waiting to see to see my little sister come out of the hospital in Santa Fe. What a disappointment! She looked like every other squalling baby I had ever seen. My excitement over her died away rather quickly. The same could not be said for Dad. She was apparently the best thing that ever happened to him even though he did have an adult daughter at the time. As it turned out, I ended up spending a good deal of my early years protecting our little sister from my brother. They apparently had a real rivalry based on a little jealousy that her presence inspired in Sammy. She replaced him as Dad's favorite. I had a grandfather and grandmother and was never replaced in my role with them.

Even though the race track did not last very long, Dad's fast and reckless driving continued all through New Mexico, leading to a number of exciting accidents. Crashing soon appeared to be worthy goal in life to Sammy and me. The more spectacular the crash, the more life points one got. At least this is the way we figured it.

The crash I remember best occurred late in this period. We were in Albuquerque in the Mercury that Mom and Dad had bought in Texas. We came up behind a long line of very slow traffic on a two-lane road. Dad had driven a dump truck in one of his previous jobs, and he announced that he was going to show us how he had dealt with traffic problems when he was driving the dump truck. He pulled into the left lane and began passing the long line of cars. No one was approaching from the opposite direction. Unfortunately, an older couple ahead of us in the line decided to make a left turn. The woman was driving, and she put her arm out the window to signal her intent as she began her turn. Her arm was still out of the window when we plowed into the driver's side of her car. Sammy and I were standing behind the front seat, and Mom was in the front with Dad. When we hit the side of the turning car, Sammy was thrown toward the front seat. Mom put her arms up and caught him and pushed him back into the back seat. Meanwhile, I hit Dad in the back of the neck and fell back on the floor behind the front seat. Sammy got up, yelling, "We got him, Daddy! We got him!"

I don't remember the events that followed at the accident scene, but I later learned that the woman in the car had suffered a serious injury to her arm. I know this because she filed a lawsuit against us, and we were still paying for the accident years later. I don't understand the details because they were not shared with me, but I imagine we had insurance. We still had to pay. I had this information because Mom shared it with me after she began confiding in me regularly.

Chapter 5

Good Times at the Ranch

Random arrangements appear and disappear endlessly; More expansion; dilution: NOTHING? SOMETHING ELSE? FOREVER? TIME? NEVER? NOTHING…

*****

As we moved around New Mexico, Sammy and I began spending significant time during the summers at the Ranch, where we began riding horseback on Punch, a horse that had been my uncle Frank's when he had lived at home. Uncle Frank had already joined the Air Force by this time. Punch was a gentle horse that was easy to ride. When Sammy and I were quite small, Grandpa would put us up on his back, often both of us together. He would walk in front of Punch, leading us around various parts of the Ranch. This was great fun for us, and Punch must have enjoyed it too. He got an extra pan of corn or oats at the end of the ride. This sometimes caused him to begin looking for shortcuts back to the Ranch House, but Grandpa always won the minor tug-of-war that ensued.

When we were not riding or otherwise playing, Grandmother would make us pull weeds around the ranch house and in her garden down by the creek. Neither of us liked this chore, but we got through it by acting like we were being tortured severely enough that we were not likely to survive.

We were very easily distracted to more pleasant adventures. For example, there were salt licks for the animals scattered about. When we would find one, we would break off chunks of salt, put them in our pockets, and lick them when no one was watching. There were times when we got down on all fours and licked the block like the cattle and other four-legged creatures. This would save having to break chunks off. When Grandmother discovered this activity, she corralled us.

Punch was sold to friends during these early years at the Ranch. Afterward, Sammy and I had no horse to ride. The problem was somewhat alleviated by a neighbor's horses who often found their way through the fence to graze on the Ranch. One neighbor, in particular, was notorious for "accidentally" allowing his horses and cattle graze on other people's property. Grandfather didn't seem to mind since he had no animals of his own to graze.

This situation led to a friendship that Sammy and I entered into with one of the neighbor's horses. The horse was young and frisky. We thought maybe he could become our horse by some means that we did not understand. We had heard of cattle rustling, but being horse thieves? We knew we didn't want to go there. "Our horse" was all black except for a white marking on its forehead. We named him Blackie. Grandpa allowed us feed Blackie corn and grain, but he did not want us to attempt to ride him. We enjoyed petting the horse while he ate the grain. Of course, this was not enough. Sammy and I wanted to ride Blackie.

One day, we miraculously found Blackie out away from the Ranch house, and we just happened to have a pan of oats and a rope with us. Well, maybe this was not so much a miracle as a charity event for hungry horses. We must have been planning to jump rope to entertain the hungry horse. Or maybe we always carried oats and a rope with us wherever we went to be prepared. Yeah, that must have been it. We were being prepared like Boy Scouts.

The plan worked perfectly to a point. We gave Blackie some oats, and then we very gently slipped the rope over Blackie's head while we scratched his ears and mane. We could tell he was somewhat nervous about the rope, and we didn't know if anyone had ever attempted to ride him. He lifted his head rapidly a couple of times and snorted. Nevertheless, the oats kept him mostly distracted. Once Blackie was enjoying the oats again as I held the pan for him, without saying anything, Sammy quickly swung himself up onto the horse's back, catching both me and Blackie by surprise. The horse reacted quickly by rearing up and dumping the small cowboy on the ground. In Sammy's defense, he didn't have anything substantial to hold onto, and he had little opportunity to settle in on the horse's back.

At the time, we didn't know whether Blackie had been ridden before. Sammy didn't care. He liked taking chances. It was no surprise to either of us that it did not take much effort on Blackie's part to dump the small, would-be bronc rider on his rump. Had I been Roy Rogers or Gene Autry, I would have sung a song to Blackie before scrambling onto his back just for the principle of it. I was older and bigger after all. However, I couldn't seem to find my saddle.

It took Blackie a while to come into our territory again. By then, we had lost interest in him. We were moving on to bull riding—well, maybe not. Not only had we learned a lesson, but Blackie had too. He never trusted us again. He mostly stayed away from the two little hooligans with the oats and the rope.

Another activity that Grandfather introduced me to was shooting rifle. I was six years old at the time. I don't remember Sammy shooting at all. He was only four after all, and Grandfather surely deemed him to be too young. Anyway, I remember Grandfather teaching me how to hold the rather small .22 caliber rifle, which was too big for me to hold properly. I had to slide the stock under my armpit. Grandpa would put a bottle up on a shelf on the side of the old sawmill building, which was located just south of the Ranch houses. I was soon hitting the bottles with almost every shot.

I enjoyed shooting, which was somewhat of a surprise to both of my grandparents. A couple of years earlier, they had given me a cap gun for my birthday, but when Grandmother had demonstrated it for me, I began to cry because I didn't like the noise. For some reason, firing the .22 was a different story. Well, I was older. I don't think I was eager to kill anything other than an empty bottle when I started shooting. The rifle was a single shot, requiring me to put a new cartridge in after each attempt on the life of a bottle. I never shot without Grandfather present. Shooting was part of growing up and becoming a man in the culture I was born into. I would begin to question this culture very early in my life. No problem; any kind of questioning was always encouraged by Grandfather.

CHAPTER 6

Cowboy Culture

NOTHING? What is nothing? No existence? Where is NOTHING? It would seem that the first step in understanding existence is would be to understand nonexistence... Nothing? Does this sound easy?

*****

Rodeo was another part of the culture that I was born into even though my grandparents were not into rodeos. Many in the family were. For many years, the big event in Las Vegas was the Cowboy Reunion and Rodeo held every summer. The rodeo would attract some of the best cowboys in the West. Part of the celebration was the reunion of the surviving members of Teddy Roosevelt's Rough Riders. There was always a parade through downtown Las Vegas before the rodeo began, and one or two cars in the parade carried the surviving, and rather elderly, members of Teddy Roosevelt's Rough Riders. Everyone looked forward to seeing them, but every year, there were fewer. They were getting very old during the 1950s. Finally, there was only one, and then there were none. I don't remember what year it was when we saw the last Rough Rider or if I was present for the event.

I began going to the rodeos when I was very small. However, my grandparents never attended. The rodeo was better in tune with the younger people in the family.

Aunt Jessie had a movie camera that allowed us to enjoy the thrills and spills of each rodeo more than once. The kids especially enjoyed watching the rodeo films run backward. It was very amusing to see the cowboys leap from a sprawled out position on the ground onto the back of a wildly bucking animal. We never seemed to tire of watching this distorted view of the bucking events illustrating the laws of physics run backward, seeming to violate the law of entropy. Well, the bulls didn't give a crap about entropy even though they were creating it with all they could muster.

It was a bit odd that Jessie took these movies and showed them because she had experienced a grim tragedy at an earlier rodeo. I was only two years old at the time. Jessie had just married a young cowboy named George F. (Teeter) Hayes. Teeter decided he wanted to compete in the bull-riding event. Aunt Jessie didn't want him near a bull, but he was determined. Bull riding was certainly the glamor event of the rodeo.

Jessie and others from the family were in attendance at the fateful rodeo. I was in Las Vegas at the time, but I was only two years old. Mom left me with Grandmother in an apartment during the rodeo. When the rodeo party returned, everyone was upset. I knew something was not right, but I was too young to understand it. I would learn the story much later in my life. However, an older cousin, Dorothy, documented the event in her book, *Audrey of the Mountains*. She had attended the rodeo with her mother and sister according to the book.

Dorothy wrote that Teeter's bull came out of the shoot and very quickly tossed Teeter over its head. As the bull continued to rampage, it landed on Teeter's chest with its front hooves. After the bull finished its wild dance, Teeter did not get up. He did not move. He was soon on his way to the hospital in an ambulance with very grave injuries. Nevertheless, he was still alive when everyone arrived back at the apartment where Grandmother was taking care of me.

Unfortunately, he only lived for two more days. His funeral services were held two days before my second birthday.

Jessie continued to go to rodeos as I was growing up. This was something I never understood. She remarried and had five children. It was common for our family to attend rodeos with her family. I noticed that Aunt Jessie always left the stands when the bull-riding event began, leaving the movie camera for someone else to operate. Mother explained to me that Jessie was underneath the stands crying, a ritual that she performed during the bull-riding event at each rodeo she attended. She always returned with her eyes teary and red. What people do and why they do it can be very difficult to understand.

CHAPTER 7

Early Days at Pot Creek

Nothing? Was it before the Big Bang? What does *before* mean? *Before* implies a clock. Was there time before the Big Bang? Or does time come into existence when the universe explodes from nothing into nothing? BEFORE?...

*****

Our next stop in New Mexico was near a very special place, Taos, a town where part of my heart still resides. Taos is and was a magical place for artists, writers, and even for a future scientist. It is also a special place for a post-scientist. It has always had a mystical air about it that attracts artists and writers. Part of its attraction is the beautiful, open mountain valley overlooked by the tall and rugged Pueblo Peak, sacred to the Pueblo People of Taos and to many privileged to reside in its shadow.

I became very connected to this special place during the seven years that we lived near Taos. I don't pretend to understand the strong feelings of connection I still have for this high mountain valley. Furthermore, I don't seem to care that I don't understand them. One could say that I was simply captured by the mystical spirit of Taos, whatever that is. Nevertheless, one should be aware of what I

mean by "mystical spirit." It is much the same for me as being captured by the mystical spirit of the universe along with the fact that
the human mind is able to comprehend and make sense of some of it.
I like to think of my "mystical" is a natural property. It is the wonder
caused by the aspect of nature that allows us to study its complexity
and almost understand it using the power of our minds. That we can
do this seems most unlikely. This is the mystical part.

*****

Shortly after my sister, Diana, was born, Dad took a job with
Pot Creek Logging and Lumber Company. The logging company
was owned by Rounds and Porter of Wichita Kansas, and the logging-and-lumber camp was situated on an old Spanish land grant
located about twelve miles south of Taos, New Mexico. Mr. Rounds,
the owner of Rounds and Porter, had purchased the land grant in
order to log it.

Rounds and Porter was a rather large company based in
Wichita, Kansas. It had logging operations in several places in the
West. During our time at Pot Creek, Mr. Rounds visited the lumber camp from time to time as did one of his sons, Bill, who often
brought his family along. However, the day-to-day management of
the logging-and-lumber operation was based at the lumber camp.

When any of the Rounds family visited, they stayed in their
private apartment that was located upstairs over the main office
building. Entrance to the apartment was provided by two outside
stairways that wound around the office building in a semi-circular
fashion. Both stairways led to an outside balcony where the entrance
to the living space was located. The apartment was very fancy by
logging-camp standards. The office building was located very near
the house we lived in for most of our stay in the logging camp. Both
were just inside the main entrance to the logging camp.

The Pot Creek operation included logging the mountains of
an old Spanish land grant and turning the logs into lumber. At the
center of the operation was the sawmill. Logs were cut, loaded, and
delivered to the sawmill by the loggers. The output of sawmill was

lumber that was sold to many places around the West. One customer was the United States Air Force Academy being built near Colorado Springs, Colorado. Lumber was delivered on large trucks that carried the lumber over the highways.

Pot Creek or, in Spanish, Rito de la Olla was one of two creeks that came down from the mountains surrounding the logging camp. The other was the Little Rio, or Rio Grande del Rancho, named after the more famous Rio Grand River that it runs into. Most important, and disappointing to some, Pot Creek was not named for a plant that grew along the banks of the creek. Rather, it was named for all the broken pottery found on the site, remnants of previous, and more legitimate, occupants. Some of these inhabitants also left the remains of an old pueblo and some pit houses that had become buried under the sands of time. Many other artifacts left by these people could be found strewn about in the mountain valley where the logging camp was located. Included were many arrowheads, spear points, and decorated pottery shards from pots that were broken during the passage of time. There were also items of kitchenware such as metates and pestles for grinding corn.

We moved to Pot Creek before the end of the summer in 1953 near my sixth birthday. My little sister had been born in June. Dad's new job was to run the mechanical shop for the logging and lumber operation. He was responsible for repairs and maintenance on logging trucks, lumber trucks, all kinds of logging equipment, and the sawmill equipment. It sounds like a lot; however, he generally had only one or two helpers.

When we first arrived at Pot Creek, we lived temporarily in a house that Mom was not happy with. She wanted a better one. Like all the houses in the logging camp, the temporary house had no indoor plumbing. In addition, it was not large enough for Mom. Her desire to move may have also been motivated by several adventures that she had while Dad was at work. I remember one of these events. It occurred shortly after Dad had departed for his shop one morning.

A "funny" man forced his way in through the front door and staggered around our living room. At least, Sammy and I thought he was funny, but the situation was more serious. Mom certainly did not think the event was funny or entertaining. The "funny" man was drunk and did not want to leave. Mom gave him a cup of coffee to try to sober him up a bit. While he drank the coffee, Sammy and I crawled around on the floor under the table, laughing and playing. We thought we were being entertained by a clown. Mother finally managed to talk the "clown" into leaving. As soon as he was gone, she locked the front door. Next, she had a little talk with Sammy and me about how serious the situation had been. The man had been a "bad man." He was not a clown trying to entertain us!

It was not long before Mom prevailed in her endeavor to get us into a different house. The logging-camp management accommodated her by agreeing to fix up a house near the main office. It was also very near Dad's shop. Like the first house, it had no indoor plumbing. Furthermore, this particular house had no outdoor facilities either. To top it off, there was no well. The creek did run right past the house. In spite of all the shortcomings, it was the house that Mom wanted.

Dad had a plan. He bought a chemical toilet that worked for us until he was able to dig a well, put in a septic field, and added indoor plumbing. I don't remember how we obtained water before we had the well. With Dad's effort, our house became the first house in the logging camp with running water. Dad had done most all of the work himself after we moved into the house. He may have received some support from the company to get the work done. Thinking about it years later, I realized that Dad put the septic field fairly close to the well. Oh well, I guess Dad either knew what he was doing or we got lucky. Our water tasted great and we never had a bad—well, you know—attitude toward life.

Further improvements included two new bedrooms that were added onto the house. Dad apparently convinced the company to make the bedroom additions. One of the new bedrooms was for Mom and Dad, and the other was for Sammy and me. Baby Diana shared Mom and Dad's bedroom. Mom was able to convert one of original bedrooms into an office where she put her ham radio equipment and did her writing. The other original bedroom was absorbed into a larger living room. In addition, the old front door and porch on the south end of the house were converted into a laundry room complete with washing machine. The main entrance, or front door, was moved to the west side of the house. It opened into the living room. The changes made sense. We had what Mom wanted. The house was surrounded by something roughly resembling a lawn. A wooden fence enclosed the rather large yard.

The house became the show piece of the hillbilly camp, which caused some of the other kids to begin calling us city hicks. We still had no telephone and would never have one at Pot Creek. There was only one phone in the entire logging camp, and it was in the main office, which was within hollering distance of our house. In fact, that is the way it worked. We would get a call at the main office, and the administrative person would come out of the office and blow her whistle to get Mom's attention. Mom would walk over and take the call. This was the way our phone calls worked the entire time we lived in the logging camp. The other residents did not seem to need a telephone although they could be summoned to the office if necessary.

All of Dad's work on the house put the other foremen in the logging camp into a state of "keeping up with the Dixons." It was not long before they were demanding equal housing, and they managed to get it, most likely by following Dad's example and doing much of it themselves.

One of the most interesting natural features of our Pot Creek residence was an old cottonwood tree that was standing next to the creek just inside of our front-yard fence. The tree was huge with a trunk diameter of more than five feet near the base. There was a makeshift ladder that had been made by nailing boards to the trunk of tree. The ladder led up to a hollow where three secondary trunks split off to continue to their skyward climb. Previous occupants had not only constructed the ladder but they had also nailed some boards around the hollow where the main trunk split into three secondary trunks. This created a wonderful tree house. It did not take Sammy and I long to take possession of the lofty gift from our predecessors. We were good climbers, and the tree house was a great place for a lookout, allowing us to keep a diligent watch on the neighborhood.

Okay, most of what we watched for was attacking Natives or cavalry. The neighborhood was on its own. It was a great place to get accustomed to climbing to new and dangerous heights. Had one of us fallen from the top rung of the crude ladder, it would have saved the lives of many of the trout residing in Pot Creek.

All was well with the new house, the yard, and the giant tree until Mom began hearing strange noises emanating from the tree during the night. The noises both concerned her and stirred her imagination, causing her to eventually write a story about the old tree and what it might have witnessed in its early existence. She attempted to get the story published without success. Many years later, I found her correspondence with a potential publisher that indicated that she could have published her story if she had given in to the agents' wishes. The story involved her imagined history of the old tree. It was inspired by the haunting sounds of the old tree creaking and cracking in the wind during the night.

Eventually, the creaking noises raised a concern in Mom that the huge tree might fall on the house. She loved the tree as much as Sammy and I did. Nevertheless, she feared that it might fall. She knew that if it fell, the roof of our house would not stop the massive trunk from joining us in our beds. Finally, she told Dad the tree had to go. He agreed, and a team of loggers showed up while Sammy and I were at school. They took the tree down. Sammy and I knew it was going to happen. We were not happy, but our votes were not properly taken into account. No provision was given to compensate for us for our tree house. Afterward, Grandfather took us over to the sawmill where the large tree had been taken. He photographed us as we posed in the hollow trunk.

Our disappointment in losing the tree house did not last long. The stump was about four feet high, and it was hollow inside. Sammy and I noticed holes bored into the trunk. We began digging into one of the holes out to see what we might find. We were surprised to dig out a spent bullet. We followed more holes to their conclusion with the same result. It was not long before we had an entire bucket full of spent ammunition.

There had been an old fort across the main road from the logging camp. It had been built in 1850 and occupied until 1860. Apparently, the soldiers from the fort, and maybe others, had used the tree as a backstop for target practice. Or could it have been the location where firing squads did their work? We did not know.

As if the bullets were not enough, Sammy found the blade of a dagger buried deep within the hollow of the stump. We managed to dig it out. A short time later, Sammy gave the first demonstration of his sixth sense for finding artifacts. He was kicking around underneath the front gate in the fence around the yard when he managed to uncover the handle of the dagger. This old two-piece relic became a family heirloom.

Meanwhile, the bullets did not survive the logging-camp kids. Some of the older boys found our bucket of bullets and turned them into ammunition for their slingshots. Only the broken dagger survived until years later when another tragedy struck at the end Mother's life, and we lost most of the material items from our family history.

During our time at Pot Creek, Sammy would use his sixth sense to find many Native American artifacts. He and I would often walk into the woods together. If I were walking ahead, he might walk behind me and find one arrowhead or spear point after another that I had missed. Well, I am exaggerating the frequency of his finds a little... Okay, I am exaggerating it a lot. Nevertheless, I think I might have found one arrowhead during the entire time we lived at Pot Creek while Sammy gathered an impressive collection. This ability never left him.

*****

Sammy and I began fishing when we were very young. Pot Creek formed the northwestern boundary of our yard, and it was full of trout. During the spring runoff, it ran under our bedroom, allowing us to fish from our bedroom window. When we were very small, Mom required us to use bent safety pins instead of real fishhooks to catch fish. She deemed the barbed fishhooks to be too dangerous.

Mom didn't want us getting barbed hook caught in an ear, nostril, or some other body appendage.

Dad would eventually demonstrate such an event for us. It was a good learning experience. He was fly-fishing at the time, drying his fly by swinging the rod back and forth. He missed on one of the drying cycles, and the fly caught in his ear. Sammy and I were somewhat older at the time, but not experienced surgeons. Nevertheless, it was up to us to cut the errant lure out of Dad's ear. The only tool available was Dad's pocketknife. We did not want any part of cutting into Dad's ear. Nevertheless, he instructed us to dig in. Very tentatively, I began trying to dig the fishhook out. He coaxed me on. Soon, both Sammy and I were enjoying the mutilation—well, maybe not. By cutting away lots of flesh, we were able to remove the barbed hook along with a lot of blood. I had originally thought that taking the entire ear off would be easiest. It turns out that Dad did not want the "easiest" solution. He took the impromptu surgery like a fish, not uttering a single exclamation of pain. I would have at least let go with a few words referring to bull excrement and the mating practices and offspring of stray dogs. I know I am right because I would eventually get my chance to outdo everyone in the ability to express pain with volume if not with literary elegance. But this is for a future chapter.

It was not long after I began fishing before I began snagging trout using the bent safety pins. It did not take me long to conclude that I would never catch a fish even though I had snagged quite a few, thrilling them with a joyride on the improvised hook and a toss through the air to a different location in the fishing hole. Bait also slipped off the makeshift hooks rather easily. I gave quite a few fish a snack along with a joyride on a bent safety pin. It seemed like it was a long time before I finally caught one of the slippery, slimy water critters.

The big event happened when I was fishing in a relatively deep pool at a bend in the creek just behind our house. I was six years old at the time and still using a bent safety pin. I snagged a ten-inch trout and yanked hard on the fishing pole. My yank managed to toss the fish onto the bank before it could wriggle free of the improvised hook. Sammy was with me. He jumped on the fish, grasping it with both hands. I paid no attention to him or the fish. Instead, I went running upstream as fast as I could and crossed a bridge that led back to our house. I was so excited that I had finally caught a fish that I could barely keep from wetting my pants. When I got near our front door, I began screaming, "Mommy! Mommy! I caught a fish!" She came to the door and looked at me. She calmly asked, "Well, where is it?" I shouted, "Sammy has it!" Indeed, Sammy had picked up the fish and was running toward the house, holding it in front of his face with both hands. He did more to complete the catch than I had done to begin it. Nevertheless, I ate the first fish caught by my own hand for dinner that night.

Up to this time, Dad had been the primary supplier of game and fish. This didn't really change, but I pretended it did even though I was not yet threatening him for the title of "provider." Well, maybe I was never a threat, but I wanted to think that he was worried about me surpassing his skills in the fishing and hunting department. The truth is that he was in no danger of losing his title, and he never would be.

Fishing continued to be a main summertime activity at Pot Creek for as long as we lived there. Sammy and I had a ritual on the first day of fishing season. If it was during the week, we would get up early and go fishing for a couple of hours before we went to school. Fishing was also a big activity on the weekends. We often went with Dad to fish the beaver-dam ponds that were upstream of the logging camp. This was great fun, but for some reason, I tired of fishing as I got older. I still liked eating fish, but I lost much of the enthusiasm I had for catching them. I guess I never considered it to be a fair fight. Nevertheless, fish was a main menu item at our house for all the years we lived at Pot Creek.

One day near the site of the first fish adventure, Sammy and I were walking along on the other side of creek from the house. As we passed the first fish bend in the creek, we found a blue bird fluttering around on the ground. It was struggling because it had a broken wing. We went home and got a cardboard box from Mom and returned to the bird. We carefully picked it up and put it in the box. By the time we got back to our house with the box, Bluey had a name. We asked Mom if we could keep the little bird and make it well. She agreed, but we could tell that she was skeptical about the "making it well" part.

We kept Bluey in the box and gave the little bird water and various insects and worms to eat. Mom was very surprised that the little bird was eating the food we provided. After only a few days, Bluey seemed to be ready to attempt to fly. We took the little bird outside, hoping it would test its wings. Bluey responded quickly by flying into a tree in the front yard. And then the little bird flew back to us, allowing us to pick it up again. We left Bluey outside, thinking it would fly off to make its fortune. This did not happen. Bluey hung around the yard and would fly down to us from its favorite tree whenever we went outside. It liked to land on our shoulders. This went on for several days. Mom was amazed. Sammy and I were pleased with ourselves. Bluey was not afraid of our friends either. This seemed wonderful. Nevertheless, Bluey's lack of fear had a dark side.

One day, Sammy and I went outside and found Bluey in its favorite tree in the front yard. The little bird flew down to see us as usual, but when it was time to go back to the tree, the small bird must have seen something interesting to investigate in the grass. It flew down and landed in the grass without taking note of a fairly ferocious dog, Jiggs, from across the creek that had just entered the yard. The dog immediately pounced on Bluey and gave the unsuspecting little bird a fatal chomp. We had failed to teach Bluey that not all creatures are friendly. Preventing Jiggs from having Bluey for lunch was the best Sammy and I could do for the little bird. Well, we also got even with Jiggs in other ways over time.

It turns out that Bluey was not our last pet at Pot Creek. For some reason, a woman in Taos who bred Sealyham terriers gave us a throwaway puppy. She had a neighbor who bred cocker spaniels. Somehow, one of her Sealyhams had managed to get mixed up with one of her neighbor's scruffy cocker spaniels. Mom agreed to take one of the half-breeds off her hands.

Sammy and I had previously adopted a stray dog that we had named Bullet. However, Bullet did not stay with us very long. He was a bit wild and overprotective of baby sister Diana. Mom was afraid he would hurt someone. Shortly after Mom expressed her concern, Bullet disappeared. My guess is that Bullet took one of his namesakes in the head. It was probably from Dad's pistol.

Sammy and I were very happy to have a new dog. We came up with the name *Doty*. I don't remember where we got this name, but it stuck. Doty turned out to be very intelligent and a great companion for two boys. She would live for more than eleven years. She had one set of puppies. We easily found homes for all of them.

CHAPTER 8

School at Pot Creek

Trying once more, what is nothing? Does *nothing* exist anywhere? Is empty space nothing? Space expands? Can nothing expand? Can it be the subject of a sentence with an action verb? NO! Maybe…?

*****

I started to school at the Pot Creek School shortly after we arrived at the logging camp. The school had grades from pre-first through the eighth grade. Older students who continued in school, and many didn't, were bused to Taos to finish their educations.

I was six years old, and I had a broken arm in a cast on my first day of school. The cast started at my hand and went to the middle of my upper arm. The arm had been broken in a horrendous teeter-totter accident—well, it seemed horrendous to me. It was my little brother's fault, or so I claim. We tended to play rough. The "accident" happened on a makeshift teeter-totter at the Ranch. Grandfather had put it together for us using a one-inch by six-inch board placed across a sawhorse. We had not read all the safety dos and don'ts that were surely attached to the underside of the sawhorse. Both of us were attempting to bounce the other off the teeter-totter by coming down hard with our end of the board and letting it slam

72

into the ground with all the force we could muster. It turns out that this is a good way to learn to ride a bull if you don't have a real one handy.

It did not surprise me that Sammy won the contest. However, it did go several rounds before coming to a dramatic conclusion. Sammy came down hard with his end of the board, and when it hit the ground, I was catapulted into the air. I attempted to quickly learn to fly. Failing this, I managed to get turned upside down with my head leading the way toward a landing on the hard ground. I instinctively put my left arm in an attempt to protect my very special brain, or maybe I just didn't want to die upside down. Well, I might have been better off landing on my head. Anyway, my left hand contacted the hard ground first, snapping both arm bones clean in two (logging-camp English) just above the wrist. I got up crying and staggered to the nearby adobe house. Grandmother had already heard the commotion and met me at the door. She asked, "What happened?" I held my left arm up, showing her my hand and wrist dangling from the end of the arm. I cried, "Can't you see?" She had probably seen worse. Nevertheless, she mobilized Grandfather and put a sling around my neck to hold the hand and wrist roughly in place. Next, the four of us got into the 1947 Willys Jeep for the long drive to town over the very rough road. Well, I exaggerate. People called it a road, but it would not qualify as a road today in most of the civilized parts of the world.

It seemed to take forever to get to town, where there was a hospital. Grandfather drove, and Grandmother held me in her lap as I whimpered. My brother sat in the small jump seat in the rear of the jeep, wondering what the big deal was. I would guess that it took close to two hours to get to the hospital in human time. However, the pain had switched me to dog time, and it was well over two weeks before we arrived as far as I was concerned.

Once at the hospital, I remember being laid out on a table. Dr. Mortimer examined me and very quickly placed a rag over my nose. Okay, it probably wasn't a rag, but we are not talking Grey Sloan Memorial Hospital here. My first thought was that I should blow my nose into the rag, but before I could turn this thought into action, my arms transformed into giant Ferris wheels spinning into a dark, starry sky. I felt myself punch Dr. Mortimer in the face with the Ferris wheel that spun at the end of my broken arm. Stars exploded from his head in all directions… I don't remember anything else. I woke up with a cast on my arm, and Dr. Mortimer seemed to be fine. He didn't even have a bruise. Ether must be quite a hallucinogen. It was all magic to me.

The cast on my arm was barely dry when Mother took me to the Pot Creek School to register me for the first grade. I remember being very frightened when she told me to go and play with the other kids while she took care of my registration. One look at "the other kids" told me they were dangerous. I was right, but I did not know how right I was. They were Arkansas hillbillies whose fathers worked in the logging camp. They had been moved to New Mexico by Rounds and Porter. I stood on the back porch of the school and cried. Little did I know that I would soon be the ringleader of the Pot Creek Robin Hood Gang. Well, this was probably two years later. I did not rise to power before I knew who Robin Hood was. Many of the other kids never figured out the Robin Hood part. Nevertheless, the boys soon accepted me as their leader. I told them what Robin Hood would want us to do to the girls' makeshift playhouses. It mostly had to do with ransacking them, rendering them uninhabitable for their dollies. Well, it never took the girls long to recover from a raid, and I noticed that they seemed to like the attention I was giving them. I did not realize how much trouble this could get me into. Nevertheless, I was secretly trying to impress them, and I apparently did. By the time I was in the third grade, several were courting me and talking marriage. They were hillbillies after all. However, I did not want to settle down in a playhouse taking care of dollies. I had other plans.

At registration, Mother was told that I could not start in the first grade because I was required to have a year of pre-first to learn to speak English. Mother argued that I already knew how to speak English. I had even started picking up hillbilly English pretty well. The intent of the law was to teach English to the many Spanish-speaking children in New Mexico who only spoke Spanish at home. But wait! There were no Spanish-speaking kids at the Pot Creek school. Nevertheless, the rule applied to me and to the rest of the kids at Pot Creek who could not speak Spanish. It was a good rule. Almost no child at Pot Creek really spoke English either. They spoke hillbilly, and that was good enough reason to teach them some English before they tackled the first grade.

I spent a year in pre-first. Mrs. Torres, a native Spanish speaker, was my teacher. The first and second grades were in the same room as the pre-first. Mrs. Torres taught all three grades. Interestingly enough, she did not speak English very well, but this had no effect on her teaching ability. I thought she was wonderful, and I did very well during the two years I spent with her. However, there were some adventures along the way.

When I came home singing a naughty version of "Peter, Peter, Pumpkin Eater," Mother asked me where I had learned the song. I told her that I had learned it in school. This began a very interesting relationship between Mrs. Torres and Mom. Mother helped her to get the correct versions of the nursery rhymes. She also helped her with English. Mrs. Torres welcomed the help. In spite of the English problem, Mrs. Torres was a great teacher. To this day, if someone asks me who my favorite teacher was in school, I never hesitate. It was Mrs. Torres. She deserves as much or more credit than any other teacher for what I eventually did with my life. (I didn't even miss the dirty songs after Mother set Mrs. Torres straight.)

I adapted to school and learning very quickly. I not only learned my lessons; I learned what the first graders and the second graders were being taught at the same time. I truly loved Mrs. Torres and everything about school. Nevertheless, it is interesting that state law required me to be in pre-first for a year to learn English from a teacher who had not quite mastered the language herself. It didn't matter. Mrs. Torres allowed me to skip the second grade, catching me up with the normal schedule for the rest of my schooling.

When I got to the third grade, which was in a different room, I had Mrs. Cardenas. The room included third through sixth grade. I was also very fond of Mrs. Cardenas, but she got pregnant and was replaced by her husband when I was in the fourth grade. This seems like an underhanded way for a man to get a job. Anyway, Mr. Cardenas became my teacher.

Mr. Cardenas had two problems: One was that he was obsessed with his muscles, and the second was that he was not a great teacher. His most annoying habit was to sneak up behind a student working on a test or an assignment, and give a hard flick to the student's ear. Besides being annoying, the flick was very painful. There never seemed to be a good reason for the flick. Nevertheless, I was in full learning mode by then, and I learned to tolerate his muscle displays and flicks.

Again, I learned ahead of my grade by paying attention to the lessons given to the fourth, fifth, and sixth graders in addition to my third-grade lessons. This is where I became aware of my talent for arithmetic. I could do multiplication and division of large numbers like the sixth graders were learning before they had mastered these operations. I simply could not resist paying attention when these subjects were being taught.

My brother was two years younger than me, but Mother started him in school one year behind me since she knew he would also have to spend a year in pre-first to learn English. This worked fine until he made it through the first grade. At that point, someone must have decided, "This is one of the Dixon boys. They are smart, so they get to skip the second grade." Sammy skipped and ended up graduating from high school a year early. He was too mean to stay another year anyway. He loved looking for trouble, and he was an expert on finding it. But I am getting way ahead of the story. For now, let's just say my brother was something special. He was not only smart, but if you wanted trouble, he could fulfill all your wildest dreams. He and I would stay very close all the way through our years in school, and we are close now. We were even close in between when he found more trouble than any normal person could deal with, but again, I am getting ahead of myself.

At the Pot Creek School, I went from crying on the back porch of the school when Mom took me to register for the first grade to being a gang leader at the school. I had started reading books fairly early. In fact, I had people convinced that I was reading even before I started to school. Mom would read children's books to me, and without effort, I would memorize every word of the book so that I could sit and read it back to Mom or someone who didn't know I couldn't read. I got every word correct and turned the pages at the right times.

In about the third grade, Mom allowed me join two book clubs to begin getting books at home. One of them was a junior book club that provided the classics such as *Robin Hood* and *Black Beauty*. The very first book I read was *Black Beauty*, followed quickly by *Robin Hood*.

It was not long before I began putting my reading to practical use by starting a Robin Hood gang at school. None of the kids knew who Robin Hood was, but I forced my version of this classics character on them. Robin Hood and his merry men became Robin Hood and his merry hillbillies, destroyers of all things girly. The main purpose of the gang seemed to lie in terrorizing the girls by destroying the playhouses they built in the woods surrounding the school. It was a little frustrating to find that the girls seemed to enjoy the attention I was giving them. Nevertheless, I have to admit that I enjoyed getting their attention in return. I wouldn't have admitted this to anyone at the time.

It was not long before I was reading books from the Science Fiction Book Club. Mom had been concerned about me joining this book club. She had thought long and hard about it before she finally relented. After I began receiving books, I remember catching Mom reading one of them before she gave it to me. She admitted that she was just checking on what I was reading. I think she was worried about the language I might encounter. Dad cussed a lot, but he only used words like *damn* and *hell* with a well-placed *god* thrown in occasionally so that we would get exposed to a little religion. Some of the science-fiction books may have been a little raunchy for a boy my age. However, I had developed a clear interest in science, and the science fiction seemed to stoke my imagination. Mom did not want to turn this off. She allowed me to read all the books I ordered. It worked. My interest in science was cultivated. Nevertheless, Mother was right with her concern about the books. I did learn some new words that I could have taught to Dad to make his cursing a little more colorful.

It is always good to improve one's vocabulary. Eventually, I was able to teach the logging-camp kids what the words they used meant. I don't know if my lessons were appreciated. They certainly weren't always accurate.

The science-fiction books encouraged my interest in science, but they were not my first exposure to the subject. The first had taken place when my Grandfather told me about the atomic bomb when I was much too young to comprehend much of what he told me. Nevertheless, this discussion had both fascinated and frightened me. Even more interesting to me, there was talk of launching human beings into space. This was a major subject of the science-fiction books. I wanted to know more and to be a part of it. The Science Fiction Book Club stirred my imagination on these topics. In addition to the science fiction novels I received from the book club, there were books that included real science. These did not hold my interest as completely as the fiction, but I did learn some science from them. One such book had the title *Satellite*. It was mostly technical, and I admit that I never read very far in it before trading it for some fiction. However, I got enough out of it to begin appreciating real scientific facts even though I seemed to need a story for most of my reading. Books such as *Vanguard to Venus* satisfied my requirement.

*****

The Pot Creek School was located on the western edge of the land grant that was being logged, lying just south of the present-day location of Southern Methodist University at Taos. I suspect that Rounds and Porter had something to do with locating and building the school. It was a little red schoolhouse with four rooms. The pre-first through the second grade were in one room with one teacher, third through sixth grades were in a second room, and seventh and eighth grades were in the third room. The fourth room was a lunchroom.

There were no defined limits to the school grounds. The Little Rio ran north behind the school. Pot Creek ran into the Little Rio from the east downstream of the school. During recesses and lunch breaks, we played in the woods on both sides of the Little Rio, wandering as far from the school as we thought we could get away with. We were often in some trouble when we strayed too far to get back in time after a lunch period or a recess. However, this trouble was never very serious. We were hillbillies after all. What would you expect?

I have already mentioned the girl's favorite activity was building playhouses in the woods. Meanwhile, the boys didn't see the point in the playhouses or the girls...or so we claimed. Yet I admit to spending a good deal of energy trying to impress those girls by acting like a tough customer, a typical male mistake. I simply did not yet understand that you don't tear stuff up to impress the female side of humanity. Well, maybe you do. It seemed to work. No wonder males behave the way they do. Tearing stuff up seems to impress anyone with a maturity problem. Anyway, the girls were not really afraid of us, but we liked to think they were. Some of them seemed to take too much note of me. Strangely, this made me feel that I was on the right track. I enjoyed their attention, but I was particular. I had my eye on two girls. One was Judy Jones. Her dad ran the sawmill. The other was Gail Lambert. Her father was a logger.

I have to admit that I didn't figure out how the girl thing worked until much later, if then. Nevertheless, I had preteen fantasies of riding a horse into the mountains with Judy Jones in the saddle behind me. I had no idea what I would do with her when the horse got tired and we had to stop. I guess that would have been up to Judy—or maybe the horse.

As a preteen boy, I secretly imagined rescuing preteen girls from dangers that were lurking almost everywhere. At least I hoped such dangers lurked everywhere. Well, it was mostly just Judy who I rescued. The rest of the girls were on their own. It was not so clear what the step following the imagined rescue would be. Roy Rogers or Gene Autry would sing a song in that situation, but singing seemed silly to me. I was more into pistols than guitars. Also for some reason, my fantasies had more to do with the horse than with the girl. It's okay for cowboys to be that way, isn't it? Maybe I shouldn't admit this. Anyway, the horse was later replaced by a fast car. These fantasies almost completely diverted my mind from thoughts of nuclear war as long as I saw Judy every day.

Clearly, I was too big for my britches at Pot Creek School, but I was never in real trouble. I was rather brilliant for a hillbilly, and the teachers took note of it. Sammy was more mischievous, but he was in the same league as me for intelligence. We mostly tried to hide our intelligence when we were around the other kids because being smart was not a desirable attribute to have in a logging camp. We managed to do fairly well for imitation hillbillies. Nevertheless, we continued to be called city hicks from time to time in spite of making an exceptional effort to become country hicks.

I had a friend, David, who attempted to teach me how to be a country hick. I paid close attention when he told me how to make the transition. It seemed that the main requirement for becoming a country hick was to fill your pockets with junk. Most any kind of hardware would do including pocketknives, rocks, and mysterious leftover parts from a junk pile or garage—anything that would barely fit in the pocket of a tattered pair of blue jeans. Also one had to leave junk lying around in one's yard. I knew that Mom and Dad would not agree to junk in the yard, so I resigned myself to carrying junk in my pockets. I was not very convincing. Part of the problem was that I could not see any practical point to filling my pockets with junk. Well, maybe the hillbillies were smarter than me.

Even though Sammy and I never quite made the grade, we managed to find ways to be engaged with the logging camp kids, and in the end, we were accepted by them.

CHAPTER 9

Mom at Pot Creek

What is space? What is outside of space? Does "outside of space" even exist? If so, how do you get there from here? Can we ask questions about it? Only if we are not afraid of a brain hemorrhage.

*****

Mother attracted all kinds of attention in the logging camp. My friends would often comment on how pretty Mom was. It was apparent that many men found her attractive. The milkman would usually make our house his last stop so that he could sit and chat with Mom as they drank coffee together. He would often stay quite a long time.

Somewhat surprisingly, Mother included a priest among her male friends. His first name was Frank, and he was a priest at the Ranchos de Taos church for a while. She had met him on the ham radio before he was transferred to the Ranchos church. He was invited to eat trout or venison at our house from time to time. I don't know if he ever visited Mother at times when none of the rest of us were around. I don't think this could have happened. However, she did visit him at his house near the Church.

The Ranchos de Taos Church was one of the tourist attractions near Taos. It was advertised as one of the oldest churches in the United States. It was built in the late 1700s. However, the main attraction in the church when we lived in Pot Creek was a painting of Jesus that glowed in the dark. In addition, a dark cross appeared above one of Christ's shoulders when the lights were turned off. It was claimed that no one understood why it glowed in the dark. The story was that the artist who painted it went crazy after he first saw the painting glowing in the dark. The old church with the painting was a favorite place for us to take people who visited us at Pot Creek.

Mr. Rounds was always welcome at our house. When he visited us, he often brought dignitaries from around the world with him to eat trout or venison that Mother had prepared. I only can imagine what they thought as they sat down to dine in our kitchen table in our very modest logging-camp shack. Well, it was almost a house due to all of Dad's work and Mother's demands of the lumber company. Anyway, it must have been quite a dining experience for them. One such guest I remember in particular was the deposed Shah of one of the Middle Eastern countries. Mr. Rounds seemed to know everyone.

Another guest that Mr. Round's brought to our house was Dr. Fred Wendorf, an archaeologist. He had come to Pot Creek at the request of Mr. Rounds to investigate the site for its archaeological prospects. Dr. Wendorf became a friend of the family.

Mr. Rounds knew he always had an open invitation to bring people to our house. If it seems unusual that Mr. Rounds would visit the home of the head mechanic in a logging camp with guests from around the world, it was. He had recognized that we were not a typical logging-camp family. Well, it was really Mother who was not typical. Mr. Rounds' distinguished friends were always impressed by her. Her intelligence combined with her looks always commanded considerable attention, and some of the time, she handled it just fine. She was perfect during our years at Pot Creek.

CHAPTER 10

Life in the Logging Camp

If space expands, what does it expand into? Does space expand into "nothing"? Is nothing outside of space and time? Does this question make sense? Do not think carefully about this question unless you are willing to risk a fall off the edge of...sanity.

*****

One of my best friends at Pot Creek was Joe White. Joe was the only one in his family who was not retarded to some extent. He was a good student. Nevertheless, I was never allowed to spend the night in Joe's tar paper shack. Joe's older brother would one day drive our school bus to Taos. The rest of Joe's family story was not happy. It involved incest and inbreeding. I was not aware of this until much later. I only knew that I was not allowed in Joe's shack or in many of the other dwellings in the logging camp. Nevertheless, Joe was allowed to come to our house. Mother preferred to have our social activities in the logging-camp play-out where she could see us. I understand why this was so now, but I only had vague notions about it then.

Although Sammy and I interacted with most of the other kids at Pot Creek, we primarily played with the Parrett, Jones, and Fisher kids. *Play* had a rather broad definition as far as the kids were concerned. It accommodated activities such as rock fights or BB gun wars. These were conducted without official sanctions from our parents and ended without treaties. They just broke out, and usually, there were no clear winners. The truth is that most of the kids got along fairly well even though bleeding was part of the culture.

While the kids socialized through rock fights and junk collecting, some of the women in the logging camp did one another's hair. Also there were Friday-night card games. However, these gatherings only included the Dixons, Joneses, and Parretts. The corresponding kids also came together at these affairs and usually played outside in the dark. We did not try very hard to stay out of trouble. However, no one seemed to care much about what we did. We all survived without too much bleeding.

*****

Dad did not like music. I think he may have been tone-deaf. If he came home and the radio was on with music playing, he would say something like "Turn that goddamned noise off!" Mother would comply. However, Mom had a record player, and she had some records. The two of us would sometimes play records when Dad was at work. She had a number of albums created by artists such as Frankie Laine and Glenn Miller. Mom had been quite a singer after all. These music sessions only included the two of us. Through them, I discovered that I really liked music. It was something that Mom and I shared in secret. Well, it was not really a secret. The record player was sitting right out in the open. It just couldn't be used when Dad was home. Listening to the music made me decide that I wanted to be a musician one day.

Mother would also listen to news and other programs on the radio from time to time. I remember hearing westerns on the radio, and during one episode of *The Lone Ranger*, I had to ask Mom what getting "beat up" meant. I imagined bloody bones lying all over the place after such an event, but Mom assured me that it was not that bad. Worse things could happen to me than getting beat up. She would turn out to be right about the worse things.

It was not long before I would learn more about fighting, shooting, and getting beat up when television invaded the logging camp. The Jones family was the first to get a television set. They invited the Dixons and the Parretts over on the first Saturday evening after their purchase to watch *The Hit Parade*. The reception was not great. Nevertheless, television amazed me. I had been to movies in a theatre or drive-in a few times, and I can remember wishing that I could have a small theatre at home that I could watch. I had heard about television before and had even seen one, but I had never seen one turned on.

It did not take long for the Parretts and the Dixons to follow the Jones' example by getting television sets. For the Dixons, it happened one day when I was at school. As I walked home, I noticed some men working to erect an antenna on top of our house. We were getting a television! It was a surprise. After it was set up, we could almost get three channels. The reception was poor, and it took a lot of fiddling with the antenna on top of the house to get anything to show up on a snowy screen. As time went on, the reception improved. There was talk of how the signal from Albuquerque had to bounce off of several mountains to reach us in our little mountain valley. We certainly had no direct line of sight to Albuquerque. Nevertheless, we could watch the three network channels—NBC, CBS, and ABC—some of the time.

Sammy and I watched *Dick Bills* and *Andy's Gang*, as well as *Sky King*, *My Friend Flicka*, and *Lassie*. It was great! Dick Bills was a young cowboy musician who hosted the kid's show. He played guitar and sang cowboy or country-Western songs on the program. Glen Campbell, whose fame lay in the future, was one of the musicians in his band at the time. Sammy and I also liked to watch cartoons. However, we were more serious about programs such as *Combat*. I still don't understand the attraction that such programs had for us. We didn't know it at the time, but we were watching Sammy's future. He loved the program.

Meanwhile, Dad was settling in front of the television every evening to watch Westerns such as *Gunsmoke, Have Gun—Will Travel,* and many more. We all liked Westerns with lots of action that mainly consisted of gunfights and barroom brawls. Before television, Dad liked to read paperback Westerns. I don't know if Dad ever read another book after we got the television.

Not everyone in the logging camp had television sets although it wasn't long before many did. Dad's many paperback Westerns occupied a shelf in the living room where they were seldom disturbed after the television arrived. This led to an amusing incident.

It was common for kids from the camp to come to the door and ask if they could borrow a cup of sugar or a cup of flour. There was a culture that people would lend or give others what they needed. Nevertheless, Mom would have never sent me to a neighbor's house to ask for a cup of anything.

One day, a neighbor girl, Patsy, who lived up the hill behind our house came to the door and asked if she could borrow a book because her father was sick and needed something to entertain himself while he couldn't go to work. Patsy's dad knew we probably had books even though reading material was rare in the logging camp. Mom retrieved one of Dad's paperback Westerns off the shelf and gave it to her. A short time later, she brought the book back and asked Mom if she had a book with pictures in it because her dad couldn't read. Mom managed to find something to give to her.

I was not fond of Patsy's father. He had traumatized me when Patsy had invited me to their house to see their bunnies. I was always eager to see bunnies, so I had gone up the road to their house. The rabbits were in hutches. I wanted to pet one of them, so Patsy went in the house and brought her father out. He opened the hutch, grabbed the rabbit I had fallen in love with by the hind legs, yanked it out of the hutch, and swung it as hard it as he could into the side of the house. The rabbit died with a dull thunk. The old man said something about eating the rabbit for dinner. If ever a kid were traumatized, I was. Apparently, I got over it without any fancy pills or special discussions with people wearing suits and ties. I still loved rabbits, but I didn't care too much for Patsy's dad.

Baseball on television provided another avenue for Mother and I to bond. As soon as we had television, Mom found baseball on it. Our reception was poor, but I could see it well enough to understand the game once Mom provided some explanation. At World Series time, Mom would watch the games and keep score on a tablet while I was at school. When I got home, she would show me the score sheet and explain what had happened in the game. It was not long before I was a real baseball fan. Mom no longer had to provide a full explanation to go with the score sheet.

I took my understanding of the game to school and explained to the other kids how baseball worked. I am not certain they appreciated my game summaries, but we did play baseball at school; and it was not long before they were asking me questions about the game. I had set myself up as one of those experts that everyone trusts even though they don't really know what they are talking about. It is likely that I spread much misinformation. Nevertheless, I was accepted as the expert. I am still a baseball fan and would like to think that I understand more of the subtleties of the game than I really do.

Dad did not care about baseball at all. Nevertheless, he saw that I had a big interest in the game. Sammy was interested also, but I was the one who was most serious about the game. Mom and Dad bought us some kid ball gloves, and we had access to bats at school. Dad decided to get more involved. He did it in the best way possible; he made a baseball bat that was the perfect size for me. I think he might have turned the bat down on a lathe. Now I wish I knew what happened to that bat. I suspect it disappeared at Pot Creek because I have no memories of the bat after I outgrew it. Nevertheless, it was one of the best gifts I received as a child.

It was not long before we had "real" bats and gloves and were playing with the kids at school. I loved the game even though I have to admit that I never had any special talent for it even though you might hear me claim I was not bad at it either. Well, I was very good at chasing down fly balls, and I liked to play first base. I had taken note of the fact that not many kids hit balls to that side of the infield since most of us were right-handed. Furthermore, it did not take long for me to learn that most balls hit on the ground on our crude field took bad hops to the chops just as one bent down to field them. I wasn't into facial bleeding and dental rearrangements. The first-base position minimized blood and tooth loss.

*****

Mother and the other wives of the social "upper crust" of the camp often got together to socialize and to cut one another's hair. The "upper crust" was more crust than upper. The group consisted of the wives of the foremen who ran the different operations in the logging camp. The three wives were Johnny Fe Jones, Ruby Parrett, and Mom. Johnny Fe's husband, Red, supervised the sawmill, while Scott Parrett supervised the logging operations; and Dad ran the mechanical shop. Dad only had one or two people working for him in the shop at any given time even though he was in high demand to keep a large number of trucks and specialized vehicles running.

The men in this group joined the women in the social activities on Friday nights when the Parrett, Jones, and Dixon adults would gather to play canasta while the corresponding kids played outside in the dark, completely unsupervised. The men would usually watch the Friday-night fights either before or after the canasta game. The kids involved were Jackie, Judy, and John Clifford Jones; Theldon, Larry, and Roy Dean Parrett; and Roger and Sammy Dixon. Little Diana Dixon and Mike Parrett were too young to join the fray created by this group of rowdies.

We often played along the banks of the creek, rode bicycles in the dark, and did things that would often lead to spilled blood. Trouble was a familiar location for us. Nevertheless, the consequences of arriving there were never too serious because our parents were busy playing cards, paying little attention to us unless there was serious bleeding or bones sticking out through our clothing. We felt it was best for them and for us that they not know what we were doing.

Sammy and I got caught straying too far afield on one of those card-party evenings. As a result, the next week, we were left at home with Jackie Jones as a babysitter. She may have been older, but she was not up to the job. Sammy and I did not do well with babysitters.

We had a special technique for dealing with them. We quickly got into a rather violent fight that Jackie could not stop. It terrified her. She didn't know that we were just playing much as we often did. Getting bruised, cut, and a little dismembered was business as usual for us. Well, maybe the "dismembered" part is a bit of an exaggeration, but unless blood was spilled, we did not consider the fight worthwhile. A little later in life, Sammy and I would occasionally fight for show. It would usually draw a crowd. We would bleed a little, and our clothing would usually be torn to shreds. This often got us in trouble with our authoritarian parents. Well, Mom was usually the one to discipline us unless we had managed to specifically irritate Dad. Otherwise, he mostly encouraged our behavior. We continued this behavior until we were nearing high-school age. At that point, Sam and I both realized that I could get killed in these frays. He didn't want that. Oh yeah, I didn't want it either.

The Fishers never really belonged in the Pot Creek social group mainly because Mr. Fisher drove a "big rig," delivering lumber to places such as the Air Force Academy. He was gone much of the time, and the Fisher family never really clicked with the Joneses, the Parretts, or the Dixons. However, Sammy and I often played with Danny, Ronnie, and their older brother Butch. They were nuts about baseball just like I was. Butch was fourteen or fifteen years old during this time and could already throw a curveball. I was one of the few eight- or nine-year-olds that got to try to hit a big curveball. This is when I first experienced the sound of a true "wiff."

We spent hours playing home-run derby since there was often not enough of us to play a real game. We would try to hit the ball over some stacks of lumber located right across the road from the Fisher's house. Clearing the lumber stacks from the Fisher's front yard counted as a home run. Hitting a passing truck or forklift meant running for cover in the woods in the back of the Fisher's house and spending some time picking wildflowers. Several years later, I heard that Butch had signed to play minor league baseball, but I never heard from or about him again.

There was an African American contingent at Pot Creek. They were also from Arkansas. *Colored* or *Negro* were the polite terms to designate the African Americans in those days, but neither was used very often in the logging camp. The term *African American* was unheard of at that time. When a respectful term was used, it was probably at our house. Mother made certain we understood and showed respect for everyone.

Mother had Mrs. Biddle, an African American woman, clean our house from time to time. The two of them became friends, and Mother started doing Mrs. Biddle's hair. Sammy and I were under instructions not to tell Dad about the hair business. It was common for Johnie Fay or Ruby Parrett to get their hair done by Mom, and they returned the favor; but this was a select group. Mrs. Biddle never made it into the group. She was Mom's friend, and that was it.

Mom allowed us to go to the Biddle's house once in a while to play with Ronnie, who was about our age. This had to be kept from Dad. However, Ronnie was allowed to come and play in our yard from time to time, and this was not a secret. I did not understand the rules, but I abided by them using Mom's exceptions as necessary.

On my visits to Ronnie's house, I could not help but notice how clean and orderly Ronnie's house was compared to those of my other logging-camp friends. Most of the houses were really just shacks inside and out. Many were covered by tar paper on the outside, and they stunk like the lower bowels of hell on the inside. I don't know for certain why, but I think it may have been due to the vittles they ate. I don't know what the vittles were, but I did not want to eat anything that smelled anything like vittles apparently smelled. Many of my friends claimed that all they ate were beans and taters. I ate lots of beans and taters that did not smell the way those houses smelled. Something else must have been going on to create the smell, and I did not care to know what it was.

The hillbillies did most of the logging, running special equipment and driving the logging trucks. They were good at it. My friend Joe's father was called a mule skinner. He was responsible for getting trees dismembered into logs and moved from where they were cut to a location where they could be loaded onto a logging truck. Moving the logs to a logging road was probably done by mules in a distant past, but at Pot Creek, special equipment was usually used to "skid" the logs. These jobs were dangerous because one could easily be killed by a falling tree or a runaway log. This did not happen very often.

The African American men got the most dangerous jobs in terms of number of accidents. They mostly worked at the sawmill and planer. Boards were fed into the planer by hand. It was less likely that one would be killed working at the sawmill and planer, but more likely that a hand and perhaps part of an arm would go missing.

One of my dad's fishing buddies, Lonnie, was an African American. He had his hand and part of one of his arms missing. (They would have both gotten a laugh out of me calling Lonnie an African American.) He and my Dad would stand outside of the yard in our driveway and talk about fishing, making plans for where to go next. There were several good trout streams in the area including Pot Creek and the Little Rio. They both knew the trout streams well, and they liked to compare notes and plan ahead for where they might go next.

One day, I asked Mom why Lonnie never came into our yard. She said something like "Oh, it's just stupid! It's the way your father was brought up." He was raised in the culture that existed in Texas and Oklahoma at the time. As it turned out, our family was subjected to this culture. Our culture was the reason we were not allowed to go into the houses of any of our African American friends. Meanwhile, Mother's family had no such notions concerning African Americans. In point of fact, there were very few African American families in northern New Mexico at the time. Consequently, there was very little experience to determine how they should be treated.

*****

My first experiences with religion occurred at Pot Creek. A Baptist preacher showed up at the logging camp and offered to conduct church services for us. Since we had no church, services were held in the living rooms of either the Jones's or the Parrett's. Most residents of the logging camp did not participate. Occasionally, when weather conditions were pleasant, the services were held outside right across the creek from our house. Folding chairs served as pews, and we got a good preaching, too, in the bright sunshine. However, weather, especially in winter, meant that the services had to move inside, alternating between the Joneses and the Parretts.

Dad was not crazy about having services at our house, and he never attended any of the church services. It was fairly clear that the Dixons really didn't want to be saved. Apparently, we were heathens. However, heathens like the social aspects of getting together that going to church provides. And good church members liked trying to "save" the heathens. So my family, minus Dad, were often part of the group.

The aspect of the services that I remember most was that a hymn was sung at the end of each service asking us to come forward and give our hearts to Jesus. For some reason, I had no inclination to do this, and I never gave in. Well, I think being taught to think by Grandfather had something to do with my reluctance to join the church, or maybe it was because it just did not feel right. All the Jones and Parrett kids were eventually "saved." After each one had given away the main component of their circulatory system, they were scheduled to be baptized. By an agreement arranged by the preacher with the Baptist church in Taos, the baptism process was carried out at the church after the regular Sunday services were con- cluded and all the regular members of the Taos church had departed. There may have also been some baptisms at Pot Creek in the Creek.

When carried out in Taos, the baptism procedure occurred in a pool of water located behind the altar of the church. The person to be baptized and the preacher waded into the water; each was wearing a loose-fitting gown. The preacher laid the person being baptized back into the water and held them under for a seemingly long time before returning them to the world of air with their souls cleansed. This was another important factor in my resistance to giving away a major internal organ to save something I could not put my finger on. What if the preacher did not pull me up in time? Instead of being baptized, I would have been terrorized and then drowned. Anyway, baptism did not look like something I wanted to have done to me. I became the only holdout when Sammy finally gave in one Sunday.

I apparently liked being a heathen, and Mother was fine with my choice.

During the summers, the Baptist preacher would organize a vacation Bible school for the Pot Creek kids. It was held in the woods near the creek. I remember enjoying the activities, which mostly consisted of painting ceramic figures and making a few other craft items.

The biggest influence on my religious beliefs came from Mom. She read us Bible stories when we were young, and she would ask us to think about them. I remember her asking why one particular group people with one particular religion would be right and all the others wrong. I thought this was a good question. The answer was obvious to me. They were all wrong, but I don't think I ever said this. There was just no reasonable path that led me to a conclusion that any one set of beliefs not based on observations and reason are any better than any other set of beliefs also not based on observations and reason. I put my faith in observation and reason. Of course, I didn't put it that way when I was ten years old. I had not yet thought much about the issue. Clearly, Mom influenced me to be more of a thinker than a believer. Nevertheless, she thought we should learn the lessons from the Bible stories because they were good lessons, and she encouraged us to think about them. Consequently, I felt encouraged to think and make up my own mind, which was what Mom was really teaching us. Sammy, and especially Diana, were not ready to think about such things. In the end, Diana came to much different conclusions than Sam and I did.

CHAPTER 11

The Pot Creek School Closes

Stuff: atoms, molecules, rocks, dirt, water, amoeba...elephants, whales, human beings? What is going on? Where did it all come from? Who would believe it? Not the elephants or whales.

*****

When I was in the middle of the fourth grade, the Pot Creek school was closed, and our parents were told that we would attend school in Talpa. Talpa was a relatively small Hispanic community lying between Pot Creek and Taos. Nevertheless, the school was somewhat larger than the Pot Creek school, and like the Pot Creek school, it only went through the eighth grade. To make the school closing even more interesting, when the plan was announced, a rumor was passed around at Pot Creek. The rumor indicated that if the Pot Creek kids showed up at the Talpa School, they would be severely beaten and maybe worse. Many of the Pot Creek kids and parents were not bright enough to be frightened by this threat. However, there were enough concerned parents to make certain this threat was not carried out.

When the time came for us to enroll for school in Talpa, all the Pot Creek kids got on the school bus with instructions from our parents not to get off the bus in Talpa. Our parents knew that the bus would go onto Taos where it normally delivered the high school students from Pot Creek. It is likely that the only kid disappointed by these instructions was my little brother, who was already beginning to enjoy a good fight. The plan called for us to attempt register for school in Taos.

A rather short caravan of parents, including Mom, followed the school bus on what was to be our first day at the Talpa school. The plan worked. We were not forced to get off the bus in Talpa, and the Taos School system allowed us register. Consequently, I attended school in Taos from the middle of the fourth grade through part of the eighth grade. Sammy did the same a year behind me, ending his four years in the middle of the seventh grade.

I had to make adjustments to get along in the Taos elementary schools. I was no longer a big fish in a small pond. Instead, I was one of the kids from the hillbilly logging camp. Sammy and I reacted to the change in very different ways. I focused on schoolwork and kick-ball, while Sammy looked for trouble at every opportunity. He found plenty. He was usually outnumbered, but this didn't seem to help his opponents much. I once had to watch from the school bus as a group of young thugs sicced a dog on him. He got chewed up a little, but I think the dog got the worst of the deal as the rest of the group scattered. He was okay, but his clothing suffered some damage. He had some explaining to do when he got home. He never outgrew his aggressive approach to life, which led to even more blood, bruises, and clothing to explain.

My fourth-grade classroom in Taos was located in an old bar-racks that had been put in place while a new building was being pre-pared. I got along well in Taos after a rather quick adjustment. The schoolwork was easy for me as it had been at Pot Creek. Outside, I learned to play kickball, a form of baseball in which we kicked a large ball instead of batting. It was fun, and I had a very strong kicking leg.

The next year in fifth grade was even better. I had Mrs. Merton as a teacher. She was a character in the true-life book *And Now Miguel* that later became a movie. She read the book to us in class. It fascinated me. I did well in the fifth grade. I like to think that the teachers in Taos were surprised that some of the Pot Creek kids were good students. I never heard about any of us being mistreated in the classroom.

I joined the school band in the fifth grade. I decided that I wanted to play the saxophone. Mom and Dad managed to buy me an alto saxophone to give me a good start. Meanwhile, Sammy decided that he wanted to play the trombone, but this choice was doomed to failure. His arms were not long enough to slide the trombone through the entire range of notes. He changed to the drums. I don't think Mom and Dad were completely happy with this choice. Loud banging could really interfere with Dad's television Westerns. Nevertheless, everyone knew that Sammy liked to bang on things. Drums were a natural for him, and he became an excellent drummer by respecting boundaries imposed by Dad's television Westerns.

The next year, I had Mrs. Madrid in sixth grade. She was the most serious and stern teacher I had experienced up to that time. She was not impressed by me, and I had similar feelings for her. By this time, I had read enough science and science fiction to think I knew all about science. Mrs. Madrid seemed to have her own version of science. I made a big mistake by attempting to correct and fix her version too often. She did not appreciate my assistance. I did well on tests and assignments, but she gave me a D on my report card in science. I should not have been surprised, but I was very naive. I could not believe that she would almost fail me in science, my favorite subject. I was crushed. When I asked her why she had given me a D, she told me that it was because my notebook was messy. I had to concede this point. I had a very messy notebook. It was a good lesson. I understood that my poor grade was the result of my frequent corrections during our science lessons. My corrections were most likely valid, but it didn't matter. I should not have embarrassed her in front of the class. I had learned a good lesson. I would never again show up a teacher because I happened to know something he or she didn't know.

The next year in the seventh grade, I had Mrs. Delgado for science. She managed to undo any harm that Mrs. Madrid had done to me the previous year. She was reserved and serious. Furthermore, she really understood science and knew how to communicate it. She encouraged and inspired me. My science fire was burning brightly again. Too bad I was just becoming a teenager, a condition leading to many competing conflagrations. In my case, these blazes overcame my love of science—for a while. To make matters worse, I was about to experience another big adventure that would set my science back for a few more years, but I am getting ahead of myself again.

Over the years, I developed many friendships with the kids at Taos. Among the memorable friendships was one that I developed with two boys from the Taos Pueblo when I was in the seventh grade. Their names were Tyrone and Herman. I don't know why they took an interest in me, but we developed a somewhat unusual relationship. They both recognized that I could help them with science and other subjects that were difficult for them. However, they also liked to beat me up. The "beating up" was not very serious, but it got a little tedious after a while.

Tyrone was huge and overweight. Herman was much smaller than me. Tyrone would hold me while Herman worked me over. My brother and I tended to draw a lot more blood when we got into one of our fights. Anyway, I was very interested in them and their culture. I wanted to learn more about it, but they were very secretive. Nevertheless, I was able to determine that *Tyrone* and *Herman* were not their real names. They just made those names up for the purpose of going to school. I wanted to know their real names, but they would not divulge them.

I have a memory of walking along the Rio Pueblo with them at the Pueblo. I don't think it is a real memory. More likely, it is a dream. Anyway, as we walked, they told me their names translated into English. I believed them because Herman's name was Beaver and Tyrone was Little Bear. In the end, they confessed that they had just made the names up to make me happy. Apparently, their real names were still secret—even in my dream.

CHAPTER 12

Archaeology at Pot Creek

Matter: Atoms: protons, neutrons, electrons, quarks, gluons; Forces: gravitational, weak, electromagnetic, strong: Force mediators—gravitons, gauge bosons, photons, gluons. Stir briskly together with a dash of space-time, and BOOM! You have a universe.

*****

During our time at Pot Creek, Mr. Rounds, who had purchased the old Spanish land grant to log, became interested in the history of his property. There were clues that there had been a significant presence of early native people in the area. Pottery shards were scattered all over the site, giving Pot Creek its name. Mr. Rounds must have also suspected that there was even more history buried on the site. Consequently, he invited Dr. Fred Wendorf, an archaeologist at Southern Methodist University, to have a look. At the time, some of the history was already known. For example, there had been an old army encampment, Fort Burgwin, right across Highway 3 from the main entrance to the logging camp. Nevertheless, there was no visible evidence that there had been any structure at that location.

Dr. Wendorf and his team began by uncovering the foundation of Fort Burgwin. The old fort had existed for a short time around 1850 to protect settlers in the area from aggressive Utes and Jicarilla Apaches. The fort laid on a side branch of the Santa Fe trail sometimes taken to avoid encounters with the native tribes that were growing tired of the invasive species. The old fort was reconstructed to become the archaeological headquarters at the site. Soon thereafter, work was underway to uncover an ancient pueblo across the creek and up the hill from our house. It had been completely buried by the shifting sands of time. Only a somewhat suspicious mound gave away its location before the digging began. The experienced archaeologists probably knew what they would find under the mound. However, none of us living at Pot Creek had even wondered why the mound was there or what might be buried beneath it. It was just a natural hill to us.

As the archaeologists dug into the mound, they began to reveal the walls of the old Pueblo. In addition, they also began uncovering a large number of pit houses in the area surrounding the Pueblo. According to the archaeologists, these dwellings were apparently occupied at the same time as the Pueblo.

When all the digging began, Mom got a job cleaning pottery shards and other artifacts. Occasionally, Sam and I would help her. It was fascinating work. What was even more interesting was watching the old pueblo and pit houses slowly emerge from the earth as digging proceeded. Graduate students were doing much of the hard labor under a hot sun. Sam and I made a little money selling cold drinks to the overheated slave labor.

This was my first encounter with graduate students. I did not understand why they were being punished so. Being a graduate student means agreeing to do what amounts to slave labor in return for a degree given at the end of the ordeal. I would one day understand the plight of graduate students much better. Fortunately, I would choose a field that allowed me to be an indoor slave who didn't have to dig under a hot sun. I admit that I am exaggerating the plight of a graduate student somewhat. However, it is true that graduate students like to claim they are slaves. It is a gross misuse of the term.

Even though our primary interest was our cold-drink business, we were also fascinated by what the archaeologists were uncovering.

They were often happy to take a break to tell and show us what they were finding. We were mainly interested in seeing the human remains that they unearthed in the old Pueblo. They also found human remains in the pit houses that were scattered around the area of the pueblo. If the excavations were happening in the present day, would they have disturbed those bones, which were sacred to the native people?

It was all incredibly interesting to Sammy and me even though the graduate students never had much time to spend explaining their finds to us. It didn't matter. We already knew that we lived in a special area for early Native Americans, and we felt close to them when we (mostly Sammy) would find arrowheads and other artifacts. I can only hope that we demonstrated the proper respect for the items in addition to the items the archaeologists found. We both felt we had a mystical connection to the land that we were fortunate enough to be born into. Well, Sammy was born in Texas. Nevertheless, it seemed that the gods had already forgiven him for this most unfortunate event by enabling an uncanny talent in him for finding Native American artifacts. In the end, he proved to be a better New Mexican than me.

From my point of view, one of the most puzzling questions arising from the discovery of the old pueblo and its neighboring pit houses was what had happened to the people who had lived in these dwellings. From the location and disposition of the skeletons, it almost looked like something drastic had happened. I was just a kid, so I did not discuss the matter with any of the graduate students or archaeologists. Nevertheless, I was curious. Why had these people disappeared, leaving their remains scattered haphazardly in the rooms of their pueblo?

Much later in my life, I stopped by the SMU Archaeological Center located at the site of Fort Burgwin and was able to get a paper written on the old Pueblo. It confirmed a suspicion that I had in my head, possibly put there by one of the graduate students or archaeologists. I wanted to believe that I heard it from some of my friends at the Taos Pueblo, but this was most likely a romantic notion. I had come to believe that the people from the old Pueblo had moved over the mountains lying south of Pot Creek where they established the Picuris Pueblo. In fact, the paper I retrieved confirmed that this is what happened. For some reason, it seemed important, and it felt good to finally have the answer to this question. However, all the mystery did not disappear. Why did they move, leaving their remains scattered about? Could it be that the pit houses were abandoned when someone died in them? Is it possible that the same rule applied in the rooms of the Pueblo? This might explain to move to the Picuris Pueblo.

Mr. Rounds was also interested in the more recent history of the old Spanish land grant. He had become familiar with Mother's considerable abilities, and he asked her to research and write up the history of his property. This request was right in Mother's wheelhouse. She loved history and could not help but write. Writing is clearly in the family genes. This was a writing assignment with purpose. Admittedly, an assignment that requires discipline is a little difficult for our family genes. Nevertheless, Mother wasted no time starting the research and beginning to write.

Meanwhile, Grandfather and I helped by taking photographs of the land grant to go with the history. I was not new to photography. Grandfather had purchased a 35mm camera for me when I was very young, and he was teaching me how to take photographs, develop film, and make prints. He bought the rudimentary equipment for me to accomplish these tasks. Mom's assignment for us was a good opportunity for me to improve my photographic skills by working on a real assignment with Grandfather. Not only did we take photographs together but I also worked with him in the darkroom to develop the film and print the photos. This turned out to be my first and only photography assignment.

For some time, Grandfather had been purchasing black-and-white film in bulk quantities to share with me. I would take photos; we would usually develop and print them together. Once we had the finished photos, he would offer his critique, both on taking the photos and on developing the film. This did not work very well because the feedback was too slow. This is my excuse anyway. (I have excuses that go way beyond the simple notion of poor protoplasm for all my failures.) Furthermore, I never became proficient at taking photos or developing and printing them even though I did get somewhat better at taking photographs as an adult. Out of the hundreds, or thousands, of photographs I have taken with good cameras, both film and digital, I might have taken three photos worth printing. Well, maybe I am being a little hard on myself. I know good photography when I see it, and I really admire the photographers who consistently take great photos even though I do have a little hidden animosity toward them and their stinking talent.

I did not feel that the photos we took for Mom's document were very good. Too many of them were scenes of the mountains taken from a distance, showing as much of the old land grant as possible, but not enough detail or features to be interesting. The mountains all seemed to run together in the photos. This was not my fault. Now I am the critic even though I cannot suggest a way they could have been made more interesting. Apparently, this is not the job of a critic.

The job was completed, and Mom finished the research and writing. It was great to be a part of a real project. Both Mom and Grandfather worked very hard on it. Unfortunately, I never knew what Mr. Rounds thought of Mom's work or if he even read it.

CHAPTER 13

The Rounds Family
at Pot Creek

Quarks, electrons, protons, atoms… Possibilities… Chemistry, biology… Biology? Whoops! Underlying it all, the laws of physics and all the associated dangers. Whose idea was this? We don't let kids play with matches after all. What was the Creator thinking? Nothing?

*****

Bill Rounds was one of Mr. Rounds' two sons. Bill had a brother named Dwight. Bill visited Pot Creek often with his family, but I don't remember Dwight ever visiting. On his frequent visits to Pot Creek, Bill and his family got to know the Dixon family. Bill was married to Carolyn Coleman. They had a daughter named Becky, who was near my age. They also had one or two sons younger than Becky. I am surprised that I remember anything about any brother or brothers. Why? Because I had trouble breathing or thinking when Becky was nearby. She was about my age and spectacular as far as I was concerned. She was not the first to induce naughty urges in me. Nevertheless, she took my preteen fantasies to a whole new level.

Bill would fly his small private plane from Wichita, Kansas, to Taos for his visits to Pot Creek. He would buzz the lumber camp and Mom, or someone in the office would arrange for him to be picked up at the small Taos airport. Bill would have rather been able to land at Pot Creek. To this end, he asked Dad to make him a short landing strip just north of the elementary school and south of the Fort Burgwin site. Dad managed to get a strip graded, but there were some power lines that provided a challenging obstacle for takeoffs and landings. Dad warned Bill about the hazards, and Bill apparently agreed that it would be too risky to land on the strip even though he had a Helio Courier at the time. This type of aircraft was made for short takeoffs and landings. Bill never attempted a landing on the Pot Creek landing strip, and I doubt that anyone else did either.

Carolyn Rounds, Bill's wife, was part of the Coleman family, well-known for their camping-gear business. Needless to say, they had an incredible collection of camping equipment that they would use at Pot Creek. They often selected a spot on the bank of the little creek somewhere near our house. When this happened, we would visit their camp and be impressed by all the fancy equipment and many other outdoor amenities. Sometimes, we would be invited to dinner or breakfast, giving us the opportunity to experience outdoor life as the wealthy do it. I liked it!

Sammy and I often played with Becky and any brothers she might have had when Bill and his family were visiting. (She did have at least one brother.) I remember an accident that Becky had while playing with us in the back of Dad's old pickup. Becky fell straddling the wall of the pickup bed and hurt herself in the most female spot of a woman's anatomy. She was obviously in pain, but I didn't know what to do. I was helpless. Fortunately, she wasn't. She managed to make her way over the short distance back to the Rounds' apartment on her own where she recovered quickly. We were playing together again that afternoon. Sure! Like I remember what happened that afternoon. Okay, I am making up some of these details to bind the story together. Since the stories are true, my stitched-in details are surely accurate, aren't they? Nevertheless, Becky was not out of action very long. We were playing together again when, and only when, Becky had recovered.

Even though I was secretly in love with Becky, the virtual romance that swirled in my head never had a chance. We never got beyond a play relationship. We were not even teenagers for crying out loud! I did not understand that my fantasies could never become real. It would not be the last time I entertained a nonexistent possibility for a relationship with the fairer sex. However, I am happy to report that I am just about to figure all this stuff out.

Bill and his airplanes fascinated Sammy and me. He had two different planes that I remember. The first was a Cessna, and the second was the Helio Courier. Of course, we wanted a plane ride from the very beginning. Neither of us had ever been in a plane before. Getting a ride seemed like it took forever, but it finally happened—twice. The first ride was in Bill's Cessna. We took off from the small Las Vegas, New Mexico, airport. Bill had come to believe that there might be uranium located in the area of the Ranch, and he thought he might detect it from the air using a Geiger counter. It should not have been a surprise that he did not detect anything. He may have thought that there could be uranium in those mountains from Grandfather by way of Mom. Anyway, Sammy and I did not go with him on the uranium-seeking flight, but he gave us a quick ride just before he began his search.

The second ride came later. It was in the Helio Courier. This time, we took off from the Taos Airport and flew over the logging camp where our friends attempted to shoot us down with their BB guns. We had tipped them off that we would be getting a ride. There was never any doubt that they would attempt to shoot us down. They didn't succeed, but after the ride, we told them that we had heard their BBs hitting the wings. We didn't really hear anything, but we wanted them to feel that their effort was not completely futile. Dad went along on each ride. Mom did not. She had been in airplanes enough in her New York days and never enjoyed flying.

Bill went on to have a number of adventures in his small planes. On one such adventure, he crashed chasing deer or antelope across a field. He did not see a barbwire fence coming up soon enough to avoid it. It is not clear why one would chase an animal in an airplane. Was he going to slice it up on the spot with the propeller? It is likely that he didn't plan that far ahead. Anyway, he got beaten up in the crash but survived with the help of a few Band-Aids. I don't remember any details of other crashes. Maybe there weren't any. If there were, he survived them also. He was like my brother in many ways. He could get away with stuff.

CHAPTER 14

Mom's Technical Bent

Possibilities: a very hot quark/gluon plasma condenses rapidly into protons, neutrons, electrons…and a seemingly endless number of meaningless, short-lived particles. Meaningless? Where did that come from? Is *meaningless* the secret of creation?

*****

Mother had Grandfather's technical bent. Both she and her sister, Jessica, became ham radio operators. This allowed them to stay in touch with Grandfather at the Ranch on a daily basis. Ham radio was free of cost after an initial investment in equipment. Furthermore, much of the equipment that they used was home-built. This form of communication was particularly useful after the old-fashioned phones disappeared from the Ranch.

Initially, the communications between father and daughters were via Morse code. All three were very good at transmitting and deciphering the code. To understand what was being received, dots and dashes were written down on a piece of paper as they came in. After the transmission, the dots and dashes were quickly deciphered into English or, perhaps, hillbilly.

There had been an effort by both Grandfather and Mother to get me to learn how to read and send Morse code so that I could get a ham-radio license. It didn't work. The same effort was made on behalf of Jessie's oldest son, Dwight. It worked better for Dwight. I don't know how far he got in the ham-radio business, but I never got anywhere. Maybe I was waiting for a little more technology. Besides, I was in school and did not want to get further into the test business than I had to. One had to pass a test to get a ham-radio license. Part of it involved being able to send Morse code at or above a specified rate. I never understood what the hurry was.

Anyway, it was not long before Grandfather and his daughters were communicating by voice rather than Morse code. They would get together on the radio early on most mornings to have a conversation. It was a good way to check on one another. My grandparents were getting quite elderly, and their only means of communication from the Ranch were via a ride in the jeep or by ham radio.

Mother also made other friends on the radio. She joined in with a group of priests who talked on most mornings. One of the ham-radio priests, Father Frank Galley, was transferred to the Ranchos de Taos Church while we lived in Pot Creek. He became a good friend of the family and was often invited to our house for holiday dinners and other occasions. He seemed to enjoy spending these occasions with a non-Catholic family where he could be something other than a priest. It was also clear that he enjoyed being around Mother due to other male urges that exist even in priests. Dad did take note of Mom's relationships with other men. It would eventually grow into a negative factor in their marriage.

Ham radio was not Mom's only technical activity. She shared Grandfather's gift for understanding technology. Besides maintaining her ham radio equipment, she decided to build a television from a kit even though we already had a television set. It took quite a while, but she eventually succeeded in putting an entire television together and making it work. The television was given to my grandparents. They used it for several years after they finally moved into town permanently. My grandfather added a remote to it before anyone had remotes. Well, it wasn't a wireless remote. Instead, it was a switch attached to the television set by means of a pair of wires. It turned the sound on and off. Grandfather was very happy with Mother's television and his innovation. He did not want to listen to the commercials. A dimmer view is that it allowed Grandfather to cheat the people who made television possible by purchasing commercials. His device required a small skip, hop, and jump to clear the wires if one was trying to cross the cluttered room while he was watching television.

*****

During our early days at Taos and the Ranch, there was considerable concern about the Cold War and the possibility that it would turn hot. I had already heard about the atomic bomb from my grandfather and had become aware of even more powerful hydrogen bombs. I suspect my concern about these terrible weapons of war was not good for me. One experience that amplified the tension and concern about nuclear war was a Civil Air Patrol (CAP) activity. Both Grandfather and Mother joined the CAP, which was presumably something any citizen in good standing could do.

There was only one activity besides the ham radio that my grandfather became active in with the CAP. He invited me along on several occasions to participate with him in the activity. I was probably around ten years old by this time.

We would drive into Las Vegas from the Ranch and proceed to the top of the bluffs on the east side of town where a telephone pole with a phone attached to it was located. We stationed ourselves at the pole. When a plane would fly over, Grandfather would pick up the phone and report the plane to someone on the other end of the line. There was no dialing involved. The report included a description of the plane and his judgement about what type of plane it was. He had a bookful of airplane silhouettes shown from underneath that facilitated the identification. I don't know if the book showed a silhouette of a Russian bomber or even a flying saucer. Many of the latter had apparently invaded New Mexico by this time. At least there were many reported sightings. I was somewhat disappointed that we never saw a flying saucer to report. The saucer pilots were apparently too clever to allow us to spot them. Maybe they had silhouettes of airplanes painted on the bottom of the saucers.

On one occasion, a Navy officer joined us at the telephone pole and observed us as we identified aircraft. He brought a super pair of binoculars to the task, and he let me look through them at the planes flying overhead. They were much better than the field glasses that Grandfather used to make identifications. I don't think I learned anything important from the Navy officer, but I really wanted his binoculars. I have since changed my point of view on this. I like using binoculars backward to make things look farther away. The world is much too crowded.

Living in New Mexico, we all guessed that the Los Alamos Laboratory would be a primary target for an attack against the United States. Planes attacking the Laboratory from the east would fly right over Las Vegas on their way to destroy the secret laboratory. Or so I thought. Why would they come from the east? I did not know. Maybe because coming from the east was the only way to fly over Las Vegas, New Mexico, en route to Los Alamos. Well, they had to come from somewhere, and east was as good a guess as any.

My imagination was not only vivid about what an attack event might be like, but I had fantasies about what I would do in the event of such an occurrence. This mainly involved running off to the mountains on a horse, riding double with the most attractive girl in school. As I mentioned earlier, that would have been Judy Jones. I had good taste. Fortunately, I never had the opportunity to try out the war scenario with her. I was only mildly disappointed. Grandfather and I never reported anything important from our observation point on the bluff. This was not disappointing at all.

*****

Apparently, putting a television set together wasn't enough for Mother. She also participated in building an airplane while she belonged to the Civil Air Patrol in Taos. I am not certain why she joined this group, but it had to do with her ham-radio activities.

Well, she was my mother after all. She was exploring the full range of life from top to bottom. At least this was not an activity that could get her in much trouble unless...she went for a ride in the plane built by a bunch of amateurs. Well, maybe they knew what they were doing. It was exciting even though I was not eager to ride in the plane, but I didn't rule the possibility out either. In any case, I wanted to be present and watching from a safe distance when it took off for the first time. This feeling was similar to wanting to see Evel Knievel jump the Grand Canyon on a motorcycle. After all, Mother would not be in it, or so I thought.

The airplane project was exciting to Sammy and me because we had already ridden in an airplane with Bill Rounds. That experience left us wanting more time in the air. Well, this is what we thought until Mother took us to see the plane. It looked impressive enough. Nevertheless, we knew it had been built by a bunch of amateurs, including Mom. She did not mention any possibility for a ride in the plane. Mother didn't have a pilot's license. Nevertheless, there were plans for the pilots in the group to fly the plane. We were fine with them flying without us. Did someone check that both of the wings were attached to the fuselage right side up? Well, that question certainly had an easy answer. But I suspected that there were more subtle questions that would not be answered until the plane flew—or didn't fly. I never heard whether anyone flew the plane or what happened to them when it augured in. Well, it most likely turned out just fine.

CHAPTER 15

Building a Cabin at the Ranch

The human brain: A BIG mistake? An amusing experiment? An attempt to entertain? Part of an incomprehensible plan? All of the above? Yes! That's it! Maybe?

*****

I don't know how Sammy and I got the notion that we would like to build a cabin at the Ranch. Maybe it was our idea or, more likely, Grandfather put the notion in our heads. I know we were enthusiastic as soon as the possibility came up. We were energetic young squirts, and our energy needed to be directed somewhere positive. At least this was so for Sammy. In my own case, I was happy to sit and think for long periods of time. It was not so clear that I had excess energy that needed to be "directed." Nevertheless, Grandfather told me that my head was in the clouds much of the time. He was wrong. My head was way above the clouds most of the time. I found many entertainment opportunities swirling in those lofty locations.

At the time that building a cabin made it onto the agenda, Sammy and I were about ten and twelve years old. A simple design and a plan were put in place before we began construction. It would be a one-room cabin that we could finish building in one summer.

It was to be located on a gradual slope roughly twenty to fifty yards above or north of the adobe house. The time constraint on construction did not prevent us from choosing a rather fancy feature that we wanted the cabin to have. We decided that we would like our cabin to be distinguished from the other Ranch cabins. To accomplish this, we decided to construct it using peeled logs.

Grandfather accepted our plan. The cabin would have only one room with the dimensions of twelve feet by twelve feet plus or minus two feet due to the uncertainty of my brain's dimensions. It would have two windows and a door. There would be no emergency exit...or entrance. Fortunately, our plan only had to be approved by Grandfather. To provide additional encouragement, Grandfather told us that he would give us an acre of land surrounding the cabin once it was successfully completed.

To facilitate the construction, we had full use of the jeep, axes, and most other tools. The only major tool we didn't have direct, or unsupervised, access to was a large chain saw that was permanently fixed in place on an outside workbench located across the entrance road from the adobe house and Grandfather's office cabin. This big saw was used to cut wood for the fireplace. If we needed to use it, Grandfather would operate it. We didn't need it.

The daily schedule that we quickly established had Sammy and me working by ourselves in the mornings while Grandpa wrote in his office. We spent most mornings peeling logs and putting them in place to create the cabin walls. We also spent some of the time selecting trees that we wanted to cut for the cabin. Grandfather had to preapprove each tree that was to be used. The tree approvals typically happened in the afternoons when Grandfather was available, and cutting trees happened in both mornings and afternoons. The cut trees were dragged to the cabin site using the jeep.

All the cutting, peeling, and notching was done with axes. Some of the logs were easy to peel, and others seemed to have the bark so tightly wrapped that we wanted to give up on peeling them. This was not allowed. None of the logs could be wasted. Each day around noon, Grandfather would walk up to our construction site to check our work and give us advice.

Many of Grandfather's tools got a good workout and suffered some damage due to our inexperience. A major case in point: Many of the trees that we selected for cabin construction were in areas where there was no road. This was not a problem since we had full use of the jeep. I would drive the jeep through the forest to get to trees that we had selected. We would cut them down and tie them to the trailer hitch so we could drag them back to the cabin site. I did all the driving. I was the oldest, but not necessarily the smartest as I would rather dramatically demonstrate.

One morning, we were dragging a tree back to the cabin site when we encountered a formidable monster lurking just beneath the surface of the sea of tranquility. This is just an absurd way of saying that I drove over some chicken wire that had been tossed into the woods for some reason—probably by renegade chickens. At first, I didn't think there was a problem. I just kept going. As the jeep continued to move, the chicken wire became wound so tightly around the front axle that it finally brought the jeep to a hard stop. I could not get the trapped vehicle to budge forward, backward, up, down, or sideways.

Initially, I didn't understand how serious the problem was. I figured that anything made to hold puny chickens could not hold a four-wheel drive jeep in place for long. However, I was wrong. When we attempted to unwind the chicken wire, we found that it had been wrapped so tightly around the axle that we could not pull it loose to begin unwinding it. The jeep was stuck firmly in the grasp of the chicken wire.

We walked back to Grandfather's cabin and described our problem to him. He shook his head, opened his tool box, handed me a pair of wire cutters (dikes), and said, "You better get to work right away." He was right. The jeep was the only means of transportation at the Ranch, and he knew that we had a difficult job before us. Meanwhile, Sammy and I did not yet appreciate the difficulty we faced.

As we began working on the problem, it did not take us long to conclude that Grandpa was right about the difficulty of our task. We attempted to get a hold of the wire with our hands and the dikes to begin unwinding it. This proved to be impossible. When we did get some wire loose that we could grab, the tangle was still so tight that we could not simply pull and unwind the wire. Our progress was extremely slow. We worked on the problem for a couple of days, making slow progress at first. It was a nightmare working under the jeep. We finally had a breakthrough after a couple of futile days under the jeep. We were able to begin unwrapping the wire, and we succeeded in getting to the end of the nightmare. The jeep was finally set free.

I had learned an important lesson: Sometimes, one finds chicken wire even where there are no chickens for miles around. Well, maybe the more important lesson I learned was to watch where you are going because even a jeep can be captured by the fixin's for a chicken pen. I also became an expert at using a pair of wire cutters, a skill that is useful for a range of activities from kluging electronics together to setting death-row chickens free.

All was going well on the cabin; and then one morning, while we were peeling the last of the logs, we noticed Grandfather walking slowly up the slope toward us. When he arrived, he said, "I have some bad news. Mr. Rounds passed away." He had received the news from Mother via the ham radio. We both knew this was very bad news, but after a relatively short pause, we continued working. We did not know what else to do.

Sammy and I did not finish the cabin that summer, but we came close. The walls were up, and we put a roof on it that was made of plywood covered with roofing material. We also put a plywood floor in place. The roof was tight, but there were cracks between the logs. It needed to be chinked. Also it still needed a door and some windows. We had cut and framed the openings for the door and windows, but finishing the job waited for a summer that never came. Life intervened.

Grandfather told us that we had completed our part of the deal, and the acre of land was ours. Unfortunately, no lawyers were involved in this agreement. It was a simple family understanding. This arrangement seemed to work fine for the rest of the time that Grandfather and Grandmother owned the Ranch. Unfortunately, they did not own the Ranch much longer. Much to Mother's dismay, the Ranch was sold to one of her older sisters, Opal. Technically, Opal was not related to Grandfather Shearer, who had homesteaded the Ranch since she was a product of Grandmother's first marriage. Anyway, Opal agreed that we had an acre of land, but she had other plans for our cabin and our original acre. Our replacement acre would not have a cabin on it, and we never even attempted to come to an agreement concerning its location. We knew we were in a very weak negotiating position. Opal had succeeded in getting rid of the little problem she had with our acre and cabin set right in the middle of her property without making an agreement with us. No deal was ever consummated.

Nevertheless, our little cabin would eventually have the last word. It represented Sammy and me very well. When I was in graduate school, a large forest fire burned much of the mountain. The Ranch property was completely burned off. Everyone was safely evacuated from the mountain even though my aunt Audrey had refused to leave her house. No problem; she was carried out of her house still sitting in her rocking chair and loaded into the back of a truck, which delivered her to safety.

Our cabin got in one last spectacular word. Opal's son-in-law used the cabin to store his black powder and other explosives. He liked to load his own ammunition and make loud noises. When the forest fire reached the little cabin, all the explosives and frustration stored in our unfinished work resulted in a spectacular fireworks display. By all accounts, it was the most spectacular show on the mountain. Needless to say, there was nothing left of our handiwork afterward except the memories. The same can be said for the rest of the Ranch and the entire area.

Years later when I was visiting Highlands University to give a talk and receive an award, a woman who worked at the university and owned the property that had been the Old Homestead Ranch asked me to come out and show her where our legendary cabin had been located. Of course, I agreed to this. She had built a fancy house on the Ranch that made me envious and somewhat angry. I was still too emotionally connected to the Ranch. Anyway, I was civil, and I had no trouble locating the cabin site. My selection was confirmed by a number of familiar boulders that had been charred black by the blast. Nevertheless, I could have easily found it using only the terrain as my guide. The site I identified was very close to the house the new owner had built.

CHAPTER 16

Driving Adventures in Taos and Pot Creek

Are the Creator and Creation one and the same? Is the answer to this question obvious?

*****

Taos was about twelve miles from Pot Creek. This beautiful little town is where we did most of our shopping and other business. There were closer and smaller communities with stores including Talpa and Ranchos de Taos. We occasionally stopped at the small stores in these communities, but the selection was limited. Consequently, Mom and Dad would often drive into Taos to buy groceries, hardware, or to do general shopping. On these shopping trips, Sammy and I would often be left in the car while Mom and Dad went into the stores. Most of the stores that they frequented were either on the plaza or very close to it. For some reason, I don't remember if Diana was ever left with us. Maybe we were supposed to take care of her, but I don't remember this.

Many Native Americans from the Pueblo frequented the plaza to just hangout. They would sometimes come near the car and gesture to us. They were being friendly as they attempted to amuse us.

Nevertheless, it scared the bejesus out of me at first. Mom and Dad would just laugh when we told them about it. They tried to convince us that the Pueblo people were not dangerous. They succeeded. After a while, it got to be a game between the Taos People and Sammy and me. For some reason, I felt that they were special. They were, but I did not understand why at the time.

We had other adventures that were not inspired by the native people on some of these shopping trips. One in particular occurred when Mom and Dad were shopping in the White Auto store, which was just off the southeast corner of the plaza. Sammy and I were left in the car, which was parked right in front of the store. At the time, we had a 1954 Buick Special with a Dynaflow transmission. Sammy and I would sometimes play like we were driving. The play could be somewhat realistic because we both had some driving experience even though we were very young. Unfortunately, neither of us fully understood automatic transmissions, not to mention Isaac Newton's theory of gravity. The parking lot in front of the White Auto store was on a fairly steep incline. The Buick was parked in front of the store at the top of the hill with the rear end pointing straight down the hill.

Mom and Dad had not been in the store very long before Sammy and I got into a discussion about whether the car would roll down the hill if we moved the gear shift out of the P or park position and into the N or neutral position. Sammy claimed it would, and I claimed it wouldn't. Neither of us had any experience with automatic transmissions. Anticipating my future career, I decided to do an experiment. This is the way science works after all. Experiments are done to resolve the puzzles. Besides, we had to see who was right.

I grabbed the gear shift and attempted to move it from P to N. It took a lot of force to get the gear shift to move, but I succeeded in making the change. As soon as the transmission clicked into the neutral position, the Buick began rolling backward down the hill. Dad hadn't put the emergency brake on! Why not, for crying out loud?

I pressed the power brake with my foot as hard as I could. This did no good with the engine off. We just kept rolling faster and faster. Sammy got down on the floor to try get more force on the brakes with his hands. The Buick rolled on, picking up speed. I tried to shift back into the Park position. I struggled mightily. It would not go. We continued to pick up speed as I continued my battle with the gear-shift lever. The struggle finally ended with a dull crunch as the Buick came to sudden stop. We had hit the rear end of a car that was parked at the bottom of the parking lot facing the other direction. Whoops!

This is why there is always a safety committee involved in the approval process for scientific experiments. And what could be worse? It was me, the future scientist, who was wrong! Of course, we were both in trouble because that is the way it worked. I don't remember the punishment, only the embarrassment. It was one of the dumbest things I have ever done in my life, and I knew it at the time. Both cars got fixed. We had insurance. This did not soften the blow for my ego. I count it as my first car accident. I would have several more in my first couple of years as a licensed driver. It is good to get experience with accidents before you get your license. After all, they can't take your license away from you if you don't have one. Also I thought about blaming Dad. Even though Dad and I were not officially connected through biology, I seemed to have his race-car mentality: "Try anything to see what you can get away with."

At roughly the same time as this driving adventure occurred, I had another adventure high in the mountains above Pot Creek. I would guess I was eleven or twelve years old. Dad took Sammy and me with him on a call to fix a bulldozer that had broken down in the logging operation. We rode up the mountain in Dad's shop vehicle, a Dodge Power Wagon. It had a large welding machine mounted behind the cab.

When we arrived at the stricken bulldozer, Dad began working on it while Sammy and I played near the Power Wagon. It did not take Dad long to get the bulldozer running. Once he was finished, he told me to get into the Power Wagon with Sammy and to follow him down the mountain where he would deliver the bulldozer to the logging crew working below. I eagerly jumped into the Power Wagon with Sammy. I was very happy to be asked to help, and I was certainly used to driving by then. However, I am quite certain that I had never driven Dad's work truck before. Nevertheless, I was confident that I could do it.

I was a little surprised when Dad headed straight down the side of the mountain in the bulldozer instead of following the logging road, which traversed back and forth across the very steep mountainside, making a number of very sharp switchback turns on the way to the canyon bottom. He had told me to follow him, so I did—straight down the mountain. He saw me coming, and he stopped the Cat at the first road crossing, jumped off, and began screaming at me. Somehow, I managed to stop the Power Wagon by turning it onto the road crossing where he had stopped. Had I tried to turn on the side of the mountain above or below the road crossing, it would have made the impending disaster manifest. The Power Wagon with two little boys in the cab would have rolled all the way to the bottom of the deep canyon. It would have required more than Band-Aids and a little plaster to repair the damage.

I got a good tongue-lashing on the spot, and my only defense was that he had told me to "follow him." I muttered this defense, but I was not proud of it. It was ignored. I followed the road the rest of the way to the bottom of the canyon, and I don't think anything more was said about the matter. Dad knew he had some responsibility for not giving me more specific instructions. I guess he thought I was smart. I showed him.

CHAPTER 17

Hunting at Pot Creek

Could there be other universes? Some cosmologists say, "Maybe." They call this notion the "multiverse." If there are other universes, where are they?

*****

D ad was a serious hunter. It was one of his favorite activities. Unlike many hunters, Dad was not just out to shoot something although he did enjoy this aspect of hunting. We ate most of what he killed, and others ate the rest. Deer were his primary targets at Pot Creek, and he only hunted them during the hunting season. On occasion, he would hunt wild turkey. More important was the fact that it pleased him that his fun put food on the table. Consequently, we subsisted mostly on venison and trout at Pot Creek. A good freezer allowed us to have game to eat year-round.

From time to time, Dad took inexperienced hunters from Texas out hunting. He had good connections to Texas, and even though his two older sons lived in New Mexico, they had many friends in Texas. By taking out hunters he did not know, he could not predict their behavior when they were first confronted by something to shoot at in the woods. There were many stories. One hunter had attempted to decimate a herd of deer before Dad could get him to stop shooting.

On another occasion, a hunting party came back to the house with a relatively small bear that one of the group had shot. It was in the trunk of our Buick, which often served as a hunting vehicle. The hunting party unloaded the bear and threw it in the front yard before coming into the house to celebrate. Dad did not shoot bear because they were not good to eat.

As dusk descended over the logging camp and all the hunters were in the house, we heard the neighborhood dogs begin to bark. Everyone went outside to see what was causing all the ruckus. The small bear was struggling to get up. One of the hunters quickly fetched a rifle and ended the little bear's struggle.

On another occasion, Dad took a group out that consisted of a "would be" hunter, also from Texas. Mr. Rounds had recently imported some elk onto his land grant, wanting to reintroduce them to an area where they had once flourished. There were none left in northern New Mexico at the time. Consequently, Mr. Rounds' elk were protected. Hunting them was illegal.

Dad was well aware that his group was inexperienced and were prone to shoot at anything that moved. He probably warned them about consequences, but I do not know this. Nevertheless, it was not a big surprise when a member of party shot and killed an elk. On second thought, it very well could have been a surprise that the hunter had managed to hit an elk in the first place.

Dad was upset that an elk had been killed. His inclination was to leave the unfortunate animal where it fell. However, the Texas hunter who shot it wanted to take the head with antlers back home so he could hang his illegally taken trophy on his wall. Dad reluctantly agreed to help him get his trophy. In addition, Dad decided that they should not just leave the meat there to waste. Consequently, they ended up taking much or all of the meat and the head with antlers down the mountain with them. When they arrived back at Pot Creek, the shooter took his head and some of the meat and headed back to Texas. Mother was not told what happened, and she did not notice anything unusual going on.

Sometime later, Dad was at work when a sheriff and a game warden knocked on our front door. Mom answered the door and was told that the meat in our freezer had to be tested. She let them in, and they conducted the tests. When the tests were complete, Mom was told that some of the meat was elk. She was both surprised and dismayed. No one had told her that an elk had been killed. The sheriff immediately went across the road and arrested Dad at his shop. Dad spent the night in jail and had to pay a big fine. Mom had to borrow money to cover it and get Dad out of jail.

We later learned that the person who had shot the elk got cold feet on his way back to Texas. He decided to throw the head and hide into a culvert. Unfortunately for him, part of the stash was in a box that had his name and address on it. When he was arrested in Texas, he provided the names of the other members of the hunting party. He spent some time behind bars in addition to paying a rather large fine. There were consequences for the rest of the hunting party as well. I suspect that everyone paid a fine.

Mom was extremely embarrassed by the incident because it had been one of Mr. Rounds transplanted elk. In the end, the best that can be said is that the dead elk was apparently not crucial for the well-being of the herd; there are elk all over northern New Mexico now. However, this success likely was more the result of the hunters' skill rather than their desire to obey the law.

CHAPTER 18

Two Little Savages
at Pot Creek

THE MULTIVERSE? Where did this notion come from? It would seem that we have enough to comprehend without going down this path. Yet the human mind refuses to be constrained. Evidence is everywhere, tempting us to leave our sensible constraints behind. The horses are not yet all in the barn on the question of multiple universes. In fact, there may not even be a barn.

*****

Early inhabitants of the Pot Creek area left many artifacts for the archaeologists who descended on the little valley in the 1950s. Arrowheads, spear points, and tools for grinding corn were among the items that documented their existence for archaeologists and others such as my little brother. Sammy seemed to be connected to these artifacts in a somewhat mysterious manner. He could find them where no one else could.

There was a hill just southeast of the sawmill. We called it Lookout Point. There was a trail to the top of the hill. It was not a long climb, and it provided an excellent view of the logging camp from the summit. Sammy and I liked to climb the hill. I liked the

125

view from the top, but he liked to look down as he ascended and descended the hill. Consequently, he found numerous arrowheads and spear points left behind by previous residents. I might have found one arrowhead during the entire time we lived at Pot Creek.

I can reconcile my shortcomings in the arrowhead search activity by noting that my inclination was, in fact, to look in the other direction. I loved looking at the view from the top of the hill. Being able to see the entire logging camp from the little summit gave me a different perspective of our logging-camp existence. Similarly, I loved looking at the brilliant night sky. The stars held a special fascination for me. They were too numerous to count in the extremely dark yet brilliant New Mexico night sky.

One could not help but wonder whether anyone or anything else was looking back. What other entities might exist in the vastness of the universe? I wanted a clue. I wished so very hard for a flying saucer to favor me with an appearance. It would provide a clue indicating a potential path to another existence. I was never concerned that another entity might be unfriendly even though the pages of my science-fiction books were filled with tales of grouchy aliens apparently too constipated from the meat of humans and lack of fiber to be friendly. Apparently, I was not discouraged by the possibility of alien beings with huge claws and gaping mouths filled with razor-sharp teeth that could disembowel a human being in less than a millisecond. No, these possibilities did not discourage me from wanting to contact other beings. And I never hid under the bed when I heard strange noises in the night either. Okay, I was as scared as anyone else. Had aliens appeared in the front yard, I would have waited to see what they did to Doty before deciding whether to hide under the bed or to offer them a cup of freshly perked coffee.

Apparently, I wished so hard to see something come into view in the brilliant darkness that I wished several UFOs into existence. All of my sightings became large meteors during the subsequent light of day when reason prevailed. I still don't understand why I wanted evidence that we were being visited from across the galaxy or at least from Mars or Venus. Based on experience with humans, visitors are not necessarily friendly. For some reason, I was willing to gamble. I guess some humans feel a bit lonely, or maybe frightened, upon real-izing that our little planet is isolated by the vastness of the deep, dark universe. After all, being alone is scary, isn't it? Nevertheless, I came to realize that when people look into the dark, twinkling night sky, they often see what they want to see even though for most, the vision is subsequently consumed by the rationality of a bright blue sky.

Sam and I spent many nights sleeping outside, sometimes with friends or visiting relatives, and many times, it was just the two of us. At first, it was difficult for us to make it through an entire night partly because we did not have sleeping bags that were substantial enough to withstand the chill and mostly due to the irrationality that looking into deep space induces. All manner of beings silently glided across the sky, becoming simple meteors by the light of day.

We started spending nights outside by sleeping on the front porch of the house. It took a while to make it through an entire night without retreating to the safety and warmth of our bedroom. The glowing eyes of the demons of darkness did not usually take long to convince us we were cold and they were hungry. The retreat often occurred before our normal bedtime. We eventually befriended the demons well enough to sleep through an entire night, and we even graduated to sleeping outside of the yard next to the babbling brook where we could hear the trout laughing at us as they snorted and farted. Well, we hoped it was the trout making the ruckus. There were certainly plenty of trout in the Pot Creek and plenty of shadows in the moonlight along the dark banks of the small creek. It was big a challenge for two small boys to make it through an entire night with all the mysterious gurgles and belches emanating from the water as it rushed over its rocky creek bed.

We also experimented sleeping out at the Ranch where we used an old tarp to make a crude tent. We slept out in it for two weeks during a period when it rained almost constantly. Maybe the rain kept the demons at bay. Our cousins Dwight and Russell joined us for a couple of nights. We had great fun trying to stay dry with a makeshift tent. We never succeeded.

Meeting challenges in the wild and the dark eventually made us believe that we were totally indestructible. It didn't last. It dissolved into the reality of daylight as we began to break and bleed. There were too many daylight dangers that could wink us out of existence in a bright flash...or a dull thud.

A real danger for two small boys lurked in a number of large sawdust piles located around the lumber camp. According to my memory, they were roughly fifty feet high and several hundred feet in diameter, so I say. We never measured them. One was located right across the creek from our house. We had been warned not to play on the sawdust piles, but it seemed that no one had told us that we could not play inside of them. Sammy and I loved to dig tunnels, but this was difficult work in the hard, rocky dirt. It did not take us long to discover that the sawdust piles were very easy to tunnel into. Soon, we had a network of tunnels that honeycombed the lower level of the sawdust pile across the creek. We were barely smart enough not to light our way through the dark tunnel network using a flame as a source of light. Nevertheless, we were not smart enough to stop extending the network of tunnels that we had created. Mom never found out what we were doing. We were very lucky that we were never trapped inside the pile by a cave-in. Also we knew that some of the big piles caught on fire from time to time, and it was near impossible to put the fires out. I still have nightmares about what could have happened.

Sawdust piles were not the only locations that provided an easy place to dig. We also tunneled into the side of the garbage dump, which was located just across the road from our house between Dad's shop and the creek. The soft dirt on the side of the dump that prevented the garbage from spilling into the creek made for very easy tunneling. We used the tunnels for hideouts. For the dump tunnels, we came to realize on our own that the dirt was very likely contaminated since it was full of refuse. We decided on our own to stop digging into the dump.

It was not long before we extended our digging to the fishing path that ran along Pot Creek to the west of our house. This was a safe place to dig—for us. Fortunately, we only dug one serious hole before we gave up this endeavor. It was barely out of sight of our house, and it gave us a great sense of accomplishment. We dug it as deep as possible. We stopped when it was three or four feet in diameter and five or six feet deep. However, we needed some purpose for the hole.

It did not take us long to come up with the notion of making it into a trap for animals. To accomplish this, we spread some branches over the hole and then found a piece of an old tarp. We spread it over the branches and covered it with thin layer of dirt. (Sammy and I had not yet been informed about the possibility of reform school for juveniles.) If a fisherman had come along and stepped on the trap, he or she could have been seriously injured. We either didn't think of this possibility or maybe trapping a fisherman was our intention.

Fortunately, the hole did not stay in its clandestine state for long. We weren't quite as dumb as we seemed. It just took a while for light to make its way from one side of our brain to the other through the winding path. When this journey through brain matter was complete, we removed the hidden cover, exposing our handiwork. This did not make Mom or others who found the hole happy. We filled the hole as best we could. Sammy and I were clearly outperforming the Arkansas hillbillies at being hillbillies.

BB gun and rock fights were also common at Pot Creek. Often, we just threw rocks at one another, but sometimes, the rocks were hurled with what city hicks would call slingshots. They were called something totally inappropriate by most of us hillbillies. We didn't know better, but Mother took exception and made certain that Sammy and I knew better. Dad was fine with the local hillbilly name for the weapons. The fights were supposed to be fun, but they could get quite serious and sometimes bloody. The more you bled, the better hillbilly you were. I was lucky that I don't recall ever getting hit upside the head with a rock, but maybe I wouldn't remember such an event.

The closest I came to inflicting a serious injury in these childhood wars was during a BB gun fight that didn't even involve any of our Pot Creek friends. My aunt Jessie was visiting along with her children including her oldest son, Dwight, and his younger brother, Russell. Sammy, Dwight, Russell, and I went across the creek to the large sawdust pile, and a BB gun fight just happened to break out.

Russell and I were fighting against Dwight and Sammy. Russell and I had Sammy and Dwight pinned down behind a small heap of sawdust. My brother, being more experienced in this kind of warfare, was telling Dwight to stick his head up to see where Russell and I were and what we were doing. Every time Dwight put his head up, I shot him in the top of his head. Finally, I hit right above his eye, and it created a good welt that could not be hidden. We were in serious trouble.

Another shooting incident occurred when I was playing with John Clifford at the Jones house one day. John Clifford was Judy's younger brother. Sammy was also present. I don't remember why, but John Clifford and I got into a scuffle on the back porch of the house. He had some kind of a rifle. It was most likely a pellet gun, but it could have been a .22 caliber rifle. He was threatening to shoot me in the foot with it. I attempted to take the gun away from him. As we tangled, each trying to gain control of the weapon, it went off, hitting me right in the center of my large metal cowboy belt buckle. It hurt like getting your ear caught in a car door but did no real harm. Nevertheless, we were all in serious trouble, yet I don't remember the punishment. I do remember thinking that I was surely innocent since I had been the victim. However, I was apparently not entitled to a fair trial. Our parents were very upset with us, but they were mostly glad that there had not been a serious injury. We all had learned a lesson: Always wear a large Western belt buckle!

CHAPTER 19

Abandoning Pot Creek
with a Pungent Adios
from the Skunks

What would separate our universe from other universes? Is it space? Is it time? If the answer to either question is yes, then these are just components of our universe, aren't they? Is there something else? Is nothing something?

*****

In 1960, things began falling apart for our family at Pot Creek. Dad was making frequent visits to the hospital in Santa Fe. Often, he would stay for several days. When Mom visited him, Sammy, Diana, and I would accompany her to the hospital and wait in the car while she went in to see Dad. He apparently had cancer, but we were not given any details. I can only guess that it was colon cancer. I don't know if my brother, sister, and I would have understood it if we had been told.

As our Pot Creek days were coming to a close and Dad seemed to be making a recovery, we began having more and more problems with skunks under the house. They had easy access into the crawl

space underneath the house where many took up permanent residence. Whenever Dad was home and would see one in the yard, he
would get out his pistol and attempt to gun it down. Often, he only
scared them, which is not a good approach to dealing with a skunk.
I remember him plugging one that had taken up a position very near
our front porch. Unfortunately, when the shot was fired, the skunk
let loose with all fragrance that it had. The odor was horrific! The
shooting gave Dad some satisfaction, but it didn't do much for the
fragrance of the house and yard. The traditional losers in the gun
battle always managed to claim their own victory by letting loose
with a healthy squirt of foul-smelling perfume right before drawing a
last breath. I imagined that they were somewhat proud of themselves
for going out this way. I certainly remember them all the way to the
present.

In spite of the skunk shootings, we seemed to accumulate more
and more of the stinky residents under the house as time went on.
Toward the end of our stay in Pot Creek, Dad got the idea that he
could seal up the crawl space and run exhaust from the mechanical
shop's Power Wagon under the house to teach the skunks a lesson
they wouldn't forget. We wouldn't forget it either. This final attempt
to be rid of them would surely kill them or, at least, encourage them
to mosey on over to another house up the road. Well, none moseyed
out, and most, or all of them, were likely killed in place by the exhaust
fumes.

The price of Dad's victory was a horrendous stench that pene-
trated to the very heart of the Dixon family essence. We stunk to high
heaven just like our house. It surely smells better in hell. I learned
what a skunk with auxiliary power provided by the exhaust from a
gasoline engine smelled like. (Maybe a combustion engine will be
the next step in the evolutionary chain for the skunk.) The odor per-
meated into every corner of the house. Skunk perfume mixed with
exhaust seemed to ooze from our clothing. Our hair smelled like
Wildroot hair tonic, skunk, and exhaust. We went to school with
clothing saturated with the disgusting odor. We had no other option.
School was a nightmare. It was very difficult to pretend you smelled
something, too, when people began complaining about the odor.

The old "Okay, who let go with that one?" did not work at all. To the school's credit, we were allowed to continue attending in all our pungency. This did nothing for the reputation of Pot Creek and the kids who lived there. And we thought we were one of the "better" families.

*****

Dad's health continued to deteriorate. When he was not in the hospital, he and Mom would fight late at night after Diana, Sammy, and I were in bed. I overheard the fights. I worried. What would happen to us? One topic they fought about was the many men who stopped by the house to see Mom. Dad thought she had too many male friends. He questioned their motives. He was probably justified in raising the question even though I never had any direct evidence that Mother got out of bounds at Pot Creek. Would I know?

Meanwhile, Dad seemed to be losing his battle with cancer. He was in and out of the hospital in Santa Fe often. I don't remember when Dad quit working. Maybe he was let go by the company. It was evident that he was spending less and less time on the job. After an operation or two, he continued to struggle. Furthermore, he and Mom continued to fight. Finally, one day in the summer or fall of 1960, he got in the Buick and drove away. He did not tell Mom where he was going. This is Mom's version anyway. We did not see anything of him for a long time afterward. As it turned out, he went to southern New Mexico where he would eventually get a job on a cattle ranch. Furthermore, he miraculously recovered completely from cancer.

Meanwhile, we were stuck at Pot Creek after he left with no visible means of support. We did not know if he would ever come back. Much later in our lives, my brother told me that Dad told him that he had planned to come back for us as soon as he found a job. I have no doubt that this is what he told Sam and Diana, but I have to be a little skeptical. I know how desperate we were, and I know that he and Mom were not getting along at all. We would have starved at Pot Creek had it not been for Grandfather. He came to Pot Creek a number of times during the fall of 1960, always arriving with a few bags of groceries and other necessities. We were very hungry and appreciative. Fortunately, the company let us stay in the house during this time. Well, with the skunks, maybe it wasn't such a bargain.

When Mr. Rounds passed away in 1960, he left Mom a Nash Ambassador that he had kept at Pot Creek for use when he visited the logging camp. It was a very fancy car by most standards. The timing of this gift was fortunate. It would be the car we used for the next few years since Dad had taken the Buick.

With Dad gone, Mom began confiding more in me. She needed a partner to help figure out how we would survive. She continued discussing her problems with me for much of the rest of her life. I think this made me prematurely mature, a different sort of preemie, if you will. Nevertheless, I still don't have much gray hair. Mom's discussions with me began before Dad left. These discussions continued all the way to the end of her life. I was clearly biased by her point of view on Dad's motivation for leaving.

It didn't matter whether Sam's version of Dad's motivation for leaving was right or wrong. We were desperate for those last few months at Pot Creek. We had very little to eat, and we smelled of skunk. I don't know how we would have survived had it not been for Grandfather's occasional grocery deliveries. He and Grandmother were living on his pension. He couldn't afford to take care of us. Nevertheless, he could not see us starve either. We were desperate. He was desperate.

Sometime during the fall of 1960, when Dad was still missing in action, Rounds and Porter came to our rescue. They offered Mom a job in Breckenridge, Colorado, where Bill Rounds planned to fulfill his dream of owning a ski area. We were soon making plans to move. The company would pay the moving expenses. All we had to do was to let Mayflower load our skunk-ravaged belongings into a moving van and then head north in the Nash Ambassador. Mom knew it was our only option, but she was frightened to make a move to what seemed like a faraway place that she knew nothing about. She confided in me when she got the offer. I encouraged her to take the job. I argued that she had no choice. It was a matter of survival.

I understood how desperate our situation was. It was evident to me that we had no other option.

The notion of a ski area came about because Bill had wanted to own one. The story I heard at the time was that he had attempted to purchase the Aspen ski area. He was told that it was not for sale. No problem; he decided to build his own ski area. This is my version of how Breckenridge began. The real story is likely a bit more complicated. This version came from Mother.

I do remember that sometime before all this happened, Bill had been concerned about people living above an elevation of 8,000 feet. Mom and Dad had discussed the issue. Without much real knowledge of the subject, they were convinced that it was not a problem. The Ranch was 7,700 feet after all, and there were many people in the world living much higher than 8,000 feet. Mom and Dad got the correct answer. They may have done a little research to reach this conclusion or, more likely, they just knew it would not be a problem. Mother assured Bill that people lived higher in many places. After all, the town of Aspen is at an elevation of about 8,000 feet.

Mother was frightened by the prospect of leaving New Mexico with her three children for a job in a place that she didn't know anything about. She was very concerned that taking the job was the wrong decision. I confess to being guilty of strongly motivating the move from Pot Creek. I had become her primary support for making decisions—the man of the family, if you will—even if I wasn't close to being a man. (In fact, I am not certain that I ever really made the cut. Nevertheless, I am apparently allowed to wear affordable men's clothing.) At the time, I thought I had some wisdom. In retrospect, I don't think it was wisdom that motivated me so much as hunger. Whatever caused it, I strongly advocated the move to the new job. I was hungry!

I was never certain that Mom told me everything. Looking back, I know that she didn't. She could never level with me concerning all the trouble she had gotten herself into throughout her life. Nevertheless, she confided in me more and more as time went on. The prospect of moving certainly frightened her. We made the move to Breckenridge because I convinced Mom that we had no choice.

It was not long before the Mayflower moving van that Rounds and Porter paid for appeared at our house and packed everything up that we were taking. It was very close to New Year's Day 1961. In fact, I seem to remember that it was New Year's Day. This seems unlikely.

I was surprised at how expertly the driver managed to cram so much into so little space in the truck. Our belongings were mostly junk with a few family heirlooms mixed in. Nevertheless, the driver treated all of it like it was important.

Loading did not take long. We did not have that much to take. Also I don't remember the driver having any issue with the skunk smell reeking from our clothing and furniture. However, he made no offer to catch the skunks and move them too.

I think we left the same day that the Mayflower van arrived and loaded our belongings. When we departed, nothing was left in the house except the linoleum flooring. Our Pot Creek days were over, and none of us were completely happy about it. It was a frightening time in our lives. I was the only one in the family who saw it as an opportunity and a big adventure. I was almost comfortable with the move. I knew it had to be done.

CHAPTER 20

North to Breckenridge

What was before existence? This question appears to be too difficult to answer without making stuff up. Is there an easier question? Yes! All other questions are easy in comparison to this one.

*****

It was a sunny January day when Blanca Peak's dramatic, tetrahedral summit slowly rose above the horizon as the Nash Ambassador made its way toward the Colorado border. The area below the summit was covered with snow, giving it a frigid appearance. As we made our way into Colorado, the Peak appeared to be blocking our path. A turn west at Fort Garland fixed the problem. We jogged west to Alamosa before heading north again, bound for Poncha Pass. Mom would come to call this part of the road the gun barrel because it did not change direction for many miles. On our right were the mountains of the Northern Sangre de Cristo Range. To the west were additional significant mountains more distant and scattered than the Sangre de Cristo's. The road was not new to me. We had taken it a few years before when we had visited Uncle Edward and his family in Grand Junction, Colorado. Nevertheless, the stark scene before me combined with the uncertainty concerning our future caused me more than a little apprehension.

On that first day, we drove to Leadville and checked into a motel for the night. It was dark when we arrived, but the snow-clad mountains were glowing in the moonlight. The scene was hauntingly beautiful. In contrast, the motel was dismally raunchy. It was more than a bit rundown, but it was what Mom could afford. We weren't very far from Breckenridge. Nevertheless, Mom had decided it would be best to drive over the last obstacle on of our journey, Fremont Pass, in the daylight. We could have taken a shorter route to Breckenridge by turning off at Buena Vista and going over Hoosier Pass. However, the road over this pass was not paved at the time. She opted for the paved route.

The next morning broke bright and sunny. The mountains were awesome, rising above timberline, projecting their whitecaps into a brilliant blue sky. We seemed very close to the summits. We were! Leadville itself is at an elevation of about 10,000 feet. I was filled with optimism. I felt like I was in my kind of country. The prospects for a new life filled me with enthusiasm. The beautiful surroundings certainly improved my outlook. I don't know how Diana and Sam felt about our surroundings, but they certainly didn't share my enthusiasm. They were not impressed by the stark, cold scenery that I thought was so beautiful. They had adjustments to make. This would take time. Their feelings were complicated because they missed Dad, and they did not understand what had happened to our life.

Meanwhile, I continued to be fascinated by all the snow along the road. The final few miles on Highway 9 from Dillon to Breckenridge were spectacular. There was no Lake Dillon in 1961 although the dam was under construction, and the original Dillon was in a completely different location than it is today. The old Dillon was located just south of the dam that was being constructed. However, it was already beginning to move because its 1961 location would eventually be well below the surface of Lake Dillon.

As we entered Breckenridge, Highway 9 turned into Main Street. There were many old abandoned buildings. Most were rundown. Torn shades fluttered from broken windows. Breckenridge had once been a mining town of some 8,000 people, but only about 300 people lived in the town on the day of our arrival.

We continued on Main Street all the way to the south end of town where Roger Grey—a Wichita, Kansas, contractor who often did work for Rounds and Porter—was constructing a bowling alley. To this day, I have no idea why a bowling alley would be one of the first construction projects in what was to be a ski town. Maybe it was the Kansas culture at work. Or better, just a fill-in job until real plans were made. Anyway, the bowling alley turned out to be a great place to hang out before there was any other recreational site in town. Well, there were a couple of bars, but these were not suitable for young people. I can't help but note that there is presently no bowling alley in Breckenridge, but there are many bars. Bowling could not compete with all the other exciting activities that became possible in the old mining town.

Roger was very accommodating. He took us to the Heeney house on Lincoln Avenue across from the school. The office for Summit County Development Corporation was to be set up in the house. In addition, it was to be a temporary place for us to live. After a new office was prepared on Main Street, we would have to find a place to live.

Our Mayflower truck arrived at the Heeney House right on schedule, and we were soon setting up a household together with an office. The office for Summit County Development Corporation was established in the dining room, which was located in front of a downstairs bedroom and behind the living room. There was also a kitchen reached through the dining room or office. It contained a small dining area. The kitchen and bedroom were connected through the office or dining room. There were three more bedrooms upstairs. Mom was the first employee of Summit County Development Corporation in Breckenridge, a name that would soon be changed to Breckenridge Lands. Additional name changes would follow.

We socialized mostly with the Greys after arriving in town. Roger and his wife, Jolene, took good care of us. They had two attractive daughters, Karen and DeAnda. Karen was a little older than me, and DeAnda was a little younger. I couldn't help but be attracted to Karen, and DeAnda was attracted to me. This was both enjoyable and frustrating. Karen was not interested in me at all. I was just a kid to her. To make matters worse, by the time I got back around to an interest in DeAnda, her interest in me had waned. I was learning how the little mating game works for immature humans, and I didn't like it one bit. Nevertheless, I could not disconnect myself from it. I had to play along. It was programmed in.

The Greys lived in a trailer house at the south end of town. We spent a lot of time with them during the first few months in town. We were at the Grey's trailer house early in the morning when Alan Shepard blasted into space on a suborbital flight, becoming the first US astronaut to be launched into space on a rocket. He did not stay long. It was just up and back with no orbiting. I was fascinated by the space program and had been since grade school at Pot Creek.

School in Breckenridge seemed right to me. It wasn't nearly as large as the Taos school I had been attending. More important, it did not have all the cultural problems inherent at Taos where three cultures were brought together in one place. Nevertheless, I did not have any teachers who I thought were memorable in Breckenridge. It was "right" only because it was easy for me to fit in socially. I was like everyone else. Taos was probably better for me.

There was an ice skating pond immediately across Lincoln Avenue from the Heeney house. Beyond the skating pond was a large red brick building that housed most of the Summit County school system. The building is now a library. All Summit County school students went to this school in this building. My little sister attended school in a lower level of the large building.

I don't remember our skunk odor ever being a problem at school. Maybe it was dissipating faster at high altitude. Fitting in at the school and the social life at ice skating pond was easy for Sam and me. Diana was too far behind and very quiet. We didn't have much to do with her and vice versa. Consequently, I don't know how she was impacted by our big change. She must have missed Dad.

CHAPTER 21

Mom's Accident

What is the most profound question that can be asked? Here are a couple of attempts at an answer: "How did we get here? What are we supposed to do?" Followed by "What will happen to the universe when all the stars are so far away from one another that it is impossible for them to detect or influence one another?" Answers: A fluctuation of Nothing to something; Nothing; and Nothing.

*****

We had not been in town long before some of the people working to make Breckenridge into a ski town decided to go on a picnic up Boreas Pass even though winter still held its grip in the high mountain valley. It was not possible to drive up Boreas Pass in winter. Consequently, weasels were used to get us up the pass. Weasels were army surplus vehicles that ran on tracks like a bulldozer. They had been used in World War II, and they were destined to become the original ski-area snowcats at Breckenridge. These vehicles were completely open with no top covering at all. They could easily carry six or seven people who just rattled around inside on makeshift seating. This made for a rather significant possibility for passengers and even the driver to fall out of the vehicle as it navigated over large snowdrifts, first climbing the drift before tipping and plunging down the far side.

As it happened, a heavy snow was falling on the day of the picnic, and the road up Boreas Pass was almost impassable even for the weasels. It took two weasels to get all of us up the pass to our picnic location that was selected on the fly. All of the Greys and Dixons went along with several of other men who were working on the ski area development. The road followed the old railroad route that led from Denver to Breckenridge. We did not go all the way to the top of the pass. Instead, we selected a location for the picnic on the fly. We stopped at an old water tower near the top of the pass that had been used by the railroad in days of yore. There was a shelter that was falling down at the water tower. Nevertheless, it looked to like a good place for our picnic. Well, it was the best place we could find. It did not have any solid walls, but it did provide a little protection from the elements with a roof that was in the slow process of collapsing. Some snow shoveling was required before we could settle in to grill our hamburgers.

I seemed to be in my element. I was really enjoying this crazy adventure in all the snow with more falling all the time. The picnic was terrific! We ate the grilled burgers sitting in snowbanks that had drifted into the bit of shelter that was left standing.

I was having a great time for a couple of reasons. One was that I had always just liked snow and cold, and this seemed to be the ultimate in snow-and-cold conditions. And the other reason was that Karen was along on the trip. However, it was DeAnda who was putting the moves on me. She kept me from falling out of the weasel at least once by having a firm hold on me.

The trip and the picnic were wonderful up to a point. Unfortunately, the trip had a big downside. When we would hit a large snowdrift, the front end of the weasel would rise up as it went over the drift, and then it would suddenly fall down the other side. This tended to leave the occupants hanging in the air for a couple of seconds on the way down. Since the weasels were open with no tops, it was not always clear that everyone would come down inside of the vehicle. DeAnda had managed to save me from falling over the side a number of times. Unfortunately, Mother did not have a similar guardian. Partway down the mountain, the weasel she was in hit one of the big drifts. Mom got suspended in the air like everyone else. Unfortunately, she came down straddling the outside edge of the vehicle. Fortunately, she tumbled into the weasel instead of falling outside. Nevertheless, she seriously injured her hip joint when she came down on the unforgiving metal sidewall of the vehicle. She was in a lot of pain, but she did not complain much. Everyone continued to have fun as the ride down the mountain continued to be rough, unpredictable, and thrilling.

Mom made it back to Breckenridge without making a big deal of her injury. Unfortunately, there was no doctor in town, and it was not clear whether she would have gone to one had it been possible. We had no insurance. In order to get by, she got some crutches somewhere. She ended up using them for a long time. This was the second time in her life that she had hip problems. The first hip problem was the one she was born with. She never went to a doctor with her Breckenridge injury even though it was obviously serious. She simply toughed it out.

CHAPTER 22

Early Days in Breckenridge

Perhaps the most profound question concerning the nature of existence is "What is nothing?" Our inclination is to define *nothing* as empty space. Yet space must be something if it is expanding. Can nothing expand? Why not?

*****

During our time at the Heeney House, an older Native American, Mr. Springmeier, often stopped in to talk to Mom in her temporary office. He liked to tell Mother stories from his days as a paratrooper during World War II. He also told stories from the early days of Breckenridge. He was almost crippled, a condition that he blamed on being a paratrooper in World War II. He indicated that his walking problem was caused by landing on his heels too hard on his jumps.

As it happened, Mr. Springmeier owned a significant amount of property in and around Breckenridge. At the time, he was becoming seriously wealthy by selling his property to Summit County Development Corporation. Nevertheless, Mom wished he would not come around quite so often to tell his many stories. She had work to do. Meanwhile, I really enjoyed his stories when I was around to hear them. It's a shame that when one googles his name, the only information one gets is about the Breckenridge ski run named after him. He was an incredible character as far as I was concerned. Unfortunately, I don't remember many details of his entertaining stories.

Mom was still walking around with a cane as summer approached. She was making small improvements in her mobility. Nevertheless, it was good that she seldom had to leave the house to do her job.

When summer arrived, everything changed. Both the Summit County Development Company office and our residence moved out of the Heeney House to Main Street. An old building on Main Street had been renovated to become the office for the company. The building that the office moved into was in the location of the present-day Rounds and Porter building. The house we moved into was another company house known locally as the A-House because it had a large *A* above the front door. It was about one block north of the company office and on the opposite side of the street. The Lincoln Mall is presently located where the A-House once stood. The front door of the A-House opened onto the sidewalk and street.

Most of the buildings on Main Street were vacant at the time. This was the case for much of the town. However, the Gold Pan Bar and the Hoosier Pass Bar both on Main Street were going strong, as were the general store and Martha's Cafe. These last two businesses were on the same side of the street as the A-house and a little south of us. Both of the bars were across Main Street from the A-House.

Sam and I had fun exploring many of the abandoned buildings in the town and some of the old mines near town. Our explorations netted us many old newspapers that were stuck to the walls in some of buildings. The papers had dates from the 1880s. We found many other interesting items in places where we probably should not have been.

One day, we found some dynamite paper along with a role of fuse. Since we were naturally creative and liked to entertain, we wrapped some of the dynamite paper very neatly around a short length of pipe. Next, we cut a length of fuse and carefully inserted it through the paper into the end of the pipe. We thought it looked like a real stick of dynamite, so we decided to see what other people thought of it. To make our case a little more dramatic, we lit the fuse and walked into the general store thinking we were being very clever. Surely, this was something that would create laughter and frivolity. In our defense, we had not watched much comedy on television, so we didn't know what was funny and what was not. Most of our sense of humor came from *Popeye* cartoons. What would anyone expect of us?

No one in the store at the time saw the humor in our ill-conceived prank. We were in big trouble with the law represented by Deputy Roger Grey. We were also in trouble with Mom. It turned out that Mother was much more severe than the law. Sam and I made a secret pact that we would not try this again until we found a real stick of dynamite—or maybe not.

On one of our explorations, we discovered that we could get into the basement of the grocery store on Lincoln Avenue. The store was located just behind our house. There was a window well located on the east side of the building. The window was cracked, but the glass had not fallen out. Under the guise of conducting an important exploration, we relieved the cracked window of its responsibility for keeping intruders out of the store basement by carefully removing the broken glass. Next, we decided that there would be no harm in entering the basement of the store. We were good boys after all. Once inside, we discovered that the basement contained a stockpile of stored groceries. We did not disturb or take anything; but someone found out we had "broken" in, and we were in trouble again.

Breckenridge was the perfect place for a couple of adventurous boys to explore the limits of acceptable behavior. We got a better understanding of where these limits lay once Mom found out what we did. This did not prevent us from continuing to explore as close to those limits as possible.

Once our first winter arrived in the A-House, Sam and I came up with a nighttime activity that would become one of our favorites. It was made possible because our bedroom windows faced Main Street and were set back so that they looked out over a glassed-in front porch. It did not take us long to notice that late-night patrons of the Gold Pan Bar seemed to stagger out and make their way south to the Hoosier Pass Bar, which was located directly across the street from our house. And there was an equal number of patrons from the Hoosier Pass Bar making the reverse trip. It seemed that there was a system where a person could get inebriated in one of the bars and be sent away only to end up in the other bar to drink until the return trip to the original bar was necessary. This system caused lots of drunken travel along the sidewalk across from our house.

After viewing this activity for a number of nights, Sammy and I decided to make the drunken evenings more interesting for the late-night bar-hoppers. We could easily crawl out of one of our two bedroom windows to a position on the top of the front porch where there was plenty of snow for making ammunition. Going from bar to bar suddenly became much more exciting for patrons of both bars.

Late at night, mostly when Mom was out doing her own evening activities, we would take up our positions on top of the front porch and create a barrage of snowballs that would pelt the alcohol-handicapped patrons of the two bars as they made their way from one watering hole to the other. Our accuracy with the snowballs was excellent, and it was apparently difficult for the impaired bar patrons to see us in our positions on the porch roof. We never got caught playing our little game, but we never slowed the traffic between the bars either. The victims were generally too drunk to figure out what was happening or to care.

School in Breckenridge was much different from what it had been in Taos. It was a much smaller school with kids from all over the county attending. Grade school through high school was all contained in one building located across the street and an ice skating pond from the Heeney House.

The ice skating pond was ideal for socializing during the evenings. The kids often had a bonfire going at the edge of the pond. This was the place where I first got the nerve to put my arm around a girl. I had been interested in achieving this major milestone since I was in the first or second grade, but as I noted before, a horse always seemed to be part of the deal. Sometimes, it can be difficult to live with one's heritage. I did fine without the horse in Breckenridge.

Being a young person was difficult back then, and I think it is even more difficult now except for the fact that there is not as much clothing in the way these days. It seems that there are just too many complications involved with the human's mating process. Animals do much better. Teenage boys are more like animals than the human beings that the girls crave. For animals, the entire process is over quickly. The animals never know what happened. If the mating involves a couple of dogs, they look a little confused after it is over. If one could read their minds, there would probably be a big question banging around in their skull, asking, "What the hell was that all about? Now where did I put my bone?"

Human fantasies, both male and female, are simply not realistic in those early years, causing the frustration to get cranked up rather quickly for the males. I don't really understand all of this. How could I? I am still wondering what the horse that was all about. Maybe I better not go any farther down this road. Also I never got around to figuring out what would happen after the act, whatever it might be, was completed. Maybe that was what the horse was for—to get out of dodge. We had Punch at the Ranch, but there were no girls to ride away from there.

Let me bring this back to Breckenridge and the beginnings of my serious interest in sex that did not involve horses. I managed to steal a girl that Sam was interested in at the ice skating pond one night. The theft got me nowhere because what is one to do out on a sheet of ice with heavy winter coats on? I never figured it out. It would have been better to be on a horse in the summertime. Anyway, I never stole another girl from Sam. We didn't have the same taste, or so I say. Apparently, I liked girls who liked horses—or maybe not. Sam liked motorcycles.

Early in the first summer we were in Breckenridge, I attempted to climb Peak 8 with Doty. It must have been early June. I had a straw cowboy hat on, and my clothing was not very warm. I could not find a trail that led to timberline. There were no ski trails to lead the way yet. I had to make my own way through heavy timber before finally emerging from the trees onto a windy and rather steep land-scape just north of the giant bowl that sits below the summit of Peak

8. There was still plenty of snow on the mountain leftover from winter. When I came to the first band of snow, I attempted to cross it. I quickly sank up to my waist in the snow. I struggle forward but didn't get very far. Doty was struggling too even though she was only about twenty-five pounds or less. She tried to leap through the snow, and it almost worked. Very quickly after entering the first snow band, my cowboy hat blew off, heading mostly north as it angled down toward the trees. Doty chased after the hat, but she could not catch it. It was lost. I still look for it every time I go skiing in Breckenridge. I could say it represents my lost youth. Baloney! I lost my friggin' hat! I did not reach the second snow band. I turned around and headed down after the first one.

CHAPTER 23

Bleeding, Twisting, and Breaking

Does nothing separate universes? If so, then nothing is not simply empty space. It is really nothing? Can we enter a region of nothing where not even space exists? Do all questions that I can ask have answers even if I don't know the answers? Could I go to jail for making up questions that don't have answers?

Sheriff: I'll ask the questions around here.
Me: Okay. Go for it.

*****

Breckenridge as a place for adventure was unsurpassed for me. I was just turning into a teenager and feeling my oats. This is another way of saying I was a bit reckless. Some of my recklessness could be attributed to certain glands that began to have an effect on my brain among other things. No one ever tells you this, but these glands can get you seriously injured; and sometimes there is an attractive girl involved—maybe even a horse.

I continued to find Karen Grey very attractive. She continued to be unaware of me. Nevertheless, one day, Karen and I were tossing a baseball back and forth behind the A-house. The backyard was a mess of old buildings and junk. There was a rundown room or shed attached to the back of the A-house. It had some large windows facing into the backyard. The view from the house in that direction was mostly old, rundown structures from the 1880s. There was not much room to play catch due to all the junk scattered about behind the "shed." Nevertheless, we began throwing a baseball back and forth. We each had a baseball glove. Karen was in the back of the yard, throwing toward the house. In spite of all the obstacles in the backyard, we managed to get a good game of catch going. Sometimes it was necessary to run down a throw, being careful to avoid the obstacles. This worked fine—until I didn't.

Her last throw that day was high over my head, but I thought I could get it if I ran back and jumped for it. I was right. I initiated my jump perfectly, going high while driving myself backward. The ball caught in the pocket of my glove so that I only had to land to demonstrate my prowess at running down baseballs. Unfortunately, her throw headed me for one of the windows on the back of the shed. I was high in the air heading backward when I snagged the ball with the glove. My body with my left elbow leading the way continued its flight backward toward the windows in the shed. My elbow entered a shed window, shattering the glass. Very quickly, there was blood everywhere. It was shooting and gushing from a long gash on the back side of my upper arm. The wound was at least six inches long, beginning on my upper arm near my shoulder and terminating just above my elbow.

The events that followed are not completely clear in my mind. Mother was summoned from work. She got some bandages around my arm that I kept pressed against the wound. There was no doctor or nurse in town. A nurse named Bonnie, who previously practiced in town, had recently moved over Hoosier Pass to Alma. Mom headed over the pass with me.

We soon arrived at Bonnie's house in Alma. We were fortunate; she was home. She examined my arm and said she thought she could close up the wound with butterfly bandages. I had thought she would stitch it up. Maybe she did not have the wherewithal in her house to do stitches. I don't know. She closed the wound with butterfly bandages instead. At the time, this solution seemed to work fairly well. Bonnie finished by wrapping a large bandage around my upper arm, completely covering the six or seven inches of the wound. The bandaging job almost stopped the bleeding. We went back over the pass to Breckenridge.

I don't remember how long the bandages stayed on, but the butterfly bandages that were spaced along the wound did not hold very well. They held in the middle but did not hold near my elbow or up close to my shoulder. Consequently, I had my first real conversation-piece scar. It would not be my last or the worst. Nevertheless, it had healed up fairly well after a few weeks, leaving only the significant scar, which still goes wherever I go.

*****

During the first winter in Breckenridge, Trygve Berge and Sigurd Rockne began teaching us to be ski racers. They were the ski resort's two Norwegian ski champions who had been hired to set up the ski school. They wanted to get some of the boys into ski racing. Unfortunately, they didn't have much talent to work with. Most of us had not spent any significant time on skis, and none of us had run gates before. They got us running gates.

When they arrived during our first summer in Breckenridge, it was clear that they were addicted to speed. They had put together a souped-up go-kart that they would race up and down Main Street, often continuing up Hoosier Pass at the south end of town. They were hitting speeds of more than sixty miles per hour going through town. Finally, the town sheriff asked them to stop their high-speed runs. A go-kart on the highway is not a good idea unless one can lie flat enough on it to slide under the cars that never saw you coming. Even this does not work if one's nose is too large.

I was sorry to see the go-kart go. It was exciting to hear it coming and to get out of the way. Seeing them go by was thrilling. I loved the speed. Maybe I was learning that I might have a speed-addiction problem.

When fall came, Sam, Diana, and I all became ski-clothing models for a fashion show and a photo shoot high on Mt. Baldy, where we had to go to get into the snow. The photos would be put into a brochure for the ski area. We also had to be models in an early-season fashion show. Even though it was fun work, I felt like a sissy doing it. Me, a fashion model? I don't think so. I did not enjoy parading around on a small stage in front of people. Nevertheless, I felt a little special. I was a male model after all! This would never happen again. I wonder why I have never included this experience on my resume. No, I don't.

Soon after the fashion show, the resort started gearing up for its first ski season. Sam and I had played on toy skis before we moved to Breckenridge, but we were not skiers by any stretch of imagination. Nevertheless, we learned fast, and we both loved speed. Once the ski area was open, we were spending most of our weekend time skiing. Lift tickets were four dollars per day, but we did not have pay for them because Mom worked for the company that owned the ski area.

At the time, Trygve was one of about five people in the world who could go off a small jump and do a complete somersault before landing. Stein Ericsson, who had brought Trygve and Sigurd from Norway, was one of the others. A postcard was made of Trygve doing his somersault with Sam and me along with a few of our friends standing near the small jump, watching him rotate through the air. This photograph can still be seen from time to time in the museum in Breckenridge and other places.

Anyway, it was not long before Trygve and Sigurd had us running gates on Thursday afternoons after school. It seemed we were learning fast, but we had a long way to go to catch up with Scott and Rudd Pyles, two of our friends from Frisco who had been skiing and racing before either could walk. Well, maybe not quite that long, but close. They were future Olympic ski-team members. They did not ski with our group at Breckenridge. Instead, they trained at Arapahoe Basin, an older ski area in Summit County that existed long before the vision of Breckenridge popped into Bill Rounds' noggin.

Thursday, March 15, 1962, became a major turning point in my life. The event that happened that day would determine my destiny, good and bad, for the rest of my life. As was usual on Thursday afternoons, we met on the ski hill after school to run gates under the supervision and coaching of Trygve and Sigurd. We were learning to be ski racers. Someone had given us a ride up to the ski area, which was at the base of the current Peak 8 area. We went to the top of the lift and ran a few gates on the slopes, coming out of the bowl located at the top of the lift.

Once we finished with the gates, our two Norwegian coaches led us to the lower part of the mountain where we went under the chairlift. The goal was to have some fun on a rather large pile of logs located underneath the chairlift near the bottom of the mountain. The logs made for a challenging ski jump for us to practice or play on. We were mostly just having fun with Trygve and Sigurd after our coaching was done for the day. Nevertheless, the log pile was good practice for dealing with big bumps that sometimes had to be dealt with in a race. Even though the jump was on rather flat terrain, it was large enough to give us a long flight where we could almost feel like we were sprouting wings. The pile of logs was to provide our last excitement of the day. It fulfilled our wildest expectations!

Trygve and Sigurd went first. They took long graceful flights after they lifted off from the log pile, showing us how profession-als did it. However, we could not see their landings due to the ter-rain. Nevertheless, we knew they always looked good flying through the air. Even though the main purpose of this exercise was fun, our coaches also wanted us to get used to airtime on skis.

I had been fascinated by jumpers flying through the air on skis since the 1960 Olympics, but I had a history of trouble getting my landing gear down properly on my previous attempts at jumping. A badly sprained ankle earlier in the year on the jumping hill near the high school attested to this fact.

By this time, I knew something about pre-jumping to prevent one from flying too far off a jump. Downhill racers do this to min-imize airtime and the corresponding loss of speed while they are in the air. I had never gone of on this particular makeshift jump before. It was much larger than the one at the school that I had sprained an ankle on. I was uncertain about what I was up against and how I would deal with it. From where I stood above the log pile, it looked almost doable mostly because it had a rather flat approach. Nevertheless, it also had a rather severe compression going into the jump. I don't remember being concerned about the compression. The landing slope was not very steep, and this was probably not good. Nonetheless, I was mostly okay with it even though I knew there would be significant airtime before the landing. I decided that I would try to pre-jump when I was in the compression to reduce my airtime somewhat, allowing me to arrive at home in time for dinner.

I watched Trygve and Sigurd as they made the jump look easy. And then a few others on the team, including Sam, went down ahead of me. They all made it look difficult for as far as I could follow them. They disappeared from view before they landed the jump. I figured most were crashing on landing since it was taking a while to get the "all clear" signal to proceed with the next jumper. It was encouraging that I did not hear any loud screaming or howling as jumpers went off the jump. Nevertheless, the delays indicated that the jump was more difficult than it looked. The debris apparently had to be gathered up after each jumper scattered poles and skis on landing. This made my decision to pre-jump look even better.

Finally, it was my turn. I somewhat apprehensive as I pointed my skis down the hill toward the log pile. I pushed off rather tentatively. I liked my plan, but it required proper execution. Afterward, I would come to the conclusion that it didn't really take enough account of the big compression that occurred just as one went into the jump. At least this is what I think was the primary source of my problem after thinking about it and reliving it for some sixty years.

I don't really remember much about my flight that day. This deficiency won't prevent me from attempting to describe it in some detail. Okay, the following description is mostly made up for the reader's amusement. I remember snatches of what happened. I simply filled in between the snatches to glorify myself as much as possible and to make the telling coherent.

As I went into the compression, I got thrown off balance. The compression was larger than I expected, causing my timing of the pre-jump to be late. The late timing gave me a long flight and an entry to airspace I was not authorized to enter. I began pinwheeling with my arms to try and get my body forward to give me the proper landing attitude. Almost no ski instructors, including Trygve and Sigurd, teach the art of pinwheeling. It didn't work for me that day. I imagine that I looked something like a tumbling, frozen chicken shot from a canon to test airplane windshields.

I continued to rotate everything I could, hoping that I would be lucky enough to have everything in a good place for the landing. Hope does not work well in such situations. I had nothing else. Hope was the only thing in my mind that was not frozen out by the drama of my situation. I became a simple passenger along for a terrifying ride, knowing full well that things were not going to end well. I was right.

One of my ski tips, the left one, dipped low just before I reestablished contact with the snow. It caught in the snow. Distorting me into a position that would not only cost me all my style points but also bent my body in ways that are illegal in most of the civilized world. Something had to give, and it did. My left femur snapped clean in two. I slid to a stop on the snow, fully aware that something catastrophic had occurred. I communicated this fact to the rest of the ski team and everyone else in the high mountain valley by means of a very loud shriek followed by a series of screams.

A real man would have struggled to his feet and collapsed again when the leg wouldn't hold him up. He would have then expressed himself with a loud curse and attempted to drag himself out of the way for the next jumper. Well, I was only a real boy, but I had the presence of mind to not curse because I did not want to get thrown off the team. Or maybe I did curse. I don't really remember.

Sam had gone off the jump ahead of me. He had survived, but I was not paying much attention to the guys who had gone ahead of me. As I lay on the snow, I was experiencing incredible pain. I wish I could say it was enlightening, but it wasn't. I just hurt like hell. I knew immediately that my injury was serious, and it would give me a good excuse for not getting my math homework done.

My left leg was completely out of kilter. The thigh muscle was contracting and pulling the two points of my spiral fractured femur into my thigh muscle. It was like being stabbed in the leg with two knives that wouldn't stop stabbing.

It did not take Trygve long to climb back up to me and wedge himself against the side of my body in an attempt to support and comfort me. It worked a little. Some of others also climbed up or came down to gather around. I didn't give a damn what they did at that point. Trygve continued to support and comfort me with words. He told me not to worry; the same thing had happened to him once. He had recovered to race again. I would be fine, he said. I paid attention to him because I wanted to hear something good and to believe it. Nevertheless, I didn't believe him.

It was not far to the bottom of the hill from where I lay, but the chairlift had quit running for the day. It had to be restarted because there was no toboggan at the top of the lift. One would be needed to transport me to the first aide room in the lodge at the base of the lift. The ski patrol had to load a toboggan onto the lift to take it to the midway point. They would then bring it down to me from there and load me into it to get me off the mountain. The toboggan finally arrived. When I was lifted into it, I let out a scream that must have been heard over the entire mountain. To this day, it is surely the loudest noise I have ever made. My thigh muscle was contracting, increasing the spearing action of the two separate parts of my femur. The pain was incredible!

Once I was loaded onto the toboggan, I was taken to the first aide room at the bottom of the ski lift. I am told that an ambulance was summoned, but it failed to show up because it crashed on the way. I did not learn about this until later. My brother, the toughest guy I have ever known, stepped outside the first aide room and vomited in the snow. Meanwhile, I just laid on a table in the first aide room. I was still in the toboggan cradle, trying to be still to avoid the pain caused by contractions of my upper leg. The ski patrol knew enough to put something substantial underneath my knee to keep the leg bent. I think this helped—a little.

I don't know how long it took, but Mom finally showed up with Roger and Jolene Grey. They had a station wagon. The plan was to transport me to the nearest hospital, which was located in

Kremmling, Colorado, about forty miles away. They loaded me into the station wagon still in the toboggan cradle. It barely fit. Mom and Jolene were in the front seat with Roger, who was driving. I continued to be in extreme pain. I don't know if I had been given anything for it in the first aide room. It probably wouldn't have made much difference either way. I attempted not to move at all because the slightest movement set off the pain and screams.

I don't remember much about the ride to Kremmling. It was dark when we arrived at the hospital. I was taken into the emergency room by means that I don't remember. I was still in the toboggan cradle. I got a morphine shot right away. This provided much needed relief for the pain.

X-rays were taken, and I heard the doctor tell my mother, "There is nothing we can do for him here. You will have to get him to a big hospital." I don't think these words fazed me much at the time. I was barely conscious, and I had already been given the morphine when I heard the doctor's words. Mother knew what to do, but she did not talk to me about it. I was too drugged by that time to understand.

I don't remember much about the rest of that first night in Kremmling. I don't even recall the transition to a hospital room and the traction device that was set up and attached to me. I would learn that it consisted of a special shoe, a pulley, and a large weight that hung at the bottom of the bed. The weight kept my thigh muscle from pulling the two spears of broken femur together, greatly reducing the pain. I was given enough morphine to put me into a state of delirium. This did not improve my memory of the events that night. Nevertheless, I do remember that whenever I complained about the pain, a nurse would give me another shot; I believe they were giving me morphine. I made it through the night with the help of the shots. I drifted in and out of consciousness.

I don't remember how long I had been in the Kremmling hospital before Dr. O'Donnell came to see me. He was an orthopedic doctor from Colorado Springs who was given free-lift tickets at Breckenridge for being on call during the weekends. I believe that he and Mom arrived together probably the first or second day that I was in the hospital. He told me that I would be airlifted to

Colorado Springs the next day. I was somewhat relieved that there was a plan. However, the next day came, and the airlift did not happen. The weather was not good, so the flight was cancelled, or so I was told. I was not looking forward to another trip anyway. I knew the traction was important for keeping me out of pain, but I did not how it would work when I was being transported. Cancellations of my flight occurred daily. After a few days, I was told that I would be transported by ambulance to Colorado Springs. This could have happened because Mom realized that she couldn't afford to have me airlifted.

During my time in the Kremmling hospital, I had only one memorable moment that stayed with me. I was in the habit of hitting my call button and asking for a pain shot when the previous one started wearing off. The nurses accommodated me with their wonderful needles. However, one morning, I hit the call button, and a nurse I had not seen before responded to my call. I told her that I was in significant pain. She listened to my complaint and looked at the traction apparatus. Perplexed, she finally said, "No wonder you are in pain," as she reached down and lifted the weight that was providing the traction at the foot of my bed. I let out a scream that surely awakened and frightened every patient in the small hospital. She let the weight go immediately. I never saw her again.

I had been in the Kremmling hospital about a week when an ambulance arrived to take me to Penrose Hospital in Colorado Springs. I was a little concerned by this development because of the complexity of the traction apparatus and my sensitivity to any changes in it. I did not know how it would work in an ambulance. When the time came, it worked, but I don't remember the details. I seem to remember that I was given plenty of morphine and loaded into the ambulance with a makeshift traction engaged. Mom rode in the front with the driver. He must have been very excited to get to drive with the red light and siren engaged all the way from Kremmling to Colorado Springs, a distance of about 155 miles. I complained along the way that his driving was causing me pain as I was thrown around. I also remember thinking that my life was not in danger from my accident as much as it was from the wild ride. I don't think that I expressed this out loud, and I don't remember Mother saying anything at all.

We arrived in Colorado Springs with no difficulty other than my pain. Unfortunately, the driver did not know where our destination, Penrose Hospital, was located. Mother had the address but did not know how to get to the hospital either. The driver stopped at a gas station and asked for directions as soon as we entered the city. The Hispanic attendant was so excited that he suddenly forgot how to speak English. He began pointing and yelling, certain that I had get there immediately because my life was in danger. I could not help but love him for it. After all, the light on the ambulance was flashing and the siren was sounding as if it were an emergency. The driver finally just pulled away without getting any useful directions. With Mom's help and a few missteps, we arrived at Penrose Hospital.

I was taken directly to surgery upon arrival. I did not know what to expect. No one had talked to me about what was to be done. I had not even been informed that I would have surgery. I was quickly knocked out.

When I regained consciousness after the surgery, I was in misery. I was almost entirely incased in plaster. I was in a body cast. It came most of the way up my chest, stopping just below my armpits, and it went all the way down my broken leg, leaving only my toes sticking out. It also went halfway down the unbroken leg, stopping just above the knee. There was a brace between my knees, reinforcing the plaster that kept my legs well apart. There were two corks on the outside of the cast located just below the knee of my broken leg. I don't remember when I learned that these covered to two ends of a pin that went through my shin bone to hold my femur in traction while I was in the cast.

I was not so much in pain when I came out of surgery as I was miserable and claustrophobic. When Dr. O'Donnell came to see me, I would not speak to him. It is probably not a good idea to put your doctor on your shit list when you are totally dependent on him or her. Nevertheless, I was upset with everyone except the nurse who brought me the pain shots. She quickly became my favorite person in the world. However, even this relationship was destined to wither in my cloud of misery and gloom.

It was not possible to keep me on morphine for long even though I would have gladly agreed to becoming a drug addict if they would just keep the shots coming. This didn't happen. Instead, my favorite nurse began bringing small white pills instead of shots. I begged her for a shot instead. She was steadfast in denying me the shot. Our relationship withered. She was a professional. Our failing relationship didn't bother her at all. Yet I still have not forgiven her for not letting me turn into a drug addict. Or maybe I have, but she surely could have given me one more shot. That's all I was asking for after all—one more little shot. I eventually adjusted and recovered from being a junkie. It is not an easy transformation to make even when it is forced on one by a jail made of plaster.

I don't remember how long I stayed in Penrose Hospital before Mom arranged for her sister, Jessie, to drive her station wagon from her home in Santa Rosa, New Mexico, to Penrose Hospital where she picked me up—body cast and all—and transported me home to Breckenridge. My grandmother came with Jessie as part of the deal. All three met at the hospital. The staff loaded me into the back of the station wagon. I was very glad to be leaving. The pain was not so bad, and I was no longer addicted to morphine. I remember driving past Pikes Peak to enter South Park, which we crossed on the way to Breckenridge. I remember Grandmother and Jessie commenting on the stark mountains that ringed the north and west side of South Park's flat expanse. It is an unusual geographical feature, but I was not into the scenery. Besides, I had seen it before.

I don't remember anything about the unloading process when we arrived in Breckenridge. Transferring me from the station wagon to the living room of the A-House would not have been simple. There was a steep stairway inside of the glassed-in porch that led up to the entrance to the living room. I suspect Mother had arranged for some men to help because she could not have carried me up even with the help of my aunt and grandmother. I don't remember this part of the process, but it must have been exciting, so exciting that I blacked out.

Mother had rented a hospital bed and placed it in the living room in front of the windows that provided a view through the glassed-in front porch. I could see Peak 8 and much of the Tenmile Range. I had a good view of the ski trails on Peak 8 from my bed. It was the best place I could think of to be in a body cast.

One can imagine that life in a body cast is constrained to the very basics. Initially, one thinks that he can't do as much as an amoeba. However, I could still read and look at the view, leaving the amoeba way behind. My bed had a trapeze affair that I could use to do pull-ups in order to exercise my arms. The pivot point was the heel of the cast on the broken leg. I had to be turned over twice a day to lay on my stomach for one half hour before returning to lying on my back. I was miserable on my stomach because claustrophobia was much worse in that position. Of course, there was a bedpan and a urinal involved. Grandmother was my constant companion, taking care of all my necessities except for the freedom part.

As I settled into my life of extreme confinement, I spent much of my time reading. This caused Mother to say that she was glad it was me and not Sam who had gotten hurt. One might think that this remark would have hurt my feelings. It didn't. Sam would not have read much. Besides, he was already building a reputation for never going full-term in a cast. He removed them himself. She must have known that he would have quickly figured out how to get out of the body cast one way or the other.

Some of the kids from school visited me, but they did not spend a lot of time with me. When one is looking at a kid in a body cast, one has seen about all there is to see in about two minutes and said about all one can think of to say. You know, stuff like "Does it hurt? How do you...you know? Can you get out of bed at all?" Most people don't think it is polite to ask "How do you, uh, well, you know, number 2?" The answer would have been "It's easier than numbers 3 and 4."

Since I was able to see the mountains by looking out of the front windows, my attitude improved somewhat, but I needed something to augment my reading. Mother realized this and arranged for an artist who painted pictures for motel rooms to come and give me a painting lesson. The two of us started an oil painting together. Well, my part in this is questionable, but I did finish the painting myself. He started by showing me how to paint trees and shadows. Even though I did not catch on, I finished the painting. It was a mountain scene of Peak 8, created by looking at the postcard with Trygve doing his somersault on skis. However, it did not have Trygve or his spectators in it. I still have the painting that we started together. I finished it while I was in the cast. One can clearly distinguish the small region in the center of the painting that the professional artist painted to show me how to do it. Looking at the rest of the painting, it is apparent that I did not catch on. The painting is not very good, but it is still amuses me. It is presently hanging in the sewing room in my Batavia house. However, I seldom go into the sewing room, and I don't show the painting off or brag about it. One only has to look at it to understand why. Nevertheless, the painting is an important part of me.

The most difficult part of my stay in the cast was constipation. This got to be a serious issue a short time after I arrived in at home. Fortunately, a doctor had just moved into town to set up a practice. Mother called him, and he came with his jackhammer, picks, and shovels. He also had some more appropriate tools, none of which worked. The concrete had apparently set. He was as frustrated as was I. Finally, he came back with a nurse who brought her special formula for an enema along. He tried it, and it worked! I would not have to be flushed into the Breckenridge sewage system in one piece after all. His nurse became my all-time hero.

While I was in the body cast, the space program was getting a good start. Earlier, we had watched the launch of Alan Shepard on a suborbital flight. Gus Grissom and John Glenn had also made their flights. I remember watching Scott Carpenter's *Aurora 7* flight on television while I was in the body cast. He was a local Colorado boy who almost made good. However, he overshot his landing site by 250 miles, which, it turns out, is not as bad as messing up a pre-jump by a foot or two. The space program was very exciting to me. However, it didn't take much to excite me in my state of existence that was right on the boundary of nonbeing.

My grandmother and I made it through the three months that I was in the body cast. I don't remember how I was transported back to Colorado Springs. I suspect my aunt Jessie was called to service again, or maybe it was the ambulance guy. By then, I was finished having memorable adventure trips.

When I arrived at Penrose Hospital, Dr. O'Donnell immediately began cutting the cast off. I was somewhat surprised that he didn't knock me out first since I expected he would also remove the pin that went through the shin bone just below my knee. Cutting the plaster was somewhat irritating to my skin. I did not enjoy it. Finally, there was nothing left of the cast except a small amount of plaster below the knee that contained the traction pin. Without warning, the Dr. O'Donnell grabbed the small chunk of plaster and pin and yanked the pin out. I felt nothing. The cast was off, and I was free. Well, not quite. I could not just jump up and run away, but it was not long before I could move around in a wheelchair. My leg had to be held straight out because the knee had not been bent in a long time. It was calcified into the straight position.

My first therapy session in the hospital came soon after the cast was removed. The plan was to put me into a whirlpool bath. I was wheeled to the pool in a wheelchair with my injured leg held straight out. When I arrived, one of the therapists told me they were going to stand me up and then put me in the pool. The first thing that was done was to drop away the wheelchair support under my injured leg. I screamed in pain as my calcified knee that had not been bent for three months attempted to bend under the force of gravity. (I always seem to get in trouble with gravity.) I immediately pushed myself out of the chair and stood straight up for the first time in over three months, allowing my injured leg to hang straight down. This did not make the therapists happy. Making them happy did not seem to be in my job description. They tolerated me and soon had me in the pool where my rehabilitation began. It was painful at times, but for the most part, it went well. I made rapid progress.

While in therapy, I had a number of roommates in the hospital. One of the first was a young boy twelve or thirteen years old who had been thrown from a horse and had a severe concussion along with a small skull fracture. He was mostly unconscious although he would say things from time to time that almost made sense. His mother, who was very concerned about him, was present in our room much of the time. I remember when the medical staff set about to insert a catheter, his mother asked if they were going to castrate him. The nurse doing the job did not laugh. She just explained what she was doing.

Even though the boy was basically unconscious, he talked much of the time. His mother tried to explain things to him, and sometimes he could almost carry on a sensible conversation. I remember his mother telling him that there was another boy on the other side of the room behind the curtain, and he responded, "Let him out!"

Later on, I had another roommate who was about my age. At first, he wouldn't tell me what his problem was, but it seemed like he had some pain in the middle section of his body. He tried to be a real cool teenager, and one day, his girlfriend came to see him. She asked him if he had told me what had happened to him. He confessed that he hadn't. She laughed. After she left, he decided that he better level with me. He told me that he had gotten into a little love spat with his girlfriend, and she had thrown his ring out into the yard. When he went to retrieve it, he bent over to pick it up, and she attempted to shoot him in the derriere with a BB gun. She sort of missed and hit one of his testicles.

When my therapy was done, I was able to get around on crutches, but I was not done with my medical adventures. When Dr. O'Donnell had removed the body cast, he discovered a bad sore on the heel of my injured leg that was originally caused by the traction shoe in Kremmling. He had dressed the wound before he sealed it up in the body cast. It had not healed during the three months in the body cast. In fact, it had gotten much worse. Gangrene had set in.

Dr. O'Donnell instructed me to put a special dressing on the sore. It did not heal. Why the heel of the cast had not been left open so that the wound could be redressed regularly is still a mystery to me. Dr. O'Donnell sent me home with instructions for keeping it bandaged and dressed. I had to go back and see him fairly often. It soon became evident that the wound was not going to heal without additional intervention. A skin graft was in order. This meant another trip to the Penrose Hospital.

For reasons that I don't understand, Dr. O'Donnell performed the skin graft himself even though his specialty was orthopedic surgery. Well, I have my suspicions that have to do with possible malpractice. He clearly felt responsible for the condition of my heel. Anyway, he made a large incision down one side of the back of my leg so that he could stretch and twist the skin over the problem area on the heel. This left a significant notch in the back of my leg near the middle of my calf muscle. Apparently, the muscle underneath had some rearrangement also. The notch was just a missing chunk of calf muscle about half an inch deep and two inches wide. He covered the notch with a thin layer of skin from my thigh, effectively creating a second skin graft. In addition, there were more than two hundred stitches down the side of my lower leg where the skin and muscle had been slipped down to cover the heel. This strange bit of surgery did not work well at all. I could not see what he had done because he put a cast on my leg that was slightly bent at the knee and covered the area from my foot to halfway up my thigh. I was in plaster and on crutches again.

Dr. O'Donnell came to our house in Breckenridge to remove the cast and the stitches. Taking stitches out was very a painful process. Many of them were wire stitches and some were thread. It was clear from looking at the wound created by the skin graft that my leg was not healing properly. The incision was a mess toward the bottom of the of my leg and around the back of my heel. When the stitches were removed, the lower part of the wound was still an open sore. I was given ointment to use. It didn't do much good. Nevertheless, the open sore eventually healed, leaving the ugly scar. My lower leg looks like the surgery was performed using a chain saw and a chisel. Even now, I am sometimes asked by those who see my scar if I was attacked by a shark. On the plus side, I have a leg that is fully functional. I still don't have any feeling in the back of my lower leg, although feeling seems to be slowly returning. At the rate it is returning, I will be about 114 years old when the process is complete. It will be time to celebrate the 100th anniversary of the accident. Fortunately, feeling in this part of the human body is not required for most normal human activities.

The most significant result of my adventure is that my left leg ended up more than an inch shorter than my right leg. Fortunately, the missing part is in the upper leg so that my foot still reaches the floor or—Never mind. It works. Most people don't notice it in my walk.

CHAPTER 24

Back in School

Black holes and white holes are places where time, space, and matter disappear and appear. Black holes are known to exist because they have been observed, most recently and spectacularly, in gravitational-wave experiments. White holes have not been observed. However, some theoretical physicists have reasons explaining the absence of their observation. Could they be places where universes are born? Do they lie on the far side of a black hole's singularity?

*****

When I got back to school at Summit County High School during the fall after my accident, the school had moved out of the classic, old red-brick building in Breckenridge to a temporary location in Frisco. Classes were held in various locations around the small town, including some churches. One had to walk around the town to move from class to class.

This situation had arisen because there had been a fight between the communities in Summit County to move the school out of the old building in Breckenridge to a new building location to be determined by the outcome of the fight. The primary argument used by the people who wanted to move the school was that the school building in Breckenridge was not safe. It was argued that it might fall down any day. One of the arguments claimed that our gymnasium could fall into the swimming pool below it. I had graduated from the eighth grade in that gym, and it seemed sturdy to me. I concluded that the nature of the battle for a new school located somewhere else in Summit County was primarily a political struggle that had nothing to do with the safety of our building. I was apparently correct. To verify this, one only has to note the fact that the old building in Breckenridge is still standing and being used as a library and a movie theatre while the new school that was built on the edge of Lake Dillon in Frisco is long gone. Politics is seldom the best way to make good decisions. Too many people want something for themselves, and the politics of numbers often leads to bad decisions.

The root of the problem was that the school served three communities in Summit County that were approximately the same size, and everyone thought that the high school should be in their community. A good solution was eventually found by building a centrally located school that isn't in any of the Summit County towns. It took too long to arrive at this solution.

I was still using one crutch as my sophomore year began in the temporary, spread-out location of our school in Frisco. Classes were distributed between churches and other public buildings in town. There were also some temporary, moveable buildings put in place. I have to admit that I do not remember having any particular difficulty getting around. I had put myself well ahead of my doctor's schedule. It was not long before I was not using my crutches at all except when I went to Colorado Springs to visit Dr. O'Donnell. Maybe this was because gravity was stronger at the lower elevation—or maybe not.

To make our school life a little more interesting, the juniors and sophomores decided they should get together and beat up the seniors. There was not much real fighting. These were not tough kids or thugs, after all. Yet they seemed to have a need for some excitement. They would have all been in real trouble in Taos or Pot Creek. There was little fighting and a great deal of talk. Nevertheless, one of my friends did get a bone broken near his temple. It happened during a scuffle that should not have been serious, but even scuffles can sometimes result in injury. It turned out to be somewhat serious because it could have caused some bleeding into his brain. This didn't happen, and he recovered quickly.

Even though I was supposed to be using one crutch, or maybe it was two, I got somewhat involved in the fighting when one of my "friends" called me out one afternoon on the school-bus ride from Frisco back to Breckenridge. I couldn't believe it. He came at me after we got off the bus. I defended myself with a crutch, and others quickly stepped in. No one was hurt, but I was certainly surprised that anyone thought they could score some social points by beating up a kid on crutches. Well, I have already admitted that I was mostly using the crutches for show by this time. Anyway, this demonstrated how silly young males can be.

CHAPTER 25

Mr. Perrin

At the end of the nineteenth century, scientists were amusing themselves by attempting to measure the speed of light in addition to the related problem of measuring the speed of the Earth moving through the ether as it orbited the sun. To accomplish these feats, they measured the speed of light in the direction of Earth's motion, in the opposite direction, and in a direction perpendicular to the Earth's motion. The results perplexed them. All three measurements yielded the same result—186,000 miles per second. Really? If you believe this, I have a team of flying reindeer you may be interested in buying. The bad news is that it takes a full bottle of tequila to get them off the ground. The good news is that the tequila is for you, not the reindeer.

*****

I was very fortunate to get a summer job working for Mr. Perrin in the summer of 1963. I don't remember how I learned about the job. Mr. Perrin and his wife drove from Philadelphia to their house in Breckenridge every summer in their Buick. After they arrived, they would hire a young person to help with a great variety of chores around their house. They were an older couple and apparently quite wealthy. The job involved doing the various chores on weekday mornings. The variety of tasks ranged from carrying out the trash to painting the outside of their house. I also cut the grass, sharpened tools, and cleaned Mr. Perrin's saddles with saddle soap. It amused me that he did not have any horses, but he had several saddles. Should a horse come by looking for work, the saddles were ready. I also pulled weeds in addition to occasionally working inside the house for Mrs. Perrin.

I spent four or five hours per day at the Perrin's house. On many days, I would only spend about half of my time doing assigned tasks, and the rest of the time was spent talking with Mr. Perrin. It seemed that these discussions were included as part of the job. The routine was that I would work for a while, and then Mr. Perrin would talk to me after had I completed the assigned tasks for the day.

During these discussions, he would ask me about my plans for the future. It seemed he wanted to make certain that I had a plan in place for my life. I told him that I thought I wanted to be an engineer, a conclusion I had only recently come to after getting to know a couple of the engineers who worked on the ski-area construction. Previously, I had wanted to be a scientist. By the time I was working for Mr. Perrin, I was thinking of becoming an acoustical engineer because I liked music, and the notion had been put into my head by one of the ski-area engineers. Mr. Perrin did not discourage me. Instead, he emphasized the importance of going to college and warned me to not let myself get sidetracked "like so many young people were prone to do." He endorsed my ambition to become an engineer.

In addition to talking about my future plans, he also tried to give me a philosophy for life. He indicated that everyone should have goals and try to make a contribution to the world by accomplishing something. In some ways, he reminded me of Grandfather, but his advice was much more explicit. His perspective of the world was much different from Grandfather's. This was not surprising since his background was also very different. I am not certain of this conclusion because I never learned much about Mr. Perrin's life. He never talked about himself. I only surmised that he was well-off from his lifestyle.

Grandfather was very good at understanding how things worked, and he had experience surviving where it was difficult to survive. He liked understanding science and the technical aspects of the world, but he also had a tendency to look outside the realm of hard science for answers to the bigger questions of existence. I could not determine where or if Mr. Perrin sought answers to the bigger questions.

I certainly enjoyed my conversations with Mr. Perrin even though I felt a little guilty about getting paid to sit on his veranda talking with him. I knew he was trying to do some good in the world by giving me guidance. I don't know if Mother was complicit in these discussions. I don't even know if he knew that Mom was a single mom. I certainly felt that he was giving me fatherly advice.

Chapter 26

Getting a Driver's License in Breckenridge

Were all the speed-of-light measurements wrong? No! Scientists don't make mistakes! They just wander off the path once in a while, or so I say. In this case, they were stumbling onto the path leading to the next big breakthrough in physics: Einstein's special theory of relativity.

*****

I turned sixteen just before my junior year in high school in Summit County. I had been driving since I was a six or seven years old, if you don't count the time I spent on my grandfather's lap steering the jeep. I also had the experiences of rolling the Buick down the hill in Taos and the Power Wagon incident at Pot Creek. Therefore, it should come as no surprise that getting a real driver's license would be an adventure.

When I reached the age when I was eligible for a driver's license, I went to the courthouse in Breckenridge and found my way to the Motor Vehicles Department. I had studied for the written part of the test, and I passed the written exam without any problem. I was soon heading out with a gruff, older gentleman to take the road test in our 1959 Ford. As soon as we got in the car, he began giving me directions for where to drive and what to do. I did as he instructed.

With the exception of Main Street, all the streets in Breckenridge were dirt streets. No lanes were marked, and I don't remember if there were any one-way streets. After we went through a couple of stop signs and turns without any problem, he told me, "Pretend this is a one-way street and you are going to make a left turn at the next intersection." I got into the left lane and put my turn signal on. When I got to the intersection, I turned onto the intersecting street. Next, he said, "Pretend this is a one-way street and the next cross street is also one-way. Turn left onto it." Once again, I moved the left-hand lane and turned into the left-hand lane of the cross street as if it were a one-way street. After making the turn, I quickly moved into the right-hand lane to avoid any cars that might be coming toward me on the street, not expecting to get involved with my driver's license test. There was not much danger of this because there was very little traffic in Breckenridge.

After a following his instructions a few more times, we returned to the courthouse. I felt confident that I had done well and would soon have a driver's license. I was wrong. As soon as I stopped the car, the gruff old gentleman announced that I had failed the test. I was shocked. I don't remember if I asked why I had failed. Nevertheless, he told me, saying, "You never disobey any traffic laws such as driving in the wrong lane or turning into a wrong lane, no matter who tells you to do it." To pass the test successfully, I should have refused to pretend. Instead, I should have told him what I would do if the street had been a one-way street. I went home without a driver's license.

I don't remember how long I had to wait to take the test again, but I passed it easily the next time. The same delightful old gentleman who had given me the first test gave me the same test the second time. He was likely the only person who gave driving tests in Summit County. He gave me a similar set of trick questions. It didn't matter. I understood the rules of the game. I passed the test. Sometime later, I read that Colorado was the most difficult state to get a driver's license in. I understood why.

CHAPTER 27

The Fall of 1963

Albert Einstein, a patent clerk who didn't have enough honest work to do, provided the explanation of the unvarying speed-of-light measurements with his special theory of relativity. Careful measurements of lengths and time intervals by different observers yield different results depending on the relative motions of the observers and the objects. This might sound trivial, but it isn't... More to come.

*****

As I entered my junior year in high school in 1963, my crutches had been ejected, and I was and feeling my oats. We went to the new school located near the edge of Lake Dillon. The lake was slowly filling as the recently constructed Dillon Dam began backing up the water from the Blue River as it flowed north from Breckenridge.

One of my best friends, Jerry Meyers, had an old Chevrolet convertible that he began driving to school. I began riding with him instead of taking the bus. We also went on at least one double date together in that old car. My social life was coming back.

During this time, Mom had managed to come up with the money to buy a house in Breckenridge. It was on Harris Street, just south of the abandoned school building and about a block away from the Heeney House where we had lived when we first arrived in Breckenridge. The new house needed some renovation, and we got some of it done. Sam and I claimed a large, unfinished room upstairs for our bedroom. It had enough room to put a workbench for our skis and other projects. Meanwhile, Diana took the only other upstairs bedroom. We had traipsed through her room to get to ours. It worked. Mom had part of the living room petitioned off with Sheetrock to make herself a bedroom downstairs. She was still having problems negotiating stairs. She never healed properly after her accident on the weasel during our first winter in Colorado. Anyway, we were good to go for a permanent stay in Summit County, or so we thought.

Shortly after we moved into the new house, Mom agreed to take a purebred Siberian husky from some friends who lived near Frisco. They bred and raised Siberian huskies. Mom made the decision to take one before she told the rest of us about it. This really surprised me. Mom was scared to death of dogs; but she understood how valuable Doty was to our security, and she was concerned that Doty was getting too old to make a good watchdog even though she was doing fine.

Doty had become a house dog in Breckenridge. She was intelligent and adapted to it very easily. Mom certainly felt better having her in the house. Doty only barked when there was something real to bark at. The new dog was just a puppy. Furthermore, Siberian huskies do not make good watchdogs. Many do not bark at all. Nevertheless, I was very excited about her, and Mother came up with the name: Princess. I don't remember liking this name, but it worked. Maybe it was Mother's attempt to make her sophisticated and gentle. Her strategy didn't work.

Doty was not happy about a new dog joining the family, but she learned to tolerate the ill-behaved newcomer who liked to chew on everything and ended up eating much of what she chewed on including shoes, furniture, and power tools. Well, maybe not the power tools. Anyway, it was not long before we heard a disturbing story about two of the other puppies from the same litter as Princess. They had been allowed to run loose. Apparently, they found a herd of sheep one day and decimated it, killing many of the sheep. They had to be put down. Princess was never allowed to run free or to have her own sheep.

We were not far into the first winter in our new house when trouble began. The plumbing failed. Nothing would drain including the toilets. We were completely stopped up. The toilet would not flush, and the bathtub would not drain. Mom could not afford to get it fixed, so we attempted to make do without a toilet and other plumbing features necessary for a normal existence. It was not easy. We used the facilities in Mom's office as much as possible. Beyond that, we had to improvise to take care of our bodily waste-disposal needs. Well, Sam and I had a spot in the backyard that worked fairly well. We used it mostly after dark. Also going to school was good place to take care of business. However, we were forced to leave to go home at the end of the school day. And then there were the weekends. They were rough to get through. I felt like a dog always trying to find a place to leave my scent. Maybe this was just a sinister scheme created by the old wise one to make us appreciate school.

In spite of these difficulties, I managed to keep some social life going at school. We were in the new school in Frisco, which was built with a floor plan that resembled two circus tents. The grade school was in one of the tent-shaped buildings, and the junior high and high school were in the other. Each building had a rotunda in the middle that all the classrooms opened into. There was no gym. There were no lunch facilities. There was not much outside other than trees. All such amenities would come much later. Most important, there were restrooms!

Rudd Pyles and I took algebra together. Neither of us was interested, and we got in trouble for having too much fun in the back of the room where we sat. One of our games was to take several deep breaths and then stick our thumbs in our mouths and attempt to blow them out while holding them firmly in place with our lips and teeth. This sometimes caused a loss of consciousness, an overturned desk, and one of us on the floor. The algebra teacher had no idea how to get us under control. We sometimes took mercy on him and attempted to behave for short spurts. I learned very little algebra in these spurts. I did not seem to be interested in learning anything in school that year.

In spite of all our many personal difficulties, I thought I was worthy of a girlfriend. I fell in love with a girl named Penny. Well, I thought it was love, but it was probably just a gland problem. I think we only had one real date together. Nevertheless, I thought this cemented our relationship for life. It didn't. I knew that most women would demand a bathroom. I still didn't have one.

Rudd, Sam, and I also got into constant trouble in Physical Education class. We had a wimpy instructor who could not control us. We frequently took over the class, completely disrupting it. When our instructor attempted to teach us to do a simple somersault, Rudd would do a forward flip. And then the instructor might ask him to do a simple somersault correctly. Rudd would do a back flip instead. Soon, all the kids were doing whatever they wanted. We were completely out of control, and the teacher seemed to have no idea what to do about it.

When the weather got better, we made up for our misbehavior. The PE teacher would take us outside to play touch football or some other activity. We enjoyed being outside. However, one day during our PE class, some tough guys came around the school in an old car, looking for our PE teacher. I am probably exaggerating by using *tough* to describe them. There weren't many "tough guys" in Summit County in those days, and I suspect there aren't that many now. It was surely some guys who had found an ad for a course in how to become a tough guy in a comic book and wanted to try out what they had learned.

Anyway, the fake thugs indicated that they wanted to give our PE teacher a beating. The entire class heard the threat. They didn't say why they wanted to beat him up, but it didn't matter to us. About ten of us surrounded their car and told the "tough" guys to stay the hell away from our teacher or else. This tactic worked surprisingly well. The result indicated that I was correct about the number of tough guys in Summit County. After all, real tough guys don't usually turn down the opportunity to take a good beating. I know that Sam never did.

President Kennedy was assassinated in November of that year. Some of us were tumbling in the designated PE room at lunchtime when the principal came in and told us that the president had been shot. There was no word on his condition at the time, but the principal indicated that he had been shot in the neck. We did not know he was in Dallas or any other details.

We all went to our first class of the afternoon once the lunch hour was over. My after-lunch class was a typing class. It was not long before the principal arrived in the classroom to inform us that the president had passed away. He also told us that the school buses were being mustered so that we could be taken home early.

Meanwhile, our English teacher was dancing around the rotunda, making joyful noises because she was delighted that the president was dead. She would have fit in much better in our present culture than she did back then. It was not long before she lost her job.

All of us were eager to go home early. We did not fully understand what the assassination might mean. I spent the entire weekend watching the news much like the rest of the country. It was a difficult weekend. I did not feel like doing anything. I was in a daze. It was hard to believe the events that had transpired. I still did not have a bathroom in my house.

CHAPTER 28

Closing Out Breckenridge

If a light beam catches you from behind, it will always pass you with a velocity of 186,000 miles per second relative to your own velocity. This is so even if you are traveling at near the speed of light yourself after drinking all the tequila offered up in a previous chapter. Who is responsible for this confusion? Jose Cuervo? No! God? Maybe. Whoever, Albert Einstein made perfect sense of the observed behavior of light in his special theory of relativity. He took note of the fact that space and time are not absolute. Distances and time intervals measured depend on the reference frame in which one makes the measurements (in addition to any tequila consumed).

*****

During our time in Breckenridge, Mom had many male friends. She often went out for dinner and other activities with them. She was still a very attractive woman. I knew that many of her dates were not appropriate, but I also knew that we were trying to survive.

Meanwhile, Sam, Diana, and I were hungry much of the time. Sam had taken the job of delivering the *Sunday Denver Post* to subscribers in Breckenridge. I helped him with this job. We would deliver the paper early Sunday mornings before we headed to the ski hill. I remember one morning, the bus carrying the newspapers did not make it over the pass until later in the morning due to the weather. Sam and I didn't think this was a problem. We would simply go skiing and deliver the papers when we got back from the mountain in the late afternoon.

Whoa! We apparently did not understand the importance of those Sunday papers. When we attempted to deliver the papers in the evening, we found all our *Denver Post* subscribers waiting for us, mouths fully loaded with foul ammunition to unleash a loud vocal barrage of frightening language upon us. Well, some of the blitz seemed to be directed at our ancestors who these people didn't even know. To avoid learning any new bad words, we attempted to sneak up on the houses where we had to deliver a paper without being seen. This didn't work at all. Everyone was waiting for us to make certain we got a piece of their mind. We had to take our punishment. It was a good lesson in responsibility.

We made enough money from the newspaper delivery job for Sam to decide that we were going to eat for a while. It seemed we never had enough to eat. Mom had more bills than she could pay and no money left to buy food. She was out with men much of the time in the evenings being wined and dined, but there was no way these experiences could be transferred to our stomachs. Consequently, Sam and I took the money to the grocery store and purchased twenty-five or thirty pounds of hamburger. Sam wanted *meat*. We were both hungry! We took the meat home on a sled. The hamburger purchase wasn't the smartest thing we ever did. But at least we weren't dogs. Had we been, we would have attempted to eat all the hamburger the first night. Come to think of it, I can't swear that we didn't try to eat it all the first night.

Sam had more aptitude for cooking than I did. He learned to bake cakes and to make other dishes. He was a great little brother to have, especially when you were hungry. After we got the hamburger, he began making up different ways to have hamburger. This was difficult because all we had was the damn hamburger. The bottom line: We survived.

During our final summer or fall in Breckenridge, Mom called a special family meeting. She told us that one of the men she had been seeing wanted to marry her and move us all to Hawaii. She had decided to take a family vote on the matter. Neither Sam nor I much cared for the man in question. I don't think that Diana knew enough to know what she wanted. Anyway, it did not take us long to vote down Hawaii. Mom accepted this decision without any debate. She wouldn't have asked us if she hadn't known how it would come out. I don't think she thought much of the man either. She surely knew the result she would get by asking for a vote. Our "No" vote most likely gave her an excuse not to accept the proposition.

It was not long after Mom turned down the move to Hawaii that she lost her job. She had gotten into trouble with the company. Money was missing, and Mom was responsible for all the ski-area receipts, which were delivered to her each morning. She shared several scenarios with me about what might have happened to the money, but none of them were well received by the company. One of them was that she always had all the cash from the ski area received the day before or during the weekend out on a table in her office where she counted it on the day she received it. People often came into the office during this time. She trusted them.

The crux of the matter was that she was responsible for the money and a significant amount of it had come up missing. She got the ax and had to pay back the missing money. She managed to borrow the money to pay back the company. I would still be helping her pay off the loan years later.

Getting the ax was not surprising because it was a common occurrence in the company. Mom was a woman. She did not make nearly as much as a man would have been paid for doing the job she was doing. This meant that we did not have a cushion to fall back on. Once again, we were playing the difficult game of survival.

I like to think that the Rounds and Porter vice president finally figured out that Mom was the one who made everything work for the Breckenridge effort. He had never wanted the company to be in the ski-resort business. This provides a convenient explanation for why Mom had lost her job. Furthermore, she had lost her pull with the Rounds family. There may be some truth in this explanation, but I don't really have any evidence that these factors were the reason she lost her job. Nevertheless, given the way the company seemed to work, it is surprising that she managed to stay as long as she did, especially since she had a knack for getting in trouble. She had always felt that her pay was not fair because it was minuscule compared to that of her bosses. She was the assistant manager; they were the managers. This could have been a motivation for her trouble.

To be sure, Mom had survived somewhere around six different general managers during her three years as the assistant manager. This was impressive. Nevertheless, this fact and a quarter would not get you more than a cup of coffee at any of the local restaurants. We did not have the quarter.

During the midst of all these problems, our toilet was still not working. After Mom lost her job, the problem became much more serious because we no longer had the bathroom facilities at Mom's office available to us. Life quickly became very difficult. Sam and I continued to use the backyard mostly after dark. There was also school during the week where we could take care of our toiletry needs. This required planning ahead. I don't remember how Mom and Diana made it through this difficult period.

Mom was able to get a job with an attorney for a while, but this did not pay enough to cover the mounting bills. Mother was confiding in me regularly, but she did not tell me everything. I knew that we were falling behind. If Mom did not get regular work, I did not know how we would survive. I soon discovered that she had a plan in her head that she had used before. It was time for her to run back home to Mom and Dad with three hungry children.

*****

We left Summit County, not quite in the dark of night. Nevertheless, our departure was without fanfare. We took only what we could fit into the car, leaving most of our belongings in the house. Mom was already falling behind on the mortgage payments. She had no plan to save the house. We headed to Las Vegas to stay with Grandmother and Grandfather in their tiny house until she could figure out what to do. This seemed like total disaster to me. Nevertheless, I attempted to be as supportive as possible.

Grandmother and Grandfather lived just north of Las Vegas near the small community of Montezuma. They had sold the Ranch and purchased the house so that they could live near town all year long. They never thought a family of four would move in with them.

I began attending Robertson High School in Las Vegas. It seemed like the last place on the planet that I wanted to be. Sam, Diana, and I all rode a school bus into Las Vegas where we attended school. I was miserable. I did not like the school, the teachers, or the other kids. Nevertheless, I survived without failing any classes.

Later in the spring or early summer, Dad, Sam, and I made a trip with a rented or borrowed truck in an attempt to rescue some of our belongings that we left in the house in Breckenridge. We loaded up anything of value that we found in the house. There wasn't much. Creditors and others had been in the house and taken everything they wanted. When we got it back to Las Vegas, we stashed what we had in Grandfather's open barn or garage. Much more was lost than was saved. In the end, Mom lost the house and most of what we had left in it.

CHAPTER 29

Back with Grandfather and Grandmother

Einstein's special theory of relativity has some rather startling consequences. One example is the twin paradox. I am married to one member of a set of twins. To illustrate the paradox, but mostly just for fun, I send my wife's sister to the Andromeda galaxy some two and a half million light years away. She accelerates away from Earth with an acceleration of one g. This acceleration continues until she is halfway to her destination. At this point, she begins slowing with a deceleration of one g. She comes to a stop at Andromeda. After getting a good night's sleep, she checks out the beaches before beginning her return trip, which she makes in the same manner as the outbound trip. The entire trip takes about twenty years and a hell of a good credit card. When she arrives back on Earth, she is eager to find her sister and tell her all about her exciting trip. Unfortunately, she discovers that her sister has been dead for five million years. Ouch!

*****

My grandparents' house was much too small to accommodate four extra people and two dogs. It had two bedrooms, but my grandfather had turned one of them into his office. This meant that

Mom and sister Diana slept on the sofa in the living room while Sam and I slept in a glassed-in front porch with no heat. It was freezing cold that winter. There was an oil stove in the living room of the small house. It was the only source of heat in the entire house unless one turned the oven on and left the door open. Before Sam and I went out to the porch to turn in each night, we would put a couple of bricks in the oil stove next to the combustion chamber so they would heat up. When they were good and hot, we would take them and put them under the blankets on the sofa bed on the porch. I seem to remember that we slept end to end where my head was at the north end of my body and his head was at the south end of the bed. Many times, it was well below freezing on that porch. Sometimes, it was even near zero. Nevertheless, we managed to stay warm with our bricks and each other. I never really wanted to get to know my brother that well!

Fortunately, Mother was able to get a job very quickly at the New Mexico State Hospital, which was just down the road from Grandmother and Grandfather's house. She was still impressive after all. Nevertheless, this did not mean that we could move into our own house right away. Mom had fallen very far behind in Breckenridge since she had been out of work for a while. In fact, she was behind before she lost her job. She had many bills to pay. I was already involved in helping her figure out how to manage.

I don't remember what her title was at the state hospital when she was hired, but it was not long before she became the personnel director or personnel administrator. Director sounds better. Administrator was probably her correct title. She would finish out her career in this position. Nevertheless, her life continued to be a mixture of some good times with significant disasters interspersed. She would eventually marry a dentist, Gordon Wickman, who also worked at the state hospital. He had come to New Mexico from Wisconsin, and he had a son that was four days older than me and a daughter that was even older. He also had a wife who was slowly dying from alcoholism.

I was very depressed to be back in New Mexico, burdening my grandparents and having to go to school at Robertson High School in Las Vegas. We rode the school bus to and from school. I think I, more or less, withdrew from social activities the first few months after our arrival. I may have made one or two friends, but I was not a happy camper. Nevertheless, I spent some time trying to get back in shape by walking on a gravel road that ran behind my grandparents' property. I also tried a little running for the first time in my life. I was still very thin and weak as I was still recovering from my time in the body cast and the complications of the skin graft. Nevertheless, my physical condition slowly improved.

I remember that I had occasion to see a couple of the local rock bands play at lunchtime in the gym. One of them was the Tornadoes, and the other was the Impalas. The latter group really impressed me. They had a saxophone, organ and lead, rhythm, and base guitars. I decided that being in a band was something that would be interesting while I was waiting out life in Las Vegas. I had already made a plan to go to the University of Alaska where I would study engineering while living with the wolves and huskies. Well, the details of this plan were rather obscure. It was an unrealistic notion that served to keep me from being too depressed. Meanwhile, Sam and Diana seemed to recover more quickly than I did. They were resilient.

CHAPTER 30

High, Cold Adventure

Grab something sturdy and hang on tight: Einstein's special theory of relativity indicates that time does not pass. Time is just one of four dimensions of space-time. Space and time mix in ways that depend on the motion of the observer. Like space, time does not pass. Whoa! What is the clock on my desk measuring? How can this be? Should I think of the clock as a ruler, a speedometer, or just worthless junk?

*****

I had been engrossed in the fantasyland that Breckenridge became while we lived there. This made it difficult to make the adjustment back to New Mexico. It all seemed so dull and hopeless to me. It was just the opposite for Sam. He got into more and more fights at Robertson High School, and he seemed to love it. He would deliberately walk into ambushes and do plenty of damage before he took a beating. I needed some excitement in my life also.

There were some good times during my final year and a half of high school. The best was with one of Sam's friends, Donald, who lived in Montezuma just a mile or so up the road from my grandparents' house. We had one of the best outdoor adventures of our lives

189

with Don. Our cold-weather sleeping on the porch had prepared us for it.

The three of us decided to hike to the top of Hermit Peak in the dead of winter and stay overnight. The summit of the Peak is at an elevation of just over ten thousand feet. The plan was to spend night in a lean-to shelter that we knew existed on the summit and return the next day. We knew it would be cold, but we were not concerned because we had our J. C. Penney sleeping bags, some coffee, a few snacks, and most important for me, Princess, our furry husky. Doty was too old for the kind of hardship we expected. We may not have been very well prepared for one of the best outdoor adventures in our life to that point, but we were enthusiastic.

We started out on a Saturday. Don's father drove us to the trailhead at the base of the mountain. We did not encounter much snow as we climbed the well-worn, but steep, trail on the southeastern side of the mountain. The trail followed a line between the two cliffs that rise to the summit on that side of the mountain. Even though we had fairly heavy loads, we reached the very broad, flat summit in the late afternoon. Several feet of snow awaited us on the summit. Princess loved jumping through the snow. One would have thought that it was the best adventure of her life.

We headed northeast from our arrival point on the summit toward a lean-to shelter we knew existed in that direction. This traverse was made by trudging through deep snow that often came halfway up our thighs. We arrived at the shelter as it was getting dark.

The shelter had a roof and one closed side. It was open on the north, east, and south sides. Best of all, it was full of snow. No problem; we were young and vigorous. We got busy and shoveled the snow out with a couple of small shovels that we carried with us, anticipating that they might be needed. It was growing dark as we shoveled. After the shoveling, we managed to put a fire together using some firewood that was in the shelter. I don't remember if we cooked any hot food, but I suspect we ate something. After our high-altitude dinner, we did not waste any time laying out the J. C. Penney sleeping bags to begin our quest to survive the icy-cold night that was already upon us.

The sleeping bags were placed on either side of the firepit in the shelter. We had shoveled the snow out of the shelter. We crawled into the sleeping bags with our clothing mostly on and our boots off. I had an advantage, or so I thought. Princess would get into my sleeping bag with me, adding warmth. Nevertheless, even I was cold as the temperature plummeted to the neighborhood of zero degrees. This is my estimate, but it could have been seventy below zero for all I know. It definitely was not thirty degrees. I would have bet it was the coldest place in the solar system. I might have been wrong on this point.

The advantage of having Princess in the sleeping bag with me turned into a disadvantage as daylight began to creep onto summit. Since I was the warmest thanks to Princess, I was nominated and seconded to get up and make the cowboy coffee after my unsuccessful attempt to cast a proxy vote for Princess.

Cowboy coffee is made in a two-pound Folger's coffee can. One dumps the coffee in the bottom, fills the can with water, and boils it all up. You can either drink it out of the can or pour it into a cup. I think I did a little of both. Drinking from the metal can is hard on the lips, but it thaws them before it quickly sears the flesh. I mastered the technique. The coffee in the can turned out to be the best coffee I have ever had, going all the way to the present day. Apparently, it doesn't take much skill to make a delicious cup of coffee at 10,000 feet on a frigid morning. Nothing ever tasted better as far as I was concerned. However, I will note that it is best to allow the grounds to settle a little, but not too long, before pouring the coffee while resisting the urge to put that sissy stuff like milk and sugar in it. Never ever do that at 10,000 feet unless you are not a sissy and have the credentials to prove it.

Breakfast was great, I think. In truth, I only remember the coffee. We were soon heading down the mountain after we ate, drank, and packed up. Once we arrived back at the trailhead at the bottom of the mountain, we began a long trek back to Montezuma. For reasons I don't remember, we did not arrange to have anyone meet us at the bottom of the mountain. Well, it would have been difficult to estimate when we would get there. Besides, we surely thought that we were tough enough to manage the long walk back to Donald's house in Montezuma. It was a very long walk. I seem to remember ten miles or more. However, I also remember catching a ride when we were partway back. Nevertheless, we were dead tired when we finally arrived back in Montezuma. It was one of my best adventures. After spending the night in the cold, we felt we could survive anything. Boys are silly that way—men too.

CHAPTER 31

The Rock Band

I have raised a mysterious notion concerning the passage of time. How can it be that time does not pass? Is it really like the other three coordinates of space-time? Given this conclusion, does it make sense to ask what happened before the existence of space and time? Is there any such place? If so, where is it, and what is it? These questions do not seem to have answers. Yet could it be that they make sense? In a first attempt to make sense of them, I made up the answers: Yes, yes, no, no, nowhere, and nothing.

*****

One thing that held my interest at Robertson High School was music. I continued to play the saxophone in the high school band. I did not enjoy the marching part. It was very difficult for me to march in time with the music and go where I was supposed to go. Nevertheless, I always arrived, sometimes early, sometimes late, but seldom in line with the others. For reasons I did not completely understand, I got yelled at even though I eventually got to where I was supposed to be. I was not a bad student in band. I was just a bad marcher, which has little to do with musical talent. In fact, during my senior year, the band teacher told me that he could get me a scholarship to study music at New Mexico State University. This was offered in spite of my tendency to turn left when marching while everyone else turned right. Don't ever ask me for directions. Left and right have no consistent distinction in my brain. Anyway, I was not interested in becoming a band teacher, which is where I figured a music scholarship would lead. However, I was interested playing music that did not require marching or having a conductor out front to yell at me when I wandered off course.

I had heard several of the local rock groups at school dances. One of the groups was very good and featured a saxophone player who I knew I could never emulate. Nevertheless, I was interested in starting a group myself. I had begun experimenting with this possibility in Colorado but hadn't gotten very far. Sam also had some interest. He was still playing drums in the high school band. We found a few other guys who were interested in forming a rock group. Soon, we had a group. We called ourselves The Shadows.

We had two problems. One was that we had two drummers. For some reason, we thought we could make this work. It didn't. The second problem was that our singer and lead guitar player had very little musical talent. I should talk. I had no real musical talent either.

It is interesting that I claim a lack of talent even though one of mother's friends had heard me banging around on the piano in Breckenridge, playing boogie-woogie and *Heart and Soul*, musical pieces that many kids played on the piano. He told Mom that I would never be good at anything other than music because once you have the talent (disease), you are done for. I suppose the lesson in this for me was that I should not have believed anything that Mom's male friends said.

Anyway, I played the saxophone in the high school band but never felt I was very good at it. However, I was good at getting people together and keeping them together. I guess that would make me an organizer.

The first attempts at forming a rock band were awkward. It would take several attempts to succeed in creating a group that could play something that was almost music. My brother was always the drummer. He was never the problem. He was an excellent drummer. In all, I organized two bands and played in three bands.

The first band I organized, The Shadows, didn't work at all. The next band was fairly good, and we called ourselves Roy and the Emeralds, or just The Emeralds, depending on when you asked. It had evolved from The Shadows. The Shadows had two drummers and a lead guitar player and singer who could do neither. It was not even good enough to be called a bad band. The most interesting thing about this first group was that the second drummer was named William Bonney. However, I am not so old that this could have been the gunslinger from southern New Mexico better known as Billy the Kid.

At one of The Shadows' few engagements, a guy named Roy Montoya got up and sang with us. This caused us to send our lead singer packing along with the gunslinger's namesake, leaving us with one drummer, brother Sam, and Roy as our new lead guitar and lead singer. Life can be so cruel. Anyway, this was the birth of The Emeralds. Roy was a very talented musician and singer. We eventually became Roy and the Emeralds.

Keyboards were becoming popular with bands, so we bought one for the band, thinking that Roy could play it while he sang. This didn't work. Roy could sing and play the guitar just fine, but he couldn't play the keyboard while singing. Consequently, I became the keyboard player. I was not very good at it, but I could play counter-melodies that the rest of the band seemed to like. It worked well enough that my saxophone turned up missing. It also gave me the opportunity to try singing background. I thought I was doing fine until I noticed that my microphone always seemed to be plugged into a dead channel of the amplifier. I got the message.

Sometime after we got going, we also lost our bass player, Floyd Lujan. He was replaced by Lou Dan Salazar, who was somewhat older than the rest of us. Lou Dan had played with the Impalas, the outstanding group that got me interested in forming my own band in the first place. Lou Dan was so poor he lived in a house with dirt floors in West Las Vegas. He had no family, as far as I could tell, and had little money. Nevertheless, he had a Fender bass and some large

Fender amplifiers. To this day, I say he is the best bass player I have ever heard. Well, I could be a little biased, but he was good.

Unfortunately, Lou Dan was an alcoholic. This did not seem to detract from his bass playing. There were times when we had to prop him up against an amplifier and watch that he didn't fall over while we were playing. He could play drunk, sober, or in between. Come to think of it, I never saw him attempt to play sober. We all loved him in spite of the problems he brought to the group.

The worst experience with Lou Dan occurred during an engagement in Wagon Mound, which is a small town about forty miles north of Las Vegas. When we picked him up to head for Wagon Mound, he was hopelessly drunk. We attempted to sober him up on the way to the job, but this did not work very well. To complicate matters even more, when we arrived in Wagon Mound and were setting up, I found a small pistol in Lou Dan's pants pocket. I took it away from him, but he pleaded with me to give it back. He said that someone in Wagon Mound wanted to kill him. I told him it was probably me. Nevertheless, I persuaded him to let me keep the gun for him. This was one of those nights when we had to prop him up against one of the large Fender amplifiers. No chairs were available on the stage. Besides, he said he couldn't play sitting down. He did fine that night a usual. When he would start to list, I kept him upright.

We got many different kinds of jobs. Sometimes, we were called on to play Mexican music, most often rock and sometimes Western. We could do it all, which allowed us to get jobs in a large area surrounding Las Vegas that extended from Pecos on the east to Mora in the north and Wagon Mound in the northeast. We had some interesting adventures along the way.

One such adventure occurred when we took a job in Mora that another band, Little Caesar and the Conspirators, had asked us to take for them. Tudy Ulibarri was the lead singer in the Conspirators in addition to being my barber. We did not ask Tudy why they could not keep their engagement. We should have. When we arrived at the south end of town, we were greeted by a large contingent of Mora's ugliest and toughest characters. They were waiting for Little Caesar with clubs, knives, chains, and other weapons of mass destruction. As we approached, they stopped us. They had noticed the band equipment piled in our cars. They were not pleased to see us. They asked us where Tudy and his band were. We told them they couldn't make it. They didn't seem to know what to do. They were clearly disappointed that Tudy's band did not show up. Fortunately, they did not take out their frustrations on us.

Apparently, Tudy's band had gotten into trouble with the town folk by messing around with some of the young women on their previous visit to Mora. They were chased out of town with a threat, which made it clear that if they ever came back, they would not get out of town alive.

Despite the town's disappointment in our arrival instead of Tudy's, we were allowed to go on to the event. Once we were set up and we began playing, we mostly used good sense by keeping our eyes on the males in the dance hall and off of the women. Nevertheless, I did catch Roy smiling and making eyes at a young woman who was dancing right in front of us. I told him to knock it off. He mostly took my advice. We successfully played the engagement and left town alive with all our body parts firmly attached and none of us even bleeding.

Another amusing incident happened when we were playing for at a noontime sock hop at school. One of the ranch kids or stompers (because of the cowboy boots they wore) threatened me for making eyes at his girlfriend. I remember that she seemed interested, but I don't think I was guilty of any flirting although women have always had a way of making me do things that I shouldn't do. Anyway, Sam overheard the threat, and it was not long before the stomper got the crap beat out of him. I have no idea who would have done such a terrible thing.

CHAPTER 32

Taken Hostage

If time doesn't pass, it would seem that everything happens at once just as all space exists at once, doesn't it? Maybe not? Nevertheless, how can this be? Could it be that the passage of time is something that occurs only in the brain? Suppose that our consciousness awareness can only be aware of a small part of space and an instant of time but can move between these small segments of existence. Then why is it that our brains seem to only move forward in an orderly manner in time whereas we seem to have the ability to move in any direction we want in space? We can also stop at any location we arrive at in space. Try as I might, I cannot seem to stop in time. The clock hands just keep moving. I will think on this problem for a chapter or two. If I can't resolve it, you may have to finish writing the book yourself.

*****

I graduated from Robertson High School in 1965. I was not a stellar student. I had plans to get as far away from Las Vegas as I could. I still wanted to go to the University of Alaska to study engineering. I didn't realize how unrealistic this plan was. I did not even know if there was an engineering school at the University of Alaska. I simply didn't understand that this plan was nothing more than a childish fantasy. I had invented it to get me far away from Mother's problems, at least in my head.

I knew I would have to earn some money in order to be able go to college anywhere. I began looking for a job that I could work at for a year. This was a little more realistic. The problem, which I had not faced up to, was that Mother was still paying off the many debts she had accumulated. She needed all the financial help she could get. Once I found a job, I would have to help her even though providing help would jeopardize my plan. I simply imagined that I would find a way to succeed.

Near the time that I graduated from high school, Mother was able to rent a state hospital house. It was great to be able to move out of my grandparents' house into our own place. Mom could almost afford the rent.

The house was adjacent to the state hospital. It was comfortable and had a good yard with a picket fence around it. This made it easy to accommodate Doty and Princess. It had a great room to work out in behind the garage. Sam and his friends used it to lift weights.

In early summer just after we moved into the hospital house, I had a somewhat unsettling adventure. It was about midmorning when I got into our 1959 Ford. I don't remember what my mission was that morning, but I may have been heading out to look for a job. I certainly remember the rest of the events that occurred that morning.

I had just backed the car out of the garage when a man with no shirt and no shoes came running across the neighbor's lawn toward me. His only attire was a pair of blue jeans. He came up to the car and flashed an Albuquerque Police Department badge at me and told me to get out of the car. I got out, and he grabbed me by the arm, forcing me back through the garage and into the house. On the way in, he asked where the phone was. As we entered the kitchen, I pointed the wall phone out to him. He sat down at our dining table and picked up the phone. At the same time, a couple of police cars went screaming down the road in front of the house with red lights flashing and sirens blaring. They came from the direction of the state hospital. I knew I was in trouble.

The man continued to hold my wrist as he picked up the phone, put it against his shoulder, and began dialing with his free hand. He told me he had to call someone in Washington state. He apparently got through to someone. As he talked on the phone, he interrupted his conversation to ask what two small children next door were doing. They were neighbor kids that had come out to play. I told him, "They shouldn't be there. I need to go tell them to leave." He did not fall for my ruse as he kept holding onto my wrist.

As he continued dialing and talking on the phone, I did not pay much attention to what he was saying. Instead, I was thinking about how I might get away from him. I came up with a simple but lame plan. I had noticed that he was barefoot. I asked him if I could get him some dry socks and shoes. He looked hesitant, but interested. He told me to get the socks. He let my wrist go, and I moved cautiously away from him as he stayed on the phone. I walked slowly to the threshold of the living room where there were entrances to the two bedrooms in the house, and the front door was straight across the living room in front of me. I only took one step into the living room before I broke into an all-out dash for the front door. When I reached it, I jerked it open, grateful that it was not locked, and ran into the yard at full speed, heading toward a surrounding picket fence. I leaped over the fence and headed up the sidewalk that led to the state hospital, located about a hundred yards up the road. When I arrived in front of the hospital, I found many squad cars and policemen near the main entrance. I went up to one and told him about the man in my house. He took me very seriously. I was put in one of the squad cars, and we returned to the house. I don't remember how many policemen were in the group that went along with us. There were several. I told them where the man was located inside. We could see him through the window still on the phone. They went in quickly with guns drawn and took him into custody. There was no struggle. He was taken away in handcuffs.

I was later told that my abductor had killed two police officers in Albuquerque, and he had subsequently been captured. He had been brought to the state hospital for a psychological evaluation. I never learned how he managed to get away from all those policemen.

Even more puzzling was his arrival at my house from the opposite direction to that of the state hospital with an Albuquerque Police badge in his hand. Also it was surprising that he made no effort to recapture me when I made my escape. Instead, he continued making phone calls. Living next to the state mental institution provided more excitement than I needed—at least on that morning.

Chapter 33

Driving Accidents

We can see in all directions of space, but we can only look backward in time while moving forward. Whose idea was this? Could it be that we are moving randomly in time? However, since we can only see in one direction, toward the past, we experience the illusion that time is passing smoothly?

*****

It was not long before I found a job with the New Mexico State Highway Department. I was to be trained to be an "office man." I would work with the team of Highway Department engineers and inspectors. Their job was to make certain that the contractors working on an interstate construction project were meeting the required design specifications as they built a section of I-25 between Las Vegas and Santa Fe. The responsibility of an office man was to keep the books for the team of engineers and inspectors.

I was not interested in a career as an office man, but I did not divulge this to anyone in the Highway Department. I was really trying to make some money so that I could get away to Alaska where I still planned to attend college. I worked with an experienced office man, Charlie, learning the job. He was part of the Highway Department crew, managing the contractor and making certain the highway was built to specifications. The Highway Department's project engineer and inspectors on the job all worked out of an office, which was located in a large old house in Las Vegas. My job responsibilities kept me almost totally in the office although I did visit the construction site a time or two.

When I took the job, I intended to keep it for a year. I thought this would be enough time to save enough money to head off to Alaska. This secret plan kept me from being a good office-man trainee. I had little real incentive to learn the job. Nevertheless, personal pride caused me to make an attempt to learn and perform the job as best as I could. Furthermore, in the back of my mind, I knew that I might have to keep the job for more than a year. I probably realized that my plan for Alaska might not be feasible, and I might need a backup plan. I did not want the Highway Department to become permanent. I knew this was a danger. I did not have a backup plan.

While I held the Highway Department job, I continued to play with the Emeralds. Maybe this was my backup plan. It was not a good one.

I began driving Mother's car to work and driving for other activities including band engagements. I was making the mistake that many younger drivers make. I thought I knew what I was doing and that everyone else knew what they were doing. It did not take me long to learn that I should spend more time hiding under my bed than driving. The first sobering incident was simple. An older gentleman ran a stop sign and hit me. Fortunately, he was going slow, and the collision resulted in minimal damage. It made me wonder how this could happen. Were people that stupid? Dad had many accidents, but they mostly seemed to be on purpose. Wait! Could that have been Dad in the other car? Some people drive for the adventure of it, and some have adventures only because they are stupid. I am not certain where this reasoning left me.

A more serious accident happened when I was driving Grandmother back to our hospital house after a shopping trip to town. The street in front of the house was four lanes, and getting into our driveway when going north required a left turn across the two southbound lanes. I put my signal on, moved into the left northbound lane, and began the turn without really being aware of all that was happening behind me. As it turned out, a woman was attempting to pass me, and she was doing it with flare. Instead of passing in the lane on my right, she crossed the centerline, entering into one of the southbound lanes. I never looked for her or expected her illegal attempt to pass. However, I felt her and heard the crunch as her car hit the driver's side of my car. She broadsided me, so to speak. She was going fast enough that the collision sent my car sliding sideways through the picket fence and into our front yard, banging up both Grandmother and me. Nevertheless, we were not seriously injured, and the woman in the other car also did not suffer any injuries. Of course, she was ticketed for attempting an illegal pass, and I thought all would be well. It wasn't.

The first problem was that Mother could not afford to fix the car. The main damage was to the back door on the driver's side. It had been bashed in, and it could no longer be opened. Nevertheless, the car could still be driven. The main problem for Mom and me was that during the accident investigation, the authorities discovered that Mother had no liability insurance. This resulted in both Mom and me losing our drivers' licenses until we could prove we had insurance.

This outcome was a bigger problem for me than Mom. My job was five or six miles from our house. I had to keep driving to keep my job. I did. Mother lived next door to the state hospital where she worked. Nevertheless, she continued to drive also. I guess that would make us outlaws sans *pistolas*. Well, we never got our faces on wanted posters. Nevertheless, we drove illegally for several months until Mom managed to buy insurance.

My most lawless action during the time when my license was suspended was done to carry out an assigned task required by my Highway Department job. I was instructed to make a trip to Santa Fe in a state car to deliver some documents to the Highway Department headquarters. I did not want my boss know I could not make the trip because I did not have a driver's license. I made the trip. I was very careful. I'm not proud of the fact that I got away with driving a state car with no driver's license. I think this might put me in competition with Billy the Kid for New Mexico's most lawless character. I concede; he wins—by a little.

CHAPTER 34

The Winds of Change

Still dancing and thinking: Is the passage of time really a problem? Yes! I need to think about it for a few chapters. I have to be very careful. I don't want to permanently damage your brain. I just want to soften it up a bit before I attempt to stretch and deform it. Then maybe it can make time pass in the other direction for you—or maybe not.

*****

My first year out of high school turned out to be very important in shaping what I would do with my life. I worked the entire year for the Highway Department. At the end of the year, boredom with the job had almost rendered me into a comatose state. I continued playing with The Emeralds to make my life a little interesting, but I knew this was not going to be a lifetime involvement. It was clear to me that my career as a musician was not going much further. Besides, most of the other members of the band graduated from high school that year and headed off to the Navy, Marines, and other points of interest.

My brother was in this group graduating a year behind me. He was only seventeen years old and physically ripped from all the weightlifting he had done with his friends at our house. He continued looking for trouble, and he continued to find it in many places. However, he was yet to find the ultimate trouble. To remedy this deficiency, he joined the Marines. Mom had to sign for him because he was only seventeen, or maybe it was Dad who signed for him. Neither of them saw any alternative. The war in Vietnam was ramping up, and Sam apparently felt he could find enough trouble there to keep him happy while doing some good for the country. He had concluded that the Marine Corps was where you went if you really wanted to get into the action in Vietnam.

I have to say that I was very proud of my little brother when I heard that he had graduated from the Marine Corp boot camp as Honor Man of his platoon. This meant that he had been the meanest and toughest son of a female dog in the platoon. It also meant that he got to march out front carrying the platoon flag at his graduation. Mom and her dentist boyfriend, Dr. Wickman, went to San Diego to see him graduate. Sam came home shortly afterward before being sent off to his preparations for Vietnam. Boot camp had profoundly changed him into someone I had trouble recognizing. I had the feeling he could kill me in an instant without breaking a sweat. He seemed to know it too. I knew that we would never brawl together again.

He told Mom and me that he was going to be a helicopter mechanic. He didn't want us to worry. As it turned out, this was not his primary assignment in the Marine Corps. Not long ago, he showed me a stash of 285 air medals that he kept in a drawer in the guest bedroom of his New Mexico house. He thinks this might be a record number of air medals. He earned the medals as a helicopter-door gunner. He got one for each combat mission he flew. He managed to get so many by volunteering for his buddies' missions. This did not surprise me. I knew my little brother too well. We have always been close, but it was difficult to maintain our relationship when he was earning all those medals.

Needless to say, he did not come back unscathed. Even though his wounds were relatively minor, the war had a devastating effect on him that many years to recover from. Besides telling me many chilling stories, he wrote songs and poetry about what it is like to kill other human beings. It is something one never gets over. What he wrote was powerful. Some of it was published in the form of songs and poems.

Meanwhile, Roy joined the Navy, and I heard that he later played in the Navy Band. I lost touch with him along with the rest of the Emeralds except for Lou Dan. After the band broke up, Mother helped Lou Dan get a job at the state hospital as an attendant who took care of patients. However, he died well before he was thirty due to all the issues in his life. I don't think he ever played in a band after he played with The Emeralds.

The Emeralds rock band was relegated to obscure, unwritten history early in the summer of 1966. However, my music career lasted a short time longer. I joined Tudy for a short time in two of his bands. One was Little Caesar Conspirators, and the other was Tudy and the Blue Notes. This was really just two versions of the same band. I could not believe that Tudy recruited me because I did not have much talent. I would soon learn that he was a fan of my countermelodies on the keyboards. I thought the melodies were overrated. I don't remember playing any engagements with Tudy. Meanwhile, a year had passed at the Highway Department without any progress on my unrealistic plan to become an engineer.

CHAPTER 35

Getting Back on Track

Okay, my brain has turned into one big knot of goo, twisting, squirming, and squirting out my ears over the passage-of-time issue. We are all allowed to make up a certain amount of stuff. Yes! That's it! I will make up stuff. This is surely the way out. Wait! Will I disappear in a puff of blue smoke when I reach my quota? Well, that would be the easy way out of my dilemma.

*****

During my second summer out of high school, I got acquainted with a young woman who was destined to become a very important person in my life. Her name was Gail Padilla. Our relationship began when she showed some interest in me at a dance. I may have been playing in the band. I could not believe that such an attractive young woman was paying attention to me. We hit it off, and I very quickly fell head over heels in love with her. I was emotionally very immature at the time. It seemed crazy, and it should have been; but it wasn't.

Gail was intelligent and ambitious. Her father was a history teacher at Robertson High School, and her mother would later become a teacher. She was going to be a senior in high school in the fall of 1966. She had worked part-time at the Carnegie Library in Las Vegas for years. I visited her in the library often after we began seeing each other.

Gail made it clear early in the relationship that she was not going to stay involved with someone who planned to spend the rest of his life working for the Highway Department. I told her I wanted to be an engineer. I don't know if this impressed her. Maybe it just gave her a clue that I might be something more. As it turned out, she completely changed my life plan. Alaska fell off the edge of my unrealistic road map. I applied for admission to New Mexico Highlands University. I would begin at this small, local university while Gail finished high school.

Not long after our relationship became serious, I told Mom about Gail. The first question she asked was "What's wrong with her?" This might seem like a strange question for a mother to ask a son under such circumstances. Nevertheless, I understood why she asked this question. The reason was an astrological prediction that Grandfather had made for me. It indicated that I would marry a person who was physically handicapped—so much for astrology. Gail had no handicaps of any kind unless you want to count being both attractive and intelligent as a handicap.

I sometimes wonder if my ski accident was added to the astrological recipe to arrive at my forecast. After the accident, one might have thought I was not a good marriage candidate for a healthy young woman. However, I was completely recovered physically. Admittedly, I had more scar tissue than your average bull rider. Yet it was barely enough to frighten a small child or cowardly puppy. I seemed to be collecting the stuff like it was a badge of honor. I didn't reveal it unless I wanted to show it off. It was useless for intimidating people, and showing it off probably indicated something important concerning my intelligence.

Okay, it should have worried any woman interested in me right out of the gate even though I had no physical handicap. It demonstrated that I was more than a little reckless and immature with an unrealistic view of life, the universe, and everything else. Meanwhile, Gail was a healthy young woman, and for some reason, Mother was surprised even though I was a healthy young man by then. She liked Gail very much, and I got along with Gail's family. Her mother was very lively and outgoing. However, her father was a little more difficult to get to know. Nevertheless, all the relationships worked.

To impress Gail, I entered New Mexico Highlands University in the fall of 1966 even though I had not been able to save any of my Highway Department salary. It all went to help Mom. Grandmother and Grandfather came to my rescue and paid the tuition for my first quarter.

I don't know what it took to get in to Highlands other than the tuition. I suppose they had to see my high school grades, which weren't great. I did not have much of a plan going, but I figured I should study physics since it would be required for engineering. There was not an engineering program at Highlands. Looking back, meeting Gail was a major turning point in my life. She was and is a very special person.

CHAPTER 36

Ambulance Work

Nothing: Another attempt to get to the heart of the matter: Since space and time are something, there appears to be nowhere in the universe where "nothing" exists... Or doesn't exist? Can nothing only exist outside of the universe? Maybe it only exists in our brains—well, some of them anyway.

*****

Sometime in the spring of 1966, Mother was notified that she would have to move out of the state hospital house. The hospital planned to demolish the house along with two houses next to it to build a new facility. Mom's sister, Opal, gave her a lead to an available apartment above a mortuary in town. Opal's husband was a mortician at the mortuary. Mom followed up and rented the one-bedroom apartment.

The small apartment almost worked for us because Sam was gone to the Marines, leaving three of us to accommodate. The living room and dining room did double duty as bedrooms. This worked for a short time when Mom, Diana, and I lived in the apartment for a short time.

During this time, Mom was not spending much of her time at home anyway. Her relationship with Dr. Wickman, the state hospital dentist, was ramping up. Sometime in this period, his wife passed away. He kept his hospital house, and soon, both Mother and Diana made the transition into it. Consequently, room in the apartment became a nonissue. Mom continued to pay the rent, and I stayed in the small apartment while I attended Highlands.

During my transition to the new apartment, a tragic accident occurred that would have an impact on my life while attending Highlands. An ambulance driver for the mortuary occupying the building below the apartment was killed in a tragic accident. In those days, ambulances turned on their sirens and went full out in response calls. The drivers assumed everyone would hear them coming and get out of their way. This did not always happen. On this driver's last call, he pulled the big Oldsmobile with the 500-plus-cubic-inch engine out of the garage and screamed up the street, heading for an accident. Ambulances could not control the traffic lights in those days. They depended on everyone hearing and seeing them coming. At the second light after leaving the mortuary, he struck a car in the intersection at high speed. The person in the other car had apparently not heard the siren or seen him coming and had entered the intersection. The ambulance T-boned the car, and the ambulance driver was killed instantly.

Mrs. Johnson, who owned the mortuary and a hardware store, was also our landlord. We had not lived in the apartment very long when she called me into her office in the mortuary to explore the possibility that I might replace the ambulance driver who had been killed. I discussed the job with her. I didn't really want it, but I needed money for college. I learned that if I took the job, I would sleep in a little bed that was separated from the main office of the mortuary by a flimsy partition. I was to be on call during the nights, and I might be called on during the day if a driver was needed. I told her that I had not had any first-aid courses. She told me that she would set up some training for me. This would never happen.

Since I was in school, I told her that I might not be able to respond. This apparently did not bother her. She wanted me primarily for the nights. She indicated that someone from her hardware store would go with me on the calls. It was not clear how this would work at night.

When Mrs. Johnson showed me the office and my sleeping quarters, she found a pair of shoes that had belonged to the deceased driver. She asked me if I wanted to try them on. I declined, but I tentatively accepted the job. I felt desperate. On my first night on the job, I attempted to sleep on the little cot in the rear of the office, not really knowing what I would do if I got a call. There were simply too many loose ends that Mrs. Johnson had not tied up for me. For example, it was clear to me that I would be going out on calls without any training—at least for a while. Furthermore, I had not even taken a drive in the ambulance. I was perplexed. I don't think I slept at all that night. I quit the next day. Unfortunately, I didn't understand that I could not quit. Quitting would have worked had I lived very far from the mortuary. My resignation did not prevent Mrs. Johnson from calling me whenever she needed someone to fill out a crew to go on a call. She never accepted my resignation. If I tried to get out of going, she would plead with me. It was difficult to turn her down when I knew that someone was in need.

Eventually, she hired another Highlands student who was officially an employee, but he could not go on calls by himself. It took a crew of two to respond to calls. I became a reluctant second person on the crew many times even though I never agreed to this. I attempted to get out of each call at first. After this went on for a while, I just went on the calls with no argument. I got paid five dollars per call.

During my time at Highlands, I worked with several different student drivers. None of us ever knew what we were doing because none of us ever received the promised training. Well, we got on-the-job training. Since I didn't officially work for the mortuary, I felt no obligation to stay in during the evening because I might get a call.

Mrs. Johnson was competing with two other mortuaries in town. The ambulance business generated business for the mortuaries. The state and city police did not play favorites. They alternated between the mortuaries when they had to call for an ambulance. If there was a death involved, an ambulance response could generate mortuary business.

Mrs. Johnson hired several married students in succession, getting them to agree to live in one of her mortuary apartments. She seldom, if ever, had a second person on call even though an ambulance crew requires two people. This meant that she never quit calling me to go out on emergencies. I was responding to calls until I graduated from Highlands University and moved away.

I picked up many people that I did not feel qualified to help. Most of them did fine. One of the first calls I went on was to pick up a stabbing victim. Another had been in a motorcycle accident. He held his leg up for the entire ride. A bone was protruding from the leg just below the knee. I did not know how to help him even though I had plenty of experience with broken legs. I had no splint or anything I thought I could use to relieve his pain. I felt helpless. Another time we had a young woman who went off the road in the Gallinas Canyon north of Las Vegas. She was in pain. I was helping a student named Wes who was on the call. Wes chose to drive. The only injury the woman had was a broken leg. However, as Wes came down the canyon road, he took the corners at crazy speeds, squealing the tires on each corner. We had not put a splint on the woman. She was sliding around on the stretcher, screaming. I was in back with her. I could tell that her life was not in danger. She had a simple, yet painful, fracture. I told Wes to knock it off with the crazy driving, adding that he was not doing anything for her survival but his driving was putting her in excruciating pain. It was just crazy! He slowed down.

The worst accident I responded to occurred about forty miles north of Las Vegas on I-25. A Plymouth Barracuda carrying three teenagers, two girls and a boy, ran head-on into a large motor home. The accident occurred at a location where the interstate narrowed to two lanes in order to pass through the small town of Springer. By the time we arrived at the scene, an ambulance from Springer had taken the survivors from the motor home to a hospital in Springer or Raton. There were no survivors in the Barracuda.

It was very late on a dark and rainy night. The state police had the Barracuda illuminated from various angles, creating an eerie scene. The body of one of the girls in the car appeared to be sitting motionless and staring straight ahead with no visible means of support. The other two victims were lying prone in the wreckage. The seats were no longer in place or even recognizable. It was the most gruesome scene that I had ever witnessed.

The state police asked us to get the bodies out of the car. However, the car was so mangled that there was no obvious way to get inside of it. The police removed some of the broken glass in the side windows to allow us to get in and remove the bodies. They had not been in the car. They just assumed that the occupants were dead. It was a valid assumption.

I was nominated to crawl into the car to remove the bodies since I was the smallest. The police helped by clearing as much broken glass out of a side window as possible. The opening they created was barely large enough to allow me to wriggle through it to get into the car. It was not so clear how to get the bodies out. I did not think it was possible, and I had wanted to wait for part of the car to be cut away. This is not what the police wanted.

I crawled through the opening the police had prepared. It took me a while to get inside. Once there, I discovered that the sitting girl had been impaled and was stuck in place. I set about attempting to free her. The other two victims were lying flat. It was grisly work and no easy task. Flesh was mixed with metal. It was grim and gruesome. Yet these words are not strong enough. *Ghastly* is not strong enough either.

After prying and pulling for a while, I had all three bodies free from the impalements and other obstacles. I dragged and pushed them one at a time to the small opening that the police had made and began stuffing them through it as best I could. My partner helped by pulling from the outside. This was difficult for both of us. After we succeeded in getting the bodies out, we loaded them into the ambulance. Two of the bodies had to be stacked, one on top of the other, in order to accommodate all three bodies in the ambulance.

For some reason, I sat in the back with them in the attendant's chair as we made our way back to Las Vegas. I don't remember why I did this. Perhaps I felt I was comforting them in death, or maybe

I just wanted to be away from my partner who was driving. I was disgusted with him along with the rest of the world. I was in shock.

When we got back to the mortuary in Las Vegas, we unloaded the bodies, taking them into the mortuary's preparation room where we laid them out on tables. Someone told us the families were on their way to make identifications. It was very late at night. We arranged the bodies as neatly as we could, but they were a mess. They should have been covered. Neither of us had thought to do this.

When the families arrived, it was awful. There were tears, shrieks of grief, screaming, and more tears. I asked myself, *What am I doing here?* After all, I had quit my job with the mortuary several years before, after only one day on the job. I felt helpless. Why hadn't we covered the mangled bodies and only revealed enough for the identifications? This might have made it easier for the parents.

After they arrived, I felt helpless because I did not know how to offer any comfort for such a tragedy. Each parent broke into wailing as soon as they recognized their child. It was traumatic to witness, but obviously unimaginably worse for the parents.

I don't remember trying to sleep that night. I can only imagine that it must have been difficult. Living and not officially working at the mortuary was a lesson in life for me. I saw how temporary existence is and how quickly and violently it can disappear.

Another lesson came to me via a woman who we picked up at least three times for trips to the hospital. She had leukemia, and her husband would ride along with us in the ambulance. We usually picked her up in the morning when she was delirious after a difficult night. One morning, we arrived, and she seemed to be suffering more than usual. Nevertheless, her husband insisted that he needed to finish shaving and getting dressed before we could take the two of them to the hospital. I wanted to hurry him along, but my partner on the call resisted this. We finally loaded her into the ambulance, and the husband got in the front seat. I rode in the back with the woman.

We began the trip to the hospital but did not seem to be in a hurry. My partner, the real employee of the mortuary, drove. The woman seemed to be suffering greatly. It seemed that I was the only one who felt any urgency. As we continued our slow crawl to the hospital, the woman stopped breathing and moaning. I did nothing. I did not know what to do. I felt that she was gone.

When we arrived at the hospital, my conclusion was confirmed. Her husband seemed relieved. It didn't take me long to understand what he had done that morning and why I was the only one who felt any urgency. As she lay peacefully on the ambulance cot, I came to the realization that the women's husband really loved her. He had helped her escape from her suffering because he loved her so much.

Wes was one of my ambulance crew partners at the mortuary. He was a student like me, but he officially worked for the mortuary. Wes was one of several partners I liked working with. Wes and I would get a call from Mrs. Johnson; we would race to the ambulance bay. The first one there would jump into the driver's seat of the big Oldsmobile ambulance with its powerful engine. Once we pulled out of the garage, it would get up to speed very quickly, and when we hit the interstate, we could cruise at about 130 mph. Neither of us trusted the other to drive at the crazy speeds we went in those days. I am still thankful that no one ever pulled out in front of us and caused the type of accident that began my involvement with the mortuary in the first place.

The residents of the five or six apartments upstairs at the mortuary and one downstairs were parked in the back. I remember pulling into the parking lot at the mortuary one day to find Dan, who was the student who covered the calls at the time, wrenching his guts out near the trash cans. I asked if I could help him. He told me that I couldn't. However, before I left him, he recovered enough to tell me that he had retrieved a body out on the interstate earlier in the morning. A man had driven off the road and down an embankment a week or two before, but no one had seen or reported the accident. The car and driver had just disappeared. The driver had been reported missing, but he had not been found until that morning when Dan was called. He had gone on the call alone.

The body was very ripe by the time Dan arrived on the scene, and the state police had offered no help in retrieving it. In their defense, it was not their job to retrieve bodies. The chore was more than Dan could stomach. He had to do it alone. Ambulance work was good to motivate the student ambulance drivers to get a good education. At the same time, it saved on grocery bills. I think it was a while before Dan could eat again.

CHAPTER 37

Draft Physical

Outside of the universe? Where is that? Where nothing exists? Apparently, one can't get there from here. Nevertheless, I am trying my best to enter this forbidden region in these pages. If I succeed, pretend this book doesn't exist. Put it down very carefully, remembering that Nothing is explosive, e.g., the Big Bang.

*****

Not long after I began my studies at Highlands University, my local draft board invited me to take a bus ride to Albuquerque, where I would be given a physical to determine the suitability of my body for disposal in the Vietnam War. The bus was filled with other less-than-enthusiastic candidates for this proposition. At the time, the Vietnam War was escalating rapidly. I had not been concerned about the draft because I was fairly certain that the injury to my leg in the ski accident would disqualify me. Dr. O'Donnell had indicated that it was not likely that I would be eligible for military service.

When we arrived in Albuquerque, I remembered being lined up around the wall of a square room with several military doctors present. They instructed us to take off all of our clothing and parade around in front of them. I was pulled out of line immediately by one of the doctors. He took me aside and told me that he was sorry, but there was no way I could get into the military. He said this as if he thought I would be disappointed. I was not. Nor was I surprised by his statement. However, I did not expect him to tell me in the next breath that the government was going to put me in a crippled children's program that would pay for all my books in college. I objected. First of all, I was not crippled. My leg was just badly scarred, but I could walk, run, and rob liquor stores with complete abandon—well, maybe not the liquor stores robberies. Furthermore, I knew that a lot of guys were putting lives on the line in the war, and my brother was one of them. It was enough that I was not going to do my part. I did not want to be made to feel even more guilty than I already did. He did not care how I felt about it, and he sent me to see another person to set it up. This person took my information and indicated someone would be in touch about the books back in Las Vegas.

It was not long after I was back in Las Vegas before the "someone" found me. I don't remember the details of how he found me. I don't even remember our first meeting. Nevertheless, he must have told me that he was running the "book program." Still feeling guilty about getting out of the draft, I told him I was not interested in the book program. He insisted that he was going to pay for my books even though I continued to object. He asked me to keep the receipts when I bought the books. I somewhat reluctantly complied. I needed the money after all. Nevertheless, I felt better after playing a little game of hide-and-seek with him at the beginning of each quarter when he would come to collect my receipts. He always got them. My effort to be elusive must have made me feel better about myself.

CHAPTER 38

Mom and Doc

Are there boundaries to existence? If so, what lies outside of the boundaries? Can you have a boundary with nothing on one side of it? Wouldn't the boundary simply fall into the nothing? Or does the curvature of space prevent a boundary from existing, much like the curvature of the Earth prevents us from arriving at the edge of the Earth? Unless we go a different way—up. Is there a different way to get out of the universe? This seems to be another question that we don't know how to answer. Yet I seem to want to know about it. Apparently, I want what I cannot have. I am never satisfied. Well, there was that one time in the janitor's closet... Never mind.

*****

During my first year at Highlands, Mother and Diana slowly transitioned to Dr. Wickman's house. His wife had passed away, and their relationship was almost legitimate. Doc's wife had been an alcoholic for much longer than Mother knew Doc. She spent most of her time in bed, or so I was told. Doc and his first wife had two children, Sally and Dale. Sally was older and out on her own. Dale was a few days older than me and attending the University of Houston, where he would eventually become an optometrist. He did not approve of his dad's relationship with Mom, but it didn't seem to matter at the time. Mom and Doc were spending a lot of time together, and a disapproval, or two, was not going to change anything.

Diana and I had moved into the apartment above the mortuary with Mom. However, Mom was not home much, and when she was, Doc was often with her. The two of them liked to drink and fish. Doc also made God's Eyes, which were large yarn wall hangings originally created by the native people in Mexico. He made them for many people. He was very skillful with his hands.

Mom and Doc eventually bought a small camping trailer that they would pull out to a lake and stay for several nights, fishing all the while. Well, I wouldn't call it fishing. They cast their lines into a lake and just leave them while they drank occasionally, pulling in a fish. The primary activity was drinking. The fish had to look out for themselves, but there was never any great danger for them.

I don't remember when Doc's wife, Arlene, passed away. It was not long afterward, when Mom and Diana moved out of the mortuary apartment and into Doc's hospital house. Sam was already in the Marines. Meanwhile, Gail and I were spending some serious time together that included all hours of the day and night. Of course, we were behaving at night as best as I can remember. Well, maybe my memory is not so good. I don't think it was very long after Mom and Diana left the mortuary apartment before Gail filled the vacancy. We would live there until I graduated from Highlands and Gail finished her junior year. Our relationship was serious. We planned to get married from a very early stage in our relationship even though we could not support ourselves while we were in school. Our car was furnished by Mom, who didn't need it because she was with Doc full-time. She may have also paid our rent for a while. I am not certain of this.

We knew it was just a matter of time before we were married. We made it official in June of 1968. My grandmother had argued that we should wait until I was twenty-one, which was less than a month and a half after our wedding date. I did not see how the month and a half would make any practical difference. We got married in June between my sophomore and junior years. Gail was a year behind me. After the wedding, we continued to receive support from our parents, who were all very understanding and wanted us both to finish college.

Attending Highlands University was a compromise for both of us. We had imagined ourselves in better places. Gail majored in journalism, while I majored in physics and mathematics. During the first summer after my freshman year, I worked at the Public Service Company as a cashier, taking money from people who came in to pay their electric bill. This helped me pay for some of my college. Gail had a scholarship, and she had worked in the public library in town for years. This experience helped her to get a job in the Highlands Library.

I did well enough in school during my first year to get a scholarship for the rest of my undergraduate studies. I don't remember when I received it, but I certainly could not have received it based on my disastrous time in high school. I remember that my grandparents had paid my first quarter's tuition. I don't remember how I paid for the rest of my first year at Highlands. Later, I obtained loans and worked in the summers to supplement my scholarships. This, with support from our parents, enabled both of us to focus on our studies at Highlands until I graduated, and Gail finished her junior year.

After Mom moved out of the apartment and into Doc's house, she continued to support us mostly by means of loan of her Volkswagen Squareback, which we used full-time while we were attending Highlands. Mom did not need the Squareback because Doc had a Squareback also. In addition, they bought a pickup after Mom moved into his house.

They used the pickup to pull a camper to various lakes where they would fish for a weekend or more. Mom seemed to enjoy this, which really surprised me. She never cared about fishing at Pot Creek. However, she was having a good life with Doc, but there was a downside. They were both drinking way too much.

I don't remember when Mom and Doc bought my grandparents' property near Montezuma. It was probably before my grandfather passed away in March of 1969. After he passed away and the property belonged to Mother and Doc, Grandmother continued to live in her small house on the property. However, there was another two acres of land available to add another house. To this end, Mom and Doc bought a double-wide trailer and put it on the property. They quickly added a family room and extra bedroom, almost making it into a real house. It was comfortable. Also it was good that they lived so near Grandmother. She needed help to get along after Grandfather was gone. Nevertheless, she never moved in with Mom and Doc. She preferred in her own little house, which was less than two hundred feet from Mom and Doc's front door.

It was during this time that Doc's drinking almost got the best of him. One day, he was making his way back home after spending too much time in a bar. He lost control of the truck on the curvy and hilly road out to their house, ran off the road, and hit a tree—crashing violently. He survived, but he was in serious condition with multiple contusions and a head injury. His face had to be rebuilt. With time, he recovered, more or less, completely from the accident, but the truck was totaled.

During Mother's transition to Doc, sister Diana lived wherever Mom was living. She continued in the Las Vegas school system through high school. She was not a stellar student, but she was very good in track. She set some school records. I don't remember her getting into any trouble. Her life during this time is mostly a mystery to me.

CHAPTER 39

Highlands University
and Summer Jobs

We see material objects by scattering light off of them and detecting the scattered light with our eyes. Our eyes code the information, or data, from the scattered light and send it to our brains where a complicated analysis is performed to complete the visual experience. We take note of patterns in the data and file them away in our brains for future reference.

*****

At Highlands University, I became reacquainted with Marsha Jo Hannah. She had been one of my classmates at Robertson High School. Marsha Jo was one of two people who had as much to do with my success later in life as any of my professors. She was brilliant. I had been aware of her incredible mathematical gift in high school, but I had not appreciated it. I simply thought of her as a geek. It had been well-known at Robertson High School that she was smarter than any of the teachers. She was completely out of my league in the intelligence department. Knowing this, I was very surprised to find her attending Highlands. She could have gone anywhere.

At Highlands, she was a mathematics major. As it turned out, her presence created the best possible situation for me. I quickly got to know her much better because we found ourselves taking the same math and physics classes together. Her genius quickly became more apparent to me.

In spite of her incredible talent, she was not very ambitious. Her long-term goal was to work at Highlands in the small computing department. Her lack of ambition really surprised me. Maybe she did not want to get far from home.

I would soon discover how very lucky I was to have her as a classmate. The fact that she was a genius did not prevent me from being competitive enough with her to get her to take note of me. The competition quickly ramped up. I was surprised that I was able to nearly keep up with her. She was pulling me along, helping me to reach my full potential. Looking back, Marsha Jo had as much influence on what I became as any of my professors.

Another fellow student at Highlands was also very important to me. His name was Louie Madrid. Like Marsha Jo, he was a mathematics major. The two of them made for very stiff, yet friendly, competition. I had trouble keeping up with both of them and felt I ranked as a distant third behind them. Nevertheless, I was put in their category by our mathematics and physics professors. The three of us were way off normal, not just for our class but also for the university.

For the first time, I really learned some mathematics. I found it fascinating. I knew this would have to happen if I were to become an engineer. Since there was no engineering program at Highlands, I also knew I would have to get an engineering degree somewhere else. However, I began to have my doubts about engineering. I liked mathematics, and during the first year at Highlands, I began to change my mind about engineering. Since I had managed to hold my own with Marsha Jo and Louie while the three of us set new standards for Highlands in physics and math, I began to think that physics would be more interesting than engineering. I don't remember when I declared a physics major, but it was probably during my freshman year even though I did not take any physics classes until my sophomore year.

The only class that I was able to handily best Marsha Jo in was an art appreciation class. We did not take the class together. It might have been different if we had. The class used a large book of art history filled with many details. The professor mostly showed examples of art in class and told us why the examples were important. We were expected to carefully read the book that went along with the class to supplement the lectures. After the professor gave us a reading assignments in the book, he would give us very detailed tests on the material in the reading assignment. The highest scores seldom exceeded 40 percent correct. This was not a big problem because he graded on the curve.

However, it became a problem when I took the class. I quickly discovered that I had the ability to read the assignments and remember all the details. This surprised me. Apparently, I had a photographic memory that I probably inherited from Roznocker the Great. However, the photographs faded after only a few days. Nevertheless, this ability allowed me to score near 100 percent on all the tests, completely destroying the professor's curve.

I could tell that he was frustrated by my ability. He watched me closely as I took the tests to make certain I had no way of accessing the material in the book. Little did he know, it was all in my head for easy access. In the end, he was forced to give me an A, but he did not penalize the other students due to my ability. Instead, he treated me as an outlier. The final exam for the course was a bit more troublesome for me because my "photographs" had faded with time. I had to refresh them as much as possible before I took the final. I ended up at the top of the curve again, but not so emphatically as I had on the weekly quizzes.

After my sophomore year, I spent the summer on a low-paying research project with Marsha Jo. We were doing some research on Fourier Analysis with Professor Conkling, who was a mathematics professor. I felt lost, but Marsh Jo managed to drag me along with her. Louis was not involved in this effort. The pay was not great, but Gail and I were surviving. She was also doing very well in school. She had a fantastic talent for writing and ended up studying journalism even though she also had an interest in biology and had some ambition to get into medicine. After I first saw how well Gail could write, I wanted to be able to write like her. This never happened. Well, maybe this skill will emerge in the next paragraph…or maybe not.

At about the time that Marsha Jo and I were doing the research with Professor Conkling, he was killed in a plane crash. He was flying with another Highlands professor in a small plane. This event was tragic. Fortunately, he had already inspired both Marsha Jo and me.

*****

During our college years, Gail and I spent many Sunday afternoons and evenings at her parents' house, having Sunday dinners. Her mother, Velma, was a fantastic cook, and we were both fantastic eaters. She was especially good at preparing New Mexican cuisine, which had been my favorite since I was a small child. I had never eaten so much good food. It was not long before our girth began to challenge our height for the largest dimension award. We were both studying hard and did not have the will to diet or the time to exercise. Nevertheless, we seemed to have plenty of time to eat. Well, we eventually got this pleasant problem under control. I have an innate need to be physically fit.

*****

Between my junior and senior years of college, I worked for the New Mexico State Highway Department again. I was assigned as a concrete and grade inspector on a job just north of Wagon Mound, which was about forty miles from Las Vegas. Mom and Doc allowed me to drive their truck to and from the job that summer. They had two other cars.

The job turned out to be an adventure. The project engineer was apparently allowing the contractor to take all kinds of shortcuts. He never specifically ordered me to let the contractor get away with anything. However, he never backed me up when I failed a test.

Another inspector, Flavio, who I had worked with on my previous stint with the Highway Department, encouraged me to stand up to the contractor. He told me not to give in by fudging the results of the tests as I was performing on grade compaction and concrete samples. We both concluded privately that our boss was on the take. This put me in a difficult situation. Flavio made it easier for me by backing me up when he could. He mostly just set a good example.

Nevertheless, the contractor made my life miserable by threatening and bullying me. He attempted to intimidate me every day as I tried to fulfill my job responsibilities. Large scrapers would come within inches of me when I was kneeling on the grade getting samples for compaction tests. The concrete crews often threatened me when I didn't allow them add more water to the concrete after I had taken my sample cylinders to be tested. It was a very difficult to stick to my guns, but thanks to the backing and encouragement of Flavio, I managed to fulfill my responsibilities. Many of the tests I conducted failed. Nevertheless, the project engineer, who was my boss, let the contractor proceed without fixing the problems.

One day, I was told by the contractor that a tough new foreman was coming onto the job. He would not tolerate any attempt by me to slow the job down; so I had better watch out, and the tests better pass because the new foreman always got what he wanted one way or the other. I was certainly frightened, but I continued to do my job. I conducted and failed tests regularly. If Flavio had not continued to encourage me and back me up, I don't know what I would have done. Of course, Flavio was in as much trouble as I was because he was causing even more problems for the contractor with the tests he was doing.

A new boss did show up, but he did not spend any time trying to intimidate me. I decided that it had all just been so much talk. Maybe they figured I was a lost cause by then and decided to wait me out since I would be returning to school soon. As a matter of fact, they weren't fixing the problems I found, so I was not slowing the contractor down by failing tests. I don't know how they dealt with Flavio. Maybe they gave up on him also. Anyway, I was very glad to get back to school.

About a year later, I read in the newspaper how a big concrete box on the job had failed, and it caused a big stir in the newspapers. Fixing the job was going to cost taxpayers a wad of cash. Meanwhile, I had applied for another summer job with the highway department for the next summer. I did not get the job. Maybe I had become the scapegoat without knowing it. I never heard anything more from the Highway Department. If I had a bad reputation with them, it apparently did not matter. Or maybe it just hasn't caught up with me yet. Wait! Is that a knock at my door? I'm not expecting anyone.

During my summer with the Highway Department, Neil Armstrong and Buzz Aldrin landed on the moon. I was enthralled by this adventure of humankind. I remember that I was driving to my Highway Department job near Wagon Mound when they blasted off. I spent the following Sunday evening watching the incredible scenes from the moon as Buzz and Neil became the first humans to do a real moon walk. We were at Gail's parents' house for this incredible event. I had watched most of the early space flights beginning with Alan Shepard's. I was in Breckenridge for the early flights, but these fantastic adventures to be continued into the period when I was in graduate school at the same institution that the first man to walk on the moon and the last man to step off the moon had attended. I guess this made me feel a little special for no good reason.

CHAPTER 40

Mountains and My Marriages

How do we see inside the nucleus and deeper into the very heart of matter? Visible light has a wavelength that is much too long to reveal details the size of an atom, much less something even smaller. We need a better flashlight that shines shorter wavelengths in addition to better detectors that can "see" the shorter, scattered wavelengths in order to peer into the chaotic, hidden, too-small-to-be-important details of the extremely tiny world hidden within our macroscopic existence. No problem; it just costs money.

*****

After Gail and I were married in the summer of 1968, we decided that we needed a honeymoon even though we did not have much money. I played the only card I had. I suggested we go to Breckenridge and stay over the Fourth of July holiday. I knew the area, and I thought we could get accommodations. Gail agreed, and we headed north so that I could show her "my" mountains.

We found a room at the Breckenridge Inn. Much of this trip has faded from my memory. Nevertheless, one adventure stuck in my mind. It would become more relevant in my life than it should have.

I not only wanted to bring Gail close to my mountains; I wanted to get her on them. I was rather foolish about my mountains after all. Anyway, I decided the two of us would attempt to climb Peak 10. I knew it would be an adventure because getting to the summit ridge requires making a steep climb on a steep scree field topping out at more than 13,000 feet and then traversing a rather narrow and somewhat intimidating ridge mostly covered with snow even in the summer.

Gail began the climb slowly. It would take a while to get up the mountain. Nevertheless, she had heart and kept going. The altitude was a big factor for her. As we climbed higher, she slowed but continued to struggle upward. Apparently, she wanted to please me even if my notion of climbing the peak seemed very foolish to her. It was foolish.

After an arduous climb, we found ourselves standing on the summit ridge. We still had a walk along the narrow ridge to reach the summit, but the steep climbing was done. Gail did not seem to be intimidated by being in such a high place. However, her enthusiasm was waning. Nevertheless, she moved slowly along the ridge with me. Finally, after the long, steep climb followed by the balancing act on the ridge, we were standing on the summit. Well, I was standing. Gail plopped herself down on the summit rock cairn, utterly exhausted. She did not look happy. Somehow, I knew I would never see her on a high summit again.

We had not been on the summit very long when I looked down the ridge and saw a woman practically dancing up the mountain. As she joined us on the summit, I recognized her as one of my Summit County High School classmates. Her name was Linda. I had thought she was very attractive in high school, but way out of my league. She was even more attractive as she joined us on the summit.

We talked, and I got caught up with her. When we were done on the summit, Gail and I waited until Linda began her descent. I did not want to slow Linda down. I knew our descent would not be fast.

I don't remember any details of our descent, nor do I remember the rest of our stay in Breckenridge. This was the last time that I would ever climb a mountain with Gail, and I knew it at the time. I don't think I let it bother me—much. Nevertheless, it did impact the way we spent our vacation time together.

CHAPTER 41

Dr. Kirkpatrick and Woodrow Wilson

Besides being small, fundamental particles have another behavioral problem. They do not come close to obeying the classical laws of physics. Instead, they obey the rather mysterious and very strange laws of quantum mechanics that were never passed by either house of congress. Even politicians have more sense than to pass laws that don't make sense... Don't they? Never mind.

*****

When I was a senior at Highlands University and coming to the end of my time as an undergraduate, one of my physics professors, Dr. Kirkpatrick, took me aside and told me that he would like to nominate me to receive a Woodrow Wilson Fellowship. He indicated that it was a very prestigious fellowship, and it would help me get into, and pay for, a good graduate school. I was flattered that he wanted to nominate me. Of course, I agreed to it. I certainly wanted to go to graduate school, but it was not clear to me how this could happen.

After Dr. Kirkpatrick submitted his nomination, proposing me for the fellowship, it was not long before I received an invitation to meet with the Fellowship Committee when they were in Albuquerque. This was not only exciting news for me; it was exciting news for the university. There had never been a Woodrow Wilson Fellow from Highlands. The provost of the university offered to drive me the 120 miles to Albuquerque for the interview. Gail was invited to ride along.

We made our trip on a Sunday morning. When we arrived in Albuquerque, we went to a hotel where the committee had a suite set up for conducting the interviews. Gail and the provost found a way to entertain themselves while I appeared before the committee.

I was rather nervous, but I tend to do well when I am nervous. Nevertheless, I could not help but wonder how a kid from Pot Creek had gotten himself into this situation. I don't remember anything about what they asked me. I do remember that I seemed to have an adrenalin kick going that enabled me to express myself without difficulty. I don't remember whether I thought the interview had gone well, but I did not think that it had gone poorly. After it was over, I decided it was an exciting experience for me no matter the outcome.

I don't remember how long it was before I heard from the Fellowship Foundation. When I did hear, it was exciting news. I was being awarded a Woodrow Wilson Fellowship. It would pay me to go to graduate school. However, there was the suggestion that came along with award. The Fellowship Foundation indicated that I might get a better offer to pay for graduate school from the universities I applied to because there was prestige that came along with having a Woodrow Wilson Fellow attending their graduate schools. Consequently, I was encouraged to take to any alternate fellowships that were offered by the universities. In doing so, I would not lose my title of "Woodrow Wilson Fellow."

I was soon getting solicitations to apply to graduate school at many schools. I had already applied to a group of schools that I was most interested in. In spite of the fellowship, I did not get into MIT or Berkeley, which were my top two choices. However, I was accepted at all the other schools where I had applied, including Purdue. In the end, I chose Purdue because I had attended a conference there for a Phi Eta Sigma, an honor society that I had been a member of at Highlands. I had been impressed by the magnitude of the school. Nothing against Purdue, but it was easy to impress a kid from Pot Creek. Also I liked the idea of going off to a place that I was somewhat familiar with. Another factor that should not have been so important was that several of my heroes had attended Purdue. Included on this list were Neil Armstrong, the first human to make a track on the moon, and Gene Cernan, another Purdue graduate who would later become the last human to leave a track on the moon. If mankind survives for a while longer, Gene could lose his title, but Neil is safe. Gus Grissom and Roger Chaffee, who came to tragic ends, were also Purdue graduates.

After I started getting offers, Marsha Jo took note. She decided to apply to two schools, Stanford and Washington State, for graduate school. She got into both and chose Stanford. We stayed in touch for a while after we went off in different directions. She had a PhD from Stanford in three years, and I believe she worked on artificial intelligence. She found a husband there. We lost touch not long after.

Meanwhile, Louie indicated he was going back home to southern New Mexico to teach mathematics in high school. I never heard from him after the three of us left Highlands University in 1970. I graduated magna cum laude, while Marsha Jo graduated summa cum laude. Louie was probably magna cum laude also, but I don't remember this for certain.

CHAPTER 42

Purdue University

Quantum mechanics dictates that extremely small fundamental particles behave like waves and particles at the same time. This means that they can be somewhat localized like a particle, but they are also smeared out by their wave behavior. The result is that they do not have definite locations and trajectories. This rather bizarre innovation is not the behavior we would expect from a transparent creator.

*****

I entered Purdue University in the fall of 1970 with fifty-one other physics graduate students. A big factor in my decision to attend Purdue had been several discussions with an administrative person in the Physics Department Office at Purdue. He called me several times while I was making my decision to emphasize that the Physics Department was very interested in having me come to graduate school at Purdue. He also indicated that if I agreed to do my graduate studies at Purdue, I would be given an NDEA Fellowship that would give me almost enough money to live on. Game over; I chose Purdue.

Gail and I did not have a good plan for making the move to Purdue. We had been driving one of Mom and Doc's Volkswagen Squarebacks, but they could not let us have it to take to Purdue.

However, they offered us a rundown MG that had belonged to Doc's son, Dale. It was in bad shape, but one of their friends had the engine expertly tuned for us, putting it in good running order. Unfortunately, it had another problem. It had been in a crash that buckled the hood. It could be latched, but it was buckled enough that there was a rather large opening that allowed a good amount of air to get under the hood. We were grateful for the car, but we had some concerns about driving it all the way to Lafayette, Indiana. There was no alternative. It was Lafayette or bust in the MG.

Our trip was not without incident. For some reason, I decided that we should stay off of the interstate highways by taking the scenic route. This was pleasant. However, the car stuttered a number of times along the way. One time, the engine was missing badly. I fixed this easily. The dipstick had twisted around and was making contact with a spark plug. We nursed the car along, stopping near Kansas City to stay overnight. We drove around the interstate loop that circled the city early the next morning as we continued eastward, staying on secondary roads instead of taking an interstate-highway route. We completed the trip in two days. I was surprised at how beautiful the countryside was, going through the small towns in Illinois and into Indiana.

We had arranged for an apartment in the low-budget, married student housing, which was very near the Purdue Airport. We were able to move into it as soon as we arrived and checked in at the housing office. It does not take long to move in when your moving van is a small, two-seater, sports car.

As we unloaded the MG, we became aware of the humidity and the heat. Our cheap apartment was extremely hot and humid even though it was early evening. We were not used to such conditions. There was a location in the wall for an air conditioner, but we had no air conditioner. We had to furnish that ourselves, but we couldn't afford to buy an air conditioner. Nevertheless, I did not feel like I could survive in the hot and humid apartment. We were desperate. For a while, I just wanted to get back in the MG and head back to New Mexico.

After the evening descended upon us, I became a little more rational. We would purchase an air conditioner. We didn't have the cash to make the purchase, but we did have a credit card. We soon had an air conditioner. Life got a little better. Maybe we could make it after all.

I don't remember whether we had planned to go back to New Mexico for the Christmas holiday, but this became our plan. The MG would have to make the trip again. We had no plan to stop overnight on this trip.

We were approaching St. Louis on the interstate when our problems began. A gust of wind got under the bent-up hood of the MG and jerked it clear off the car. I stopped and retrieved it. I tied it on as best as I could with a piece of rope. The rope must have been in the car due to my cowboy heritage. Once the hood was secured, we drove on.

We continued driving through the night and arrived in Las Vegas the next morning. The MG had made its last trip. We gave it back to Mom and Doc. After the holidays were over, we rode the train back to Chicago. Getting from Chicago to Lafayette was easy in principle. Nevertheless, it was an adventure.

We went to the bus station and caught a bus to Lafayette. It was after dark, and the weather was bad. Snow was falling and blowing. As if this weren't enough, the driver was very reckless. When some of the passengers began to comment on his driving, he got even more reckless. As the comments continued, I began to think it was unlikely that we would ever see Lafayette again. Miraculously, we arrived safely.

A taxi got us from the bus station to our apartment. We were in Lafayette with no transportation. Fortunately, there was a small shopping mall at the edge of campus that was in easy walking distance from our apartment. We survived by walking everywhere. I don't remember if we ever took a cab anywhere. We had very little money for such things. Fortunately, most of our needs could be had near the campus.

We were eventually saved because Gail's grandmother passed away and left her enough money to buy a very used Volkswagen. This occurred only after the weather got better. We were destined to have one more adventurous trip across the country in this car. We made it, but not without trouble. It was not any more reliable than the MG had been.

*****

After arriving at Purdue in the fall, it did not take the fifty first-year graduate students long to get to know one another. We compared notes and sized one another up as we quickly determined what we would have to deal with at Purdue. We took note of the fact that there were sixty physics professors, and many of them began making it clear that they were looking for a graduate student or students. This was good.

One of the first things I noticed is that most of my new friends had to teach recitation sessions, grade tests and homework, or other activities to support the very large physics department. They were paid as graduate teaching assistants. Purdue is a large engineering school, and engineers need to take physics courses. The basic physics classes were huge, and the professors needed lots of help to grade tests and homework and to teach recitation sessions. I felt very fortunate to be out of this loop thanks to my fellowship.

Another item all the new grad students quickly became aware of was the qualifying exam or qualifier. This was a test that had to be passed to get into the PhD program. We learned that we would only be given two opportunities to pass the qualifier. Failing the test a second time meant one had to be satisfied with a master's degree. We also noticed that Purdue was giving about ten to fifteen PhDs in physics per year, while they were accepting about fifty new graduate students. It didn't take us long to figure out how most of us would disappear from the program. It was the qualifier. Of course, this had us buzzing as we got samples of past qualifiers and tried to figure out how to beat the game.

I admit that the qualifier had me concerned. It was not scheduled until near the end of our first year of graduate school. We could take it a second time if we failed on the first attempt.

Many of the first-year grad students were getting together to practice qualifier problems. Meanwhile, I adopted a different strategy. While they were looking at previous tests and figuring out how to solve the problems, I was drinking beer with my feet up on the coffee table. Well, that is a bit of an exaggeration. I only had one foot on the coffee table while they were studying for the test constantly. To be honest, I was focusing on the physics courses I was taking while trying not to think too much about the qualifier. However, I did not ignore the qualifier problem completely. I probably looked at some sample tests, but I decided that since we had two chances to pass it, I would take it the first time in a totally relaxed mode to see what it was like and what I would have to do to pass it. I did not join the frenzy of group study that my fellow first-year graduate students disappeared into.

The most difficult aspect of my strategy was that my friends were studying for the qualifier day and night, causing me to think that I could be making a serious mistake. I reassured myself with the knowledge that I would have two chances to pass it. This made it possible for me to almost relax enough to do my reconnaissance on the first test.

Well, I was never completely confident in my strategy. I adopted it partly because I did not want to focus my life so completely on trying to pass that one test. The challenge depressed me. Besides, I thought the whole idea of the test was silly. I figured that I could get along without a PhD if need be. After all, I had made it all the way to Purdue University from Pot Creek elementary school and Mrs. Torres.

The first attempt at the test for my class arrived in the late spring or early summer of my first year at Purdue. I was relaxed going into the large lecture hall where the test would be administered. I sat down, took a deep breath, and focused on staying relaxed. As I made my way through the problems, I was very calm. I found the test difficult, but I was not concerned. I attempted to do the best I could with each problem. My strategy was to construct a solution to each problem that would score points even if I could not come up with the complete solution. I wrote everything down that I thought was relevant to the problem and worked it out as best I could even if I did not feel that I had correctly solved the problem. In some cases, this technique led me to a solution. Sometimes, it didn't. When I finished after about three hours, I felt like the exercise had been useful. However, I felt that there was no way that I had passed the test. The problems were difficult, and there was a limited amount of time to work on them. Nevertheless, I felt my reconnaissance was successful.

I don't remember how long it was before we were informed of the results of the qualifier. All I remember is that I passed the test on that first attempt. I was elated. I don't even remember how many in my group of friends passed it. It was not many. However, I remember that two of them passed it later.

Of course, as I think about it many years later, I have to ask whether I passed because I was a Woodrow Wilson Fellow, which preordained me to pass. Or was it because I was one of the dangerous kids from Pot Creek that everyone was afraid of? Well, I was not all that dangerous anymore. Besides, being "dangerous" is overrated. Maybe I had the right idea when I confronted the first attempt totally relaxed about it. Okay, I admit that there was no danger that I was going to fall asleep during the test. I couldn't help being a little intimidated and exercised by the challenge.

Once the qualifier was passed and before the coursework was done, professors began talking to those of us who had passed the qualifier, making their pitches to get us to work with them on their research. I had declared that I want to do a PhD in theoretical physics. The person who I was most interested in working with was a very mature professor who worked on general relativity. Fortunately, he was not inclined to take any students at the time although I think one of my early friends did end up working with him. I decided that theoretical particle physics was very interesting even though I knew nothing about it. A theoretical particle physicist, Professor Fuchs, was assigned to be my advisor.

Not long after I began to think about problems I might want to work on, Professor Fuchs called me into his office. He said something to the effect, "I see you want to do particle physics theory." I told him he was correct. He responded by telling me, "That is good, but I want to be certain you understand all the requirements we have for our theory students." I was listening intently as he continued, "Since it is so difficult to find a job in theory after one gets a PhD, we require that our theory students have a backup profession." I shrugged, wondering what point he was trying to make. Then he said, "I want you to learn to drive a taxi. That way, you will be certain of finding a job after you get your PhD." It took me a moment to realize that this was his way of telling me that only the best and the brightest should attempt theoretical physics. I got the message. I was disappointed, but not discouraged. I would get a PhD in experimental physics.

I already knew that the experimental groups were actively recruiting students. I still had an interest in particle physics, and once I let this be known, I was recruited enthusiastically.

The problem with particle physics at Purdue was that all the professors were involved with bubble-chamber experiments, and bubble chambers were being phased out in favor of "counter" or electronic experiments. I don't know how many professors I talked to, but they were all eager to recruit me into their groups. It became abundantly clear that following the experimental career path would insure that I would be a passenger in the taxi instead of the driver.

In December of 1971, professors Art Garfinkel and Virgil Barnes organized a field trip to the Argonne National Laboratory and the National Accelerator Laboratory (NAL) for two or three graduate students, including me. Both laboratories were in the Chicago area. NAL had recently been established at a 6,800-acre site near Batavia, Illinois, for the purpose of building the highest-energy particle accelerator in the world. Construction was just getting underway as I entered graduate school. The original design consisted of large synchrotron that would accelerate protons to 200 billion electron volts BeV or GeV, depending on your ancestry, or the day of the week or something like that. Argonne, on the other hand, was an older laboratory that was involved in a wide range of scientific investigations including chemistry, physics, computing, and on and on. Particle physics was done at the Zero Gradient Synchrotron (ZGS) at

Argonne. The ZGS had a maximum-beam energy of a comparatively scant 12.5 GeV.

The new Laboratory would be a single-purpose laboratory. The purpose was high-energy particle physics. Particle physics investigates fundamental nature of matter and energy by accelerating protons or electrons to high energies by passing them through oscillating electric and magnetic fields in radio frequency (RF) cavities many times. This is done in large, approximately circular machines. The high-energy beams produced in an accelerator are extracted and "shined" on various targets, ranging from simple hydrogen to more complex atoms or molecules to illuminate and reveal the basic nature of matter. Is it really that dramatic? As a matter of fact, it is.

Typically, the protons, or electrons, are accelerated and then extracted from large synchrotrons and delivered through external beam lines to targets where they interact to produce secondary beams of particles for use by the experiments. The secondary beam is incident on a target surrounded by the experimental apparatus that includes scintillation counters that register the passage of a particle and wire chamber that register the points on the track. This allows the scattering event to be reconstructed. Some experiments use the "primary" protons instead of secondaries off a target. It is also possible to make storage rings where particles of one beam collide with particles in a counter-rotating beam. This has a great energy advantage at the cost of interaction rate.

How does all this work? When a high energy proton, or other particle, hits or interacts with a nucleus or another proton or fundamental particle, some of the energy is used to create new particles that only last for very short intervals of time. Typically, experiments in high-energy physics view the interactions of high-energy particles with targets or counter-rotating particle beams by tracking the particle debris coming out of the interaction region where the collisions of the fundamental particles occur. This process is fundamentally the same process that humans and other creatures with eyes use. Light scatters off of an object, and our eyes detect the scattered light or debris from the collision, which carries information about the object it scattered from. Our brains do a complicated analysis of the information contained in details of the scattered light transmitted to it from our eyes. Through this analysis, we learn some details about the object being examined. For example, the brain may tell us that the object scattering the light creates a familiar pattern that we associate with a known object such as a pencil. Or it could tell us about something we have never seen before such as a woolly beast with large teeth and an overdeveloped set of jaws. In this case, we should check that our detectors (eyes) are working properly. If they are, we must quickly decide to run like hell. Our judgments based on our eyes result from a complicated analysis performed by the brain comparing new visual data with data stored in the brain to conclude that large jaws and teeth mean trouble for tasty human morsels with large brains, crappy teeth, and tasty brain matter—i.e., a bite fight is not a suitable recourse in this situation. Fortunately, nothing so dramatic happens in particle physics experiments.

The sun, light bulbs, and flashlights provide the beams for the daily observations carried out in the normal course of our lives. Our eyes are the detectors while our brains provide the analysis. Similarly, tracks that result from scattering a particle beam from a simple target reveal information about the target and the beam. The tracks of the scattered particles are analyzed to obtain this information. The scattering experiments not only reveal details of the internal structures of the target and beam but can also be used to determine additional properties of any newly produced particles created out of the energy available in the collisions.

Examples of properties that can be ascertained include probabilities that beam particles will be scattered in certain directions, energy or momentum of scattered particles, masses and energies of particles produced, and lifetimes of the unstable particles coming out of the collisions. Also decay products of particles produced in a scattering event can be determined. Most particles are unstable and eventually end up as either photons, electrons, protons, or neutrons. Even a neutron decays when it is not embedded in a nucleus. I know these details are overwhelming and mysterious. Don't worry over them too much. There will not be a test on them for most of you. Just remember, learning to deal with the great mysteries can be extremely satisfying, boring, or…terrifying.

By carrying out high-energy particle physics experiments, we have explored deep inside the protons and neutrons that make up the nucleus and determined the nature of the fundamental constituents of these particles and their interactions. It turns out that the higher the energy, the smaller the details that can be investigated. The most powerful accelerator in the world when I entered graduate school was in the Soviet Union. Its energy was 70 GeV. A GeV is a billion electron volts. One electron volt is the energy that an electron gains by passing through an accelerating field of one volt. Fermilab would soon exceed the energy of the Soviet accelerator if all went as planned.

This was all very exciting to me. I was looking for the true nature of existence. I was naive. There is no such thing lurking at the business end of a powerful accelerator. Instead, there is an endless parade of new information that leads to even more fascinating questions.

The construction of the large synchrotron at the National Accelerator Laboratory (NAL) had just begun when I entered graduate school. Newspaper clippings relating the progress of the construction of what would be the largest and most powerful synchrotron in the world were posted on the bulletin boards on the third floor of the physics building. The giant machine that would be almost four miles in circumference and more than a mile across stirred my imagination.

A trip to NAL was organized by some of the high-energy physics faculty in order to recruit graduate students to work on high-energy physics, possibly at the new Laboratory or more likely at other existing Laboratories engaged in particle physics research. It did not make sense to wait for construction and commissioning of a new Laboratory and a new accelerator to get data for a PhD thesis.

The first stop on our trip was at Argonne National Laboratory, where we toured the Zero Gradient Synchrotron. I was impressed by the size of the Laboratory and the experiments, in addition to the tight security at the lab. One could not just drive into the site. One had to have identification and a purpose in life. Well, maybe it was good enough to want to visit the Laboratory as a purpose although there was some classified work going on at the Laboratory.

I was most impressed when we visited an experiment led by a University of Chicago professor named James Cronin. We could look down from a mezzanine and see the wire chambers light up with tracks as charged particles passed through them. At the time, this was one of the most profound experiences in science.

We also visited the twelve-foot bubble chamber at Argonne. It was pulsing impressively, shaking the ground as it expanded to create bubbles along the particle tracks after each pulse of beam entered the chamber. We could not see much from the control room. Nevertheless, we felt the rumble, and we knew that an unknown aspect of nature was being revealed with each earth-shaking expansion.

After we visited Argonne Laboratory, we drove some thirty or forty miles west to visit the construction site of National Accelerator Laboratory. The new Laboratory was being built on 6,800 acres. Most of it had been farmland, but it had also included the newly founded town of Weston, Illinois. Weston and the 6,800 acres had been given to the federal government by Illinois to ensure that the new accelerator would be built in Illinois. Okay, it was a bribe. Many states attempted to bribe the government in order have the new Laboratory located inside of their borders.

We entered the large site from the east after having lunch at a restaurant located less than a mile from the east entrance to the Laboratory site. As we entered, we had to show IDs and have a purpose for getting onto the site. It wasn't good enough to say we were recruiting talent for our blues band. (As it turned out, much of the *Blues Brothers* movie would be filmed much later near this entrance to the Laboratory.) Fortunately, our professors had the required credentials.

Immediately after arriving on site, we entered the NAL village, which had originally been the town of Weston, Illinois. When the government obtained the site in order to create a national laboratory, houses in the town were converted to Laboratory buildings containing offices and laboratories. The village houses were all painted bright-blue and orange. There was a large machine shop in a building constructed from large corrugated metal arcs. It looked much like Dad's shop at Pot Creek. Components for the large machine were being designed and fabricated in the village. Relatively small laboratories for building and testing accelerator and detector components were also located in the houses that had formally been part of Weston.

We received a simple orientation lecture in the village before we continued west across the 6,800-acre site to view the ongoing construction of the large accelerator. The construction of underground enclosures for the large machine and its beams that would be extracted from the accelerator were underway. We also toured the experimental areas where large experiments were being assembled. The central laboratory building was under construction at the time. It would eventually have fifteen stories, but it rose only a few stories on the day of our visit.

Robert Wilson was the first director of the laboratory. He had been a professor at Cornell and was charged with getting the new laboratory built. The Laboratory offices had originally been located in Oak Brook, Illinois, but had moved to the NAL site by the time of our visit.

My first impression was one of awe. My imagination went wild. I liked the open space, but being a child of the mountains, I felt uncomfortable with the extreme flatness of the Illinois prairie. Nevertheless, it was clear that something very special was being undertaken on this very flat expanse of Illinois farmland.

We visited the bubble-chamber area at the end of the beam lines. This facility was still under construction. We also visited the site where the excavation for the big accelerator was underway; some of the concrete tunnel sections were being installed. The large ring was almost four miles in circumference. It seemed impossible to me that I could one day be a part of this magnificent endeavor. I was and always would be the kid from Pot Creek after all. Nevertheless, I think the die for me was cast that day.

It was not long after our visit to Argonne and NAL before I was officially a student of Professor Art Garfinkel. There was no plan for me to get involved at NAL. That would have been risky for a graduate student because one could get stuck for years waiting for data, which could only come after the construction was completed. Nevertheless, I wanted into the field. I figured this would happen if I worked with Professor Garfinkel.

Like all the other experimental particle physicists at Purdue, Professor Garfinkel was involved in getting data from bubble chambers, such as the one at the ZGS at Argonne Laboratory. The data came in the form of photographs that were taken in stereo by multiple cameras when beam had passed through the chamber, and the pressure had been quickly reduced in the chamber through an expansion mechanism. Three cameras allowed the tracks to be reconstructed in three dimensions. The pressure reduction caused bubbles to form along the paths of the charged particles that had passed through the chamber, ionizing the hydrogen along the way. The 3D photos showed the ionization trails or tracks left by charged particles as they passed through the chamber. Collisions of the beam particles appeared along the tracks. In such events, one particle track would turn into many at the collision site, providing a complete 3D picture of the beam particle interacting in the chamber and producing a number of particles leaving the collision site. The photographs made it possible for scientists to study the details of the collision in detail to determine what had happened and eventually why it had happened that way. The beam entering the bubble chamber could be protons, electrons, or long-lived mesons or muons as beam particles. One could also send a beam of ghostly neutrinos into the bubble chamber to look at the resulting interactions. In this case, no beam particle would be evident in the chamber. Instead, an explosion of particles would appear with no evident cause in the chamber.

All of this was very exciting to me. I agreed to become Professor Garfinkel's student, but this would not be the end of the story.

The Purdue experimental particle physics group was aware that the usefulness of bubble chambers was waning as many of the measurements that could be made with them had been completed. The major problem with a bubble chamber is that there is a limit to the number of particles that can enter it during each cycle. A cycle was typically a few seconds long. This made the bubble chambers useless for studying rare processes. Consequently, there was a movement underway in the Purdue High Energy Physics Group to move toward doing electronic experiments or counter-experiments.

The scintillation counters and wire chambers could track the particles almost as well as a bubble chamber and could electronically record many more collisions in a short amount of time than a bubble chamber, allowing the use of higher-intensity beams in the experiments. The higher intensities result in higher interaction rates in the experiment. Interesting events could be sorted out, or triggered on, in these experiments. Different types of events could be selected by the electronic triggers, enabling a much greater data rate for studying rare events or processes.

The Purdue group was late in making the move toward counter-experiments even though they were aware they would have to make the transition. The transition had already occurred at many other big research institutions involved in particle physics research.

To facilitate the transition to electronic experiments, the Purdue high-energy group hired a young Harvard PhD who had been doing a post-doctoral stint at the University of Michigan. All of his research experience involved electronic experiments. His assignment in the Purdue High Energy Physics Group was to lead the transition to electronic or "counter" experiments. His name was Ken Stanfield.

I met Ken in the spring of my second year at Purdue. He and Art Garfinkel decided that it would be a good idea to send me to Brookhaven National Laboratory (BNL) on Long Island, where Purdue was becoming involved in a relatively large electronic experiment. I would work at Brookhaven for a while to get some experience on a high-energy experiment that was taking data. Ken was already involved Brookhaven and was eager to have me join him.

I was soon making trips in a Purdue car from West Lafayette, Indiana, to Brookhaven. I would stay for about a month before returning to West Lafayette. Meanwhile, Ken would fly out as often as he could. In addition to his research, he had teaching responsibilities at Purdue. My assignment seemed to be to spend as much time away from home as I could get away with. I quickly learned that this was typical in the life of a high-energy physicist. I was initially fine with it, but it did not take long for it to get tiresome. It helped that Ken and I bonded very quickly after our relationship began. Surprisingly, the bond did not break even after I discovered that he had been born and raised in Texas. I did have to ask myself whether a true-blue New Mexican could make things work with any kind of Texan. Fortunately, the answer turned out to be yes. I guess the experience with Dad and my brother helped.

It was not long before Ken began talking to me about proposing an experiment at Argonne National Laboratory. I was very enthusiastic and wanted to be a part of it. I quickly imagined that this effort could lead to my PhD research. Ken told me his idea for the Argonne experiment. I was eager to join him and to help write a proposal that would be submitted to Argonne Lab. However, I was not Ken's student at the time. I was Art's student. I talked to Ken about this potential issue, and we decided that it would be best for me to remain as Art's PhD student. Art would be asked to join the experiment also.

Since Ken did not have tenure, he had to be careful. Stealing another professor's grad student would not have been a great idea at that stage in his career. Nevertheless, I became Ken's student for all practical purposes.

During this time, I discovered that the lifestyle of a high-energy physicist was not particularly conducive to a good marriage. I was not eager to be away from Gail for long periods of time. By then, she had a full-time job in the Purdue Library. Her paycheck was making our life much more pleasant than it had been during the first year of graduate school. She had managed to easily transfer her credits to Purdue, and she finished up her last year of college without difficulty. She had a degree from Purdue about a year before I would get my master's degree. Furthermore, it did not take long for her to find a good-paying, full-time job in the Purdue Library. Our standard of living suddenly increased substantially. I contributed a small part of this increase when I became a research assistant in the Physics Department. This position paid considerably more than my fellowship had paid. Like other graduate students, I was paid to work on my research project.

Everything seemed to be falling into place. As a result of our new wealth, we were able to move into an upscale married-student apartment. Like the first apartment, it had only one bedroom, but it was in a beautiful location on campus with a great view across to the band shell and the athletic fields. It was also much more comfortable inside. We also bought a brand new Plymouth Duster that would get us to New Mexico for visits much more reliably than the MG or Volkswagen had.

CHAPTER 43

PhD Research

Another way to probe the details of fundamental particles is to scatter a beam of particles off of a simple target such as hydrogen. The quantum wavelengths of particles with mass can be made very short by accelerating the particles to very high energies. In principle, we can make the wavelength as short as we want. It only takes money to build larger particle accelerators or super flashlights. Shorter is more expensive than longer. However, this only applies to wavelengths.

*****

Ken succeeded in getting the Purdue High Energy Group involved in electronic experiments by collaborating on the experiment at Brookhaven National Lab and by proposing an experiment at Argonne National Laboratory. The Argonne experiment would become my PhD research experiment. My official PhD thesis adviser continued to be Art Garfinkel even though I was really working for Ken. This would eventually cause some problems for Ken in the department, but it was never a problem for me.

Meanwhile, Ken and I continued at Brookhaven for a while. I would drive a Purdue car to Long Island and back while Ken usually flew back and forth. I think we made one trip to BNL together in a

Purdue car. The rest of the time, I would pick him up at an airport out on Long Island.

During this time, Ken and I became close friends. It was an interesting experience for me because Ken looked younger than I did even though he was quite a bit older. We would go into a bar, and he would get carded while I wouldn't. I wanted to exclaim, "Wait a minute! He's my professor!"

While we were spending time at Brookhaven together, he began talking to me about the ideas he had for an experiment that he would propose. I made it clear to him that he could count on me to be all in for what he was thinking. We got along well, and I could see working with him to get a PhD. He wanted to do something relatively simple and quick that would serve both of our purposes. I was sold. It was not long before we were working on a proposal to submit to Argonne National Laboratory to do backward elastic scattering of pions from protons in a liquid hydrogen target. Professor Garfinkel was good with the plan, and the entire High Energy Group supported the idea. They saw it as a way for them to get involved in an electronic experiment, which they knew was the wave of the future.

With all the travel, I soon discovered that being a high-energy particle physicist was hard on a marriage. Furthermore, it was hard for me to endure living in a small dorm room. It was not any easier for Gail. Maybe it was more difficult. I was constantly with the other graduate students and professors in the experiment working and eating out with them whereas Gail spent much time alone.

Ken's proposal for a small experiment to be done at the Zero Gradient Synchrotron (ZGS) located at Argonne National Laboratory near Chicago was approved. Art remained involved in principle, but he was not doing much for the experiment. It was not long before Ken succeeded in getting Purdue to hire a young MIT PhD into the group. His name was Ed Shibata. He was originally from New Mexico, giving the two of us something in common. Our relationship took off very quickly in a positive direction. It was not long before I was working for Ken and Ed, mostly at Purdue to build chambers and counters for the experiment at Argonne Lab.

All agreed that it would be my PhD thesis experiment. I was really enjoying the work.

Ken continued to make additions to the group. Besides Ed, two other graduate students, Sam Mudrak and Mike Fletcher, both a year behind me at Purdue, signed on with Ken and Ed. All of us were soon working together at Purdue, building wire chambers and counters we would need for the Argonne experiment.

It was not long before Ken's proposal was approved, and a postdoc, who had just received his PhD from Northeastern University, was hired to work with us. His name was Yau Wu Tang. In addition, Ken knew we needed a collaborator at Argonne to help give us a little more insight and pull with the Laboratory. Earl Hoffman, a staff scientist at Argonne, enthusiastically filled this role. He was an excellent addition to our group because he knew where all the Laboratory's valuables were hidden. Well, most important was that he knew the Laboratory inside and out.

We began constructing wire spark chambers at Purdue to track particles through a spectrometer that would view events originating in a hydrogen target. The incident beam would contain pions and kaons. We would look for hard scatters that would send particles into the backward direction. Scintillation counters would be used to tell when an interesting event might have occurred. When this happened, the trigger electronics would pulse the tracking chambers to record the tracks in the event.

We also had to make scintillation counters that would tell us when there were particles in the apparatus that scattered into backward direction so that we could trigger the tracking chambers for these events. When a signal from the scintillation counters indicate that something interesting might have happened, the trigger electronics would fire the spark chambers in order to record the tracks in them. All went well, and we were soon spending a lot of time at Argonne Laboratory putting the experiment together.

We were rather poor since we were a new group. We did not have everything we needed, but we were lucky that right next to the ZGS beam where we were installing our experiment, there was a junk heap that had once been a propane bubble chamber. It would not be used again. We found many items that we could use in the junk pile.

We also needed a Cerenkov detector to identify forward going particles so that we would know when a backward scattering event had occurred. This is the type of event that the experiment would look for and study. We would fire, or pulse, the spark chambers to record the tracks when we detected the proper particle going forward through the Cerenkov counter.

A Cerenkov counter was leftover from a University of Michigan experiment. It needed to be reconditioned. This became my job. I had to make a new curved mirror for it that would collect the Cerenkov light. I also had to put new photomultiplier tubes that would detect the Cerenkov light, which would be reflected from the mirror into the photomultiplier tubes.

A Cerenkov counter works by a mechanism similar to that for detecting a supersonic jet passing overhead. The jet creates a sonic boom in the air as it travels faster than sound. A Cerenkov detector works in a similar fashion, except that the boom is not made in sound. It is made in light. When a particle travels faster than the speed of light in the gas, a burst of light is created. It is important to note that the absolute speed-of-light speed limit is not violated in a Cerenkov counter since the speed of light in the gas is less than the speed of light in a vacuum. It turns out that one can tell the mass of the particle, creating the light cone by looking at the cone angle of the burst of light created in the gas. Since the fundamental particles have unique masses, the Cerenkov light provides information for determining the type of particle that created the light cone.

This all came together in rather short order. While the graduate students were putting together the detectors we would need, Ya Wu was writing the code for the data-acquisition computer, which completely filled a trailer-sized port-a-camp. This computer was not nearly so powerful as the iPhone I carry in my pocket now. Well, we did buy one of the original iPhones for the experiment. It was expensive and very easy to carry off. We chained and locked it to the desk in front of the data-acquisition computer. We all shared it for quick calculations.

Another port-a-camp contained the electronics that would make decisions concerning which events were interesting to trigger on and which weren't. The interesting events were written on large 9-track tapes by the data-acquisition computer.

It was my responsibility to set up all the electronics that would make the quick decisions during beam pulses to trigger on interesting events that would be written to tape. I accomplished this task by putting rather standard electronics modules into racks and connecting them in a fashion so that input signals would create the triggers we wanted. Interesting events would register in our detectors, causing a trigger in the electronics that would result in the details of the event to be written to tape. If this sounds complicated, it wasn't. We used standard modules off the shelf, cabled together in a certain manner in order to make the trigger decisions. We just had to cable them up properly.

My main problem in getting the experiment set up was to stay out of the electricity. It seemed that every piece of electronic equipment in the experiment was just waiting for me to get to close to it so that it could strike out at me. I was bitten often. I did not have the proper fear for electricity. My grandfather would not have been happy with me. Everyone in the counting room would notice when I got zapped because I would jump and shout something totally inappropriate that I had learned from hillbilly loggers. My run-ins with electricity happened frequently enough to convince me that I could not be seriously hurt by electricity. I was wrong and very lucky.

We succeeded in getting the experiment set up, and then we commissioned our apparatus rather quickly. Well, if I remembered more details, I might make a different conclusion about the ease of getting it all up and running. I know that I spent months at Argonne during the commissioning and running of the experiment. The particle-physics life continued to be difficult on my marriage. I would be gone from Lafayette for weeks at a time. Sometimes, Gail and Mike Fletcher's wife, Sharon, would drive to Argonne together to spend the weekend with us. Meanwhile, Gail continued working at the Purdue Library.

Finally, after more than a year of running off and on, the data taking was complete, and it was time for me to go back to Purdue to analyze the data and write up the results for papers to be published. Eventually, I would do a complete write-up for the experiment and data that would be my PhD thesis. I succeeded with this endeavor rather quickly, especially when compared to the time it seems to take these days. However, during the time that I was analyzing data, I had a couple of adventures that slowed me a bit.

Gail got pregnant. This was not planned, but it was good news to both of us—at first. It would soon turn into a nightmare. For birth control, Gail had been using a Dalkon Shield. It was not good to get pregnant with a Dalkon Shield, but this was not well-known at the time. She went into labor about six months into the pregnancy. The delivery was extremely difficult. It came close to killing her. The baby was stillborn. We were both shattered, but Gail took it particularly hard. I paused in my thesis writing. As soon Gail was able, we went to Kentucky for few days to try and recover. It helped, but we were both still struggling long after we returned to Lafayette. Without talking about it, I think we both knew that there was only one way to get over our loss. I knew the solution was against doctor's orders for Gail. We didn't talk about it. Nevertheless, I cooperated with her, and I think we both knew precisely when the magic event happened. It occurred on a weekend afternoon. We both felt the magic. Afterward, we went to the physics building so that I could put a deck of punch cards into the computer to run some analyses. As we rode the elevator to the third floor of the physics building, we looked at each other. No words were exchanged. I could see the magic in Gail's eyes. Something very special had occurred.

Gail soon received confirmation of her pregnancy. It would not be an easy pregnancy, especially toward the end. To prevent her from delivering early, her doctor had her quit working and had her spend her days lying down while having a drink or two of scotch per day. This sounds crazy these days. Nevertheless, Gail went full-term and then some.

Near the end, her doctor kept telling her that the event would occur any day now but the days would come and go. Finally, we were both at home in the middle of the day when the doctor called and told her to come in. They were going to induce labor. What a disappointment to me! I had been diligently practicing my race course to get across the river to Lafayette where the hospital was located. Well, maybe the practice was only in my mind. After all that, here we were leisurely driving to the hospital and stopping to mail a letter along the way.

Gail was induced. I was with her the entire time, I think. I was certainly present when the most beautiful little gift to the world I could imagine appeared. The nurse handed her right to me and told me to put her on a table that was along one wall of the delivery room. She would be cleaned up and dressed on the table. The beautiful little girl had not dressed for the occasion.

As I carried her across the room to the table, I looked into her big brown eyes. She was not crying at all. She looked into my eyes as if studying me intently. A very special light was shining from behind those beautiful eyes. It was the most profound moment in my life. We were fully bonded by the time I laid her down on the table. To this day, holding Kelly for the first time remains the most profound experience of my life. Our bond has never weakened.

After the big moment passed, Gail made a good recovery. We were both ecstatic to have such a beautiful little girl join the adventure of life with us. We both have many special memories of those early days with Kelly.

Mother came to visit shortly after Kelly's birth. I picked her up at the Purdue airport and brought her to our apartment. Kelly was lying on the sofa when Mom arrived. Mom looked down at her new granddaughter and said, "They are such beautiful little things, but they grow up to be big, ugly people." This made me laugh, and I never forgot it. Kelly did not live up to her prophecy. She is neither "big" nor ugly.

*****

The work on my data analysis continued through this period, and it went smoothly. I used an IBM 360 at Purdue to read data tapes made at Argonne and analyze their content. This took lots of punch cards that my analysis programs lived on, and it took lots of time mounting data tapes and looking at results of the analysis. However, another bump in the road awaited me before I could finish my analysis.

I became aware of the problem when I went to a conference in Washington, DC, to present some of the results of our experiment. The presentation went well, but when I was in my hotel room, I looked in my mouth for no particular reason and saw a swelling in the back of my throat. There was no pain associated with it. It just looked like a big lump off to one side. It concerned me.

When I got back to Purdue, I went to the University Medical Offices and got an appointment to see a gruff, old, former Army doctor. He looked in my mouth and said, "I have to lance your throat." This didn't sound pleasant, and it wasn't. He got out an intimidating-looking weapon that he seemed to think was the best tool for the job. I was sitting in a normal chair against the wall. He swabbed my throat with something, most likely to reduce the pain, and then he had me tip my head back against the wall and open my mouth. Next, he told me to hold still as he held his weapon high above my head and told me, "This is going to hurt a little." He quickly stabbed downward into my mouth as if he were attempting to kill me. I thought he was. The pain was excruciating! He was not satisfied. He said, "I am going to have to stab you again. Try to keep your feet on the floor this time." He raised his arm above his head, reminding me of a horror movie, and stabbed downward very quickly and hard. The pain was so excruciating that I swear I saw my footprints on the ceiling. He looked again and said, "I think I might have to stab it again, but we are through for today. Gargle with salt water and come back in a week."

When I got back to the apartment, I noticed that he had made a large wound in the swelling, which was still present even if it did look a little worse for the wear. I went back to see the doctor in a week as I had been instructed to do. He took a look in my mouth and said, "I am going to have to lance it again. It is still there." I said, "Wait a minute. I think I would like to see a specialist." He looked at me like I was some kind of a sissy but then agreed to recommend someone.

The someone was Dr. Trout, who had an office across the river in Lafayette. I made an appointment right away. I did not have to wait long after I arrived at his office. Dr. Trout saw me right away. He took one brief look in my mouth and said, "You have to have your tonsils out." I agreed to this, and he scheduled me to come back into his office in only a few days to have the procedure done. I believe he did the procedure with only a local anesthetic. As I remember it, I did not have to spend any time in the hospital.

After the tonsil removal was done, he called me back in to tell me that he had looked in my mouth and immediately concluded that I had cancer. The tonsil removal was a ruse to get a biopsy. Without taking a breath, he told me, "You don't have cancer, but you have a tumor. It is benign. Nevertheless, it needs to come out."

He scheduled me for surgery, and the tumor was removed. This was almost a happy ending, but it didn't quite make the cut. After the tumor was removed, I had a large cavity in my throat that caused me to talk like I had a dirty athletic sock stuck in the back of my mouth. I thought I sounded like an idiot. This lasted long enough to make me think that I would never get my normal voice back. During this time, Gail did a lot of talking for me. I don't remember how long it was before I quit sounding like I had a severe speech impediment.

CHAPTER 44

Writing a PhD Thesis

Particle accelerators can be used to accelerate charged particles to very high energies, giving them very short wavelengths. The high-energy particle beams can penetrate inside the nucleus and even farther into the very heart of protons and neutrons, revealing details of the internal structure of these seemingly important components of existence. And these giant machines don't even make much noise. Well, that is a little disappointing.

*****

Finally, I was ready to begin writing my PhD thesis. This went slowly at first even though I liked writing. Nevertheless, I already knew that writing a scientific document was not something that came naturally to me. Nevertheless, I was eager to get it done. Once I got some momentum built up, it went smoothly. I don't remember whether there were many changes that were required by Ken or Art, who both read the thesis and had to agree to it. To complicate matters, they were no longer getting along with each other. The source of the problem was that Ken refused to put the names of the bubble-chamber people on the papers from the Argonne experiment because they had not contributed to making the experiment happen nor had they worked shifts during the data taking.

Art, for example, had come to Argonne on some weekends and sat in the experiment control-room trailer while he graded papers. Ken did not think this justified authorship on our papers. Consequently, Ken lost favor in the High Energy Group. During this time, I recall being in High Energy Group meetings where they called Ken out and talked about things with him that I didn't think I should be hearing. It was fairly clear that he was in serious trouble with the Purdue faculty. It was not a good place to be when trying to get tenure. Nevertheless, he stuck to his principles.

The High Energy Group did not hold their feelings about Ken against any of the students on our experiment. We all got our PhDs without any problems associated with the departmental politics and disagreements.

I don't remember much about my final oral exam. This occasion is where the PhD student gets up in front of a committee chaired by the student's thesis adviser and defends his or her PhD thesis. Members of the committee are allowed to ask any physics questions they want. I don't remember this event very well, which surprises me. I may have given a small introduction concerning the research I had done. I do remember there were questions, but I don't remember being grilled. I must have answered the questions satisfactorily. I passed the test. I was a PhD.

By this time, I had already accepted an offer from Cornell University for a postdoctoral position or postdoc. This is a typical position for a new PhD. It is temporary, and it is supposed to be an opportunity to prove one's worth as a PhD. Imagine that! The kid from Pot Creek heading off to Cornell, PhD in hand.

CHAPTER 45

Cornell

What lies at the heart of matter? Quarks and gluons have been inferred by scattering beams of high-energy protons, electrons, muons, mesons, or neutrinos produced by high-energy particle accelerators.

*****

As I was finishing my PhD thesis at Purdue, I had begun looking for a postdoctoral position at another university. I had good connections to some excellent places such as Harvard where Ken had received his PhD, Michigan, Michigan State, and quite a few other places. I interviewed at Harvard, Cornell, MIT, Michigan State, and Northeastern University. I received offers from Michigan State, Northeastern, Michigan, and Temple (even though I had not applied), and Cornell. The Cornell interview and offer was a result of my interview at Harvard with Frank Pipkin who had been Ken's PhD adviser. He told me that he wanted to make me an offer, but he did not have the funds to do it; so he would get Cornell to make an offer to work on an experiment that he was involved with at the Cornell Electron Synchrotron.

When I interviewed at Cornell, I really liked the people and the place. Ithaca, New York, is beautiful; and Boyce McDaniel (Mac), the director of the Laboratory of Nuclear Studies, did not waste any time letting me know that they would make me an offer. He attempted to sell me on Cornell, telling me that I could not go wrong by coming to Cornell for a postdoctoral stint because Cornell took care of postdocs and helped them get their next job. Also on the plus side for me was the fact that Mac and I had New Mexico in common. He knew my land and my people because he had worked on the Manhattan Project as a graduate student. He told me that he was responsible for monitoring the neutron flux in the first bomb before the test. He said he was the last person on the tower before the bomb was detonated at Trinity site in the New Mexico desert.

I enjoyed the Cornell interview very much. The decision was simple. I would go to Cornell for my postdoc, a place that was farther from Pot Creek than any other place I had lived.

Soon, Gail and I were making plans to move to Ithaca, New York. It was the fall of 1975. I had to finish up my PhD thesis first, and this took more work than I had imagined. I also had to pass my final orals. This was not so difficult. It all happened on cue, and I was on my way to Ithaca in late October 1975. Kelly was only a few months old at the time.

Cornell agreed to pay for our move. A major moving company was selected to transport our rather small load of belongings to Ithaca. The moving van appeared right on time. Our modest load of belongings was carefully packed into a truck that contained belongings from other people making moves. The driver was very diligent, getting things packed properly and put in good order in the truck. He told us that our items would stay on his truck all the way from West Lafayette to Ithaca, indicating there was nothing to be concerned about.

Since Cornell paid for our move, we did not have a place to live until after we arrived in Ithaca. We quickly found an apartment in an apartment complex. The complex was at the northern edge of the small town. We had only been in the apartment a couple of days when our belongings arrived.

As it happened, the arrival of our modest load of furniture and other items was one of the more amusing adventures that we had in

Ithaca, but only when viewed from a very distant future. It was not so amusing as it happened. The moving van arrived very late on a Saturday afternoon. In fact, darkness was already settling in over the Finger Lakes region of New York. The truck that arrived was not the same truck as the one our belongings had departed in from West Lafayette. Furthermore, the driver and his helper gave every indication of having visited a very good tavern before they arrived at our apartment.

Many of our items, such as Kelly's crib, had been disassembled somewhere in route, and screws and other parts necessary to put the items back together were missing. If this weren't enough, our belongings were mixed in with at least one other family's items.

When the crew was nearly finished separating out our belongings and bringing them into the apartment, there were still some items strewn about in the complex parking lot, and many of our items were still missing. I remember one of the men asked me if a green stuffed chair that they had unloaded was ours. I told him that it wasn't, and then he asked, "Do you want it?" I told him that I did not want the chair.

Our move had turned into a nightmare. Nevertheless, we were able to get Kelly's crib back together ourselves. Many items were just flat missing. Gail filed a complaint with the moving company, and we got a large settlement. Nevertheless, this was not a happy way to begin our stay in Ithaca.

After we had been in Ithaca for a while, Gail got a part-time job working on a book of the *Letters of Lafayette*. Since she was so proficient at languages, the job was perfect for her. She worked on translating the original letters of Lafayette into English for a book that was being prepared. This was intellectually satisfying work for her, but it did not pay much. The book later won a Pulitzer Prize.

Meanwhile, I was assigned to Professor Al Silverman. He was an older professor who seemed very glad to have me join the electro-production experiment that was running at the Cornell electron synchrotron. The synchrotron was part of the Laboratory of Nuclear Studies. The experiment was done in collaboration with Harvard University. The first thing Al did after I arrived was to sign the two of us up for all the owl shifts for as into the future as the shift schedule went. These shifts ran from midnight to eight o'clock in the morning.

Besides running shifts, my duties included learning how the trigger and readout electronics worked so that I could maintain the system after the current postdoc, Dave Larsen, who was in charge of this system, left Cornell. Dave would soon move on. I was not completely happy with either assignment. My expertise was not electronics, and working all the owl shifts seemed excessive.

Dave showed me the electronics drawings that were stuffed in a disordered pile behind the electronic racks in the experiment's control room. This was not a good start. Nevertheless, Dave had some time left at Cornell. I concluded that he would get me up to speed before he left. To this end, he managed to overlap a little with me during the evenings. I would come in for my owl shift about four hours early, and Dave would be there to help me with electronics. Well, about all the help I got was to be shown where the disheveled pile of drawings was stuffed behind the electronics racks.

Meanwhile, my boss, Al Silverman, always arrived for our owl shift at approximately eight o'clock in the evening while the evening crew was still operating the experiment. Our shift did not officially begin until midnight, but I figured coming in early was a good way for me to learn the details of running the experiment before I had responsibility.

The first night, Al left well before our shift began at midnight. He did not say why. He simply left. I thought this was a little unusual to leave the shift in the hands of a person who was just becoming familiar with all the details of running experiment, but I imagined that he wasn't feeling well even though he had said nothing.

The Harvard guys were running the evening shift, and one of them, Siegbert Raither, stayed with me. We talked, and I began learning how to run the experiment. Siegbert did not stay through my entire shift. The experiment was left in the hands of a person who knew very little about running it.

The next night, the same thing happened. Al came in early and left early. This behavior quickly became routine. He never stayed for a single one of the owl shifts that he had signed the two of us up for.

In fact, he never stayed past about 10:00 p.m. Our shift was not supposed to begin until midnight.

The Harvard guys helped out on what became my shift, but they tended to leave toward the middle of the shift. This was fine with me. They could not be expected to work a double shift every evening. The one exception to this was Professor Frank Pipkin, who had been Ken Stanfield's thesis adviser at Harvard. He seemed to require very little sleep. When he was in town, he would come to the experiment control room during the evening shift and stay all the way through my owl shift with me. I was certainly very thankful for the Harvard group during this time. Frank was not in Ithaca that often since he had duties at Harvard.

Meanwhile, I was working twelve to fifteen hours a day to try to get caught up so that I could do something useful on the experiment. Being useful was on the experiment was something I would never achieve. I never became a useful member of the collaboration.

To make matters worse, it was not long before I came down with pneumonia. I went to a doctor, and he prescribed some drugs and bed rest. I tried to get a little rest, but I was falling further and further behind at the lab. I went to work with my pneumonia.

One day when the machine was not running and I was in our control room, a group of people came through. A man and a woman were being escorted on a tour, and I could tell that they were important people. I was not introduced to them, but this would not matter. The woman would become very important to me a little later in life.

Meanwhile, I never got up to speed on the electronics. I tried to do some analysis, but I was on my own with this. I suppose I stayed in this state for more than six months before I was rescued by Maury Tigner, who was in charge of operations for the Cornell synchrotron. He must have seen that I was having a disastrous postdoctoral experience, or maybe he was told. I know the Harvard guys all knew what I was happening to me. Maury asked me if I wanted to work with him and a PhD electrical engineer named Dave Morse to develop a fast-kicker magnet for a new electron-positron storage ring, CESR, that was being planned. The kicker magnets would be used to stack the positrons between the electron bunches stored in the ring. I eagerly accepted his invitation even though I intended to continue working on the analysis of data from the experiment I had been hired to work on. The analysis was never done.

I ended up working mostly with Dave. He was a superb PhD electrical engineer, and the kickers were a real challenge because they had to be powerful and work in the short interval between beam bunches. Dave and I spent most of our time working in the basement of Newman Laboratory, which housed the Physics Department, or at least a good part of it. The kickers we were working on ran in the one-hundred-thousand volt range, and they had to get up to voltage in less than one hundred billionths of a second. Dave and Maury had a good notion of how to solve this difficult technical problem. Their concept had to be turned into hardware and tested.

Dave and I spent a lot of time working in a large oil bath where we tested the prototype kickers we put together. We pulsed the prototypes that we built with more than one hundred thousand volts. This work was a little dangerous. Other people, such as the Radio Frequency (RF) group, worked in the basement also, and they had to pass near our test area to get to their work area. The kicker test area contained a large "horse trough" partially filled with oil where prototype kickers magnets were submerged in order to test them. We had a high-voltage power supply and strip lines that were used to power the prototype kickers. The entire area was cordoned off with ropes and signs. Dave and I ducked under the ropes to get in and out of the area.

We tested various designs of the kicker and were making good progress on getting a kicker that would work. I was mostly learning. Dave was brilliant and very innovative. I certainly learned a lot of high-voltage engineering from Dave. Maury was also very good at all things that had to do with accelerators. I learned much from him.

I was still working on the kickers for CESR, approaching my second anniversary at Cornell when Maury came to me and told me that he could get me a job at any of the national labs in the US. I understood that he was inviting me to leave my situation at Cornell to do something that would be better in the long-term for my career.

I suspect there was some guilt on the part of the Physics Department management that I had been given a such a raw deal.

Cornell was a like a big family that took care of its own. Gail and I were often invited to socialize at the house of Boyce McDaniel, Mac, who had recruited me and was the head of the Laboratory of Nuclear Studies. Mac seemed to be very concerned about me. After all, he was the one who had talked me into coming to Cornell. Don Hartill was another professor at Cornell. I did not work with him, but he and his wife, Marianne, invited us to dinner at their beautiful home in the woods any number of times. Clearly, Don was very concerned about me. He would have a big impact on my career much later in my life.

I told Maury that I would be interested in a position at the National Accelerator Laboratory. I might have told him that Los Alamos National Laboratory would also be interesting to me. The latter was close to my roots, but I don't think I really wanted to end up there. I updated my resume, and on my own, I applied for an assistant professor position at Notre Dame University, which might seem like a very strange thing for a guy with Purdue credentials to do. I ended up interviewing at Fermilab and Notre Dame. I gave a colloquium at Notre Dame, but I don't remember much else about the interview. However, I do remember dinner with some professors and priests. I was asked if I had a problem working for a Catholic university. I surely said that I didn't, but I don't remember this. Maybe I wasn't convincing. I did not get an offer.

When I interviewed at Fermilab, the person who was looking to hire someone was Helen Edwards, who had gone all the way from freshman to PhD at Cornell. She was the VIP who had passed through our counting room at Cornell on the tour. The two days of my interview at Fermilab were rigorous. I started off with Helen and talked to people in her group in the Accelerator Division. She and I seemed to hit it off even though she was all business and not very talkative. In addition to Helen, I talked to many people in both the Accelerator Division and the Research Division. I don't remember whether I talked to anyone in the Director's Office.

The interview was exhausting. In spite of my fatigue, it became very clear to me during the interviews that Fermilab was where I wanted to be. Jeff Appel, who worked for Helen at the time, took charge of me during the interview and made certain I got around to all the interviewers in addition to getting all my questions answered. There was only one interview that crossed over into negative territory. The person attempted to discourage me from thinking I wanted to work at the Laboratory. He described the place as pure chaos.

I returned to Cornell exhausted. After a few days, Maury Tigner came to see me in my office at the synchrotron lab. He told me that he had just talked to Helen Edwards. Since they had been graduate students together at Cornell, he knew her well. He confessed to me that he had told Helen that he didn't think I was up to the job that she wanted me to do. I did not have enough experience. Apparently, she was looking for someone who would take over her role in the Accelerator Division so that she would be free to work on a big new superconducting machine that was being planned at Fermilab. Helen led the group that was responsible for extracting the beam from the large accelerator and dividing it up between the beam lines to the various experimental areas. It was a position at the pressure point in the Laboratory. Maury had told her that I was not ready for that yet.

I was very disappointed. I really wanted a job at Fermilab. I don't remember if I gave up all hope or how I felt at the time. I may have been waiting to hear from Los Alamos.

I kept working on kickers for three or four days, and then I got an unbelievable lift. I received an offer in the mail from Fermilab. The assignment would be to work for Helen. I don't know if Maury was surprised, but I would learn very quickly that Helen had a mind of her own; and she knew what she wanted, and it was the kid from Pot Creek. This was the best thing that happened to me in my entire career.

It was not long before Gail and I were arranging to move back to the Midwest. Kelly was two years old. Once again, it was necessary for us to have our limited belongings moved—this time, to the far western suburbs of Chicago. Unlike the move to Ithaca, this move went smoothly even though it was necessary to put our belongings in storage while we looked for a house to buy near Fermilab. During our search, we stayed in a motel. It all worked out reasonably well. We bought a tricycle for Kelly that she could use at the motel. She was so excited that one would have thought we bought her a new red sports car. Okay, maybe that would have excited me, but Kelly would not have been impressed even if we had let her begin studying for her driver's license test at two years old.

It did not take us long to find a small, inexpensive house in Aurora. It needed work. We felt we were up to it. The new house was almost conveniently located at roughly eight miles from the Laboratory. We immediately began working to make improvements. This would pay off when we made our next move to Batavia in a few years.

At the Laboratory, Helen wasted no time in getting me up to speed. Jeff Appel was my first mentor, but he would only be in the Helen's group for a short time after I arrived. It didn't matter. Helen made certain I got oriented properly for the job that she was grooming me for. She wanted me to come up to speed quickly. I began working with the Switchyard operations specialist in the Main Control Room, learning how to tune extraction and the primary beam lines. At first, this was Bob Weber, a former accelerator operator with considerable experience at tuning extraction and the external beams. Bob Weber was soon replaced by Bob Mau, who had recently been promoted from operations crew chief to Switchyard specialist. Bob Mau and I got on very well, and I learned much from him.

However, this was not the entire job. Another part of my training was to learn how maintenance and improvements were done in the extraction and switchyard systems. To accomplish this, Helen took me into the accelerator tunnels on a maintenance day soon after my arrival. She found the switchyard vacuum crew working on an improvement. She interrupted their work and introduced me to the technicians on the crew. They were installing a new radiation shield in front of some Lambertson magnets in one of the beam-splitting stations. The primary proton beam had to be divided into three beams so that it could be sent to the three main experimental areas simultaneously. Once I was introduced, she told the crew leader that

I was working for him. He was to teach me the fundamentals of his job. Over a rather short period of time during my first weeks at the Laboratory, Helen did this with each subgroup that worked for her. It felt good to me. I liked working shoulder to shoulder with the people who had their hands on the hardware that made up the beam lines. They all had a great deal of respect for Helen and were determined to do a good job of getting me up to speed. Well, to be honest, some of them were terrified of her. One had to be outstanding at his or her job to gain favor with Helen.

The electronics group was a little more complicated for me. Helen had an extremely bright electrical engineer, Jack McCarthy, heading the group. His sidekick was a character named Robert Oberholtzer, or Obie, who was in charge of a small group of electronics technicians. Like most members of the switchyard group, Obie was extremely clever and competent while being little unconventional. Well, most of the people Helen's group did not color inside the lines.

Meanwhile, Jack was one of the brightest people I have ever known. He could do everything from tuning the beam to designing a new device to help control the spill quality of the beam. If one had a really difficult problem that involved an accelerator or beam, he was the go-to guy.

Jack and Obie were skeptical of me. Nevertheless, I felt like I was fitting into the team very well. I was certainly very enthusiastic and working crazy long hours that frequently had me at the lab for twenty-four hours or more without going home. The beam had to keep running, and I had to learn the details of the extraction and switchyard systems.

It was not long before I had more responsibility. Helen seemed to trust me. I knew she could become very volatile, but I learned there were certain people that she would never blow up at. Jack was one of them. Another was Mike Harrison, who was another physicist she hired a couple of months after I was hired. I felt very fortunate to be the third member of this untouchable group. We were "Helen's Boys," according to the word on the street. This meant we were not to be messed with.

One member of the survey crew that I worked with often to reconfigure beam lines was determined get me in trouble with Helen. One day, he finally thought he had me when a section of beam I designed did not match up with the downstream-section beam as it headed out of my territory into the experimental areas. The problem was discovered when I had the survey crew position a device at the elevation that I had calculated for it. When we put it in place, it was one inch off from matching up with the downstream magnet and beam line. He said, "What's Helen gonna think about this, Mr. Junior Scientist?" I laughed and told him I would find out.

I went straight to Helen and told her about the problem. She asked me to meet her late that evening in the service building above the section of the beam line in question. We would take a look at the problem together. It was about 11:00 p.m. when she was finally free for our investigation. She grabbed a large wrench out of a toolbox in the service building that was located above the problem area, and we went down into the meson beam line to the location of the beam mismatch. She looked at the misfit magnet while I explained how I had calculated the elevation. We had the survey equipment that the crew had been instructed to leave in place for us. We shot the entire beam line together and could not find the source of the mismatch.

Helen went back to her office and worked through the night. Meanwhile, she sent me home to get some rest. The next morning, she told me that she had traced the problem all the way back to the Booster Synchrotron nearly a mile away from the problem area. Apparently, the entire Booster was one inch off with respect to the meson beam line. This seemed to amuse her. She had known there was a problem for some time. The one-inch discrepancy I had found revealed the source of the problem. She told me to fix the beam so it would work. We weren't going to move the Booster.

I quickly developed a solution. It was simple. I changed the operating current of a few magnets, and I moved the target hall magnets to match up with the downstream magnets. The alignment crew chief was only mildly disappointed that Helen's solution didn't involve any loud shouting at me. He liked to play his games, and he figured he would get me eventually.

All went well during my first few months at the Laboratory. I was called in often after hours. It felt good to be needed at all hours of the day and night. All was going very well. I was in my element.

I finally experienced the full wrath of Helen one morning. She and I had been working together all night, attempting to get the beam extraction losses under control. Okay, she was doing most of the tuning. I was learning from her, which was a little difficult because she did not spend much time explaining what she was doing. We were still in the Main Control Room (MCR) early in the morning. I told her that I had to close on a house, so I would have to leave. She was fine with this as she continued to work on the extraction problem.

I took care of the house business as quickly as I could before heading back to the lab even though I had been there the entire night before. I knew Helen would still be working on the extraction problem, and I planned to rejoin her.

When I arrived at the east entrance to the Main Control Room (MCR) and looked through the window, I could see Helen leaning against the Duty Assistant's desk, which was located in an anteroom just outside of the MCR proper. There were glass doors that led into the MCR from the anteroom. This allowed people to see what was going on in the control room without disturbing the operators. I opened the door and headed across the anteroom toward Helen, wondering what was happening. As I made my way to Helen's position, I saw that a television camera was set up inside of the MCR, and the glass doors were open with bright lights illuminating the entire control room. I saw and heard a man just inside the MCR in front of the television camera talking into a microphone. He was saying something like "We are in the Main Control Room of the University of Chicago's National Accelerator Laboratory..." I continued toward the Duty Assistant's desk and Helen, wondering why the television crew thought we belonged to the University of Chicago.

When I arrived at the Duty Assistant's desk, I parked my tush right next to Helen's on the front edge of the desk. And then I leaned over and whispered in her ear. "Helen, what's going on?" I may as well have lit a stick of dynamite and tossed it on the floor. Helen went into a rage, beginning with the words, "This goddamned bullshit…" Margaret Pearson, the public affairs person at the lab, attempted to calm her down, but Helen would have none of it. The more Margaret said to try and assuage Helen, the more Helen would scream and rave. Finally, the television crew was forced to pack up their gear and leave. Of course, I was feeling a little guilty for touching off the bomb. Nevertheless, it was amusing. Helen and I got back to tuning extraction after the television crew left.

Helen certainly had a fiery personality. This event was the first time I experienced the full fury of her volatile personality. Over the years, I saw it in action a few more times. Fortunately, the flames were never directed at me.

It was not long before I was told that I would be replacing Helen as head of the Switchyard Group. This was not a surprise. After all, she had told Maury that she wanted someone who could take her job so that she could focus on getting the Tevatron built. I agreed to take the reins of the group, feeling a little trepidation. After all, I was almost the most junior person in the group. The only exception was Mike Harrison, who had been hired a short time after me. I remember being confident I could do the job even though I knew, as did everyone else, that I was no Helen Edwards.

The day when I would assume my new responsibilities finally arrived. I was shown the letter from the division head that would go to the group, announcing the change. It looked good to me except maybe for my name being in it. Yet I still had confidence that I could carry it off.

On the morning when the letter appeared in the mailboxes, I was particularly interested in the reaction of Jack McCarthy and Obie. I needed them on board, and I knew I they could be tough customers. It might take some effort to convince them I was legitimate.

Jack's office was down the hall from mine. I didn't have to wait long before I looked up and saw both Jack and Obie walking toward Jack's office, each reading a copy of the letter that had been placed in their mailboxes. I decided I would talk to them right away. I waited a couple of minutes to give them time to read the letter before I walked down the hallway to Jack's office.

I found them sitting in front of Jack's desk with their feet up on it, each studying a copy of the letter. When they looked up and saw me, they each wadded up their copy of the letter and slam-dunked the crumpled documents in the waste basket. I laughed. I was not rattled because I had expected this kind of show. A few friendly words were exchanged, and we were off and running. There was no doubt in my mind that they would work as hard as ever. They both had their pride, and I would benefit from it. This was our first and only mildly tense moment. We had sailed right through it.

With Jack and Obie fully on board, they quickly became my go-to guys for the most difficult problems. The transition worked well because I didn't have the philosophy that I had to turn everyone's desk around in order to demonstrate that I was boss. It also worked because I made it clear that I had complete confidence in everyone in the group. The transition of Switchyard leadership went smoothly leaving no scars or marks of any kind other than Jack and Obie's shoe prints on Jack's desk.

CHAPTER 46

Head of the Switchyard and Extraction Group

Quarks and gluons have not been directly observed, but our giant accelerators indicate that these objects lurk inside of the protons, neutrons, and other observed particles. They are not included inside the electron or other leptons.

*****

Russ Huson, the Accelerator Division Head, was my new boss when I became head of the Switchyard Group. The group was responsible for extracting beam from the Main Ring Accelerator and dividing it up for distribution to the experimental areas. Russ was very supportive; but he never fully understood what Helen did, and he did not understand what I did. Nevertheless, he was a good boss. He knew what he had to know.

Early in my tenure as Switchyard group leader, I asked Russ what my budget was. He said, "Don't worry about it. Just buy what you need." Wow! Those were the days! I took him up on it and bought what I needed. I never got called on any of it. It probably helped that I never bought anything that I didn't need.

I had to make some major changes in the switchyard beams to enable them to deliver and target the higher-energy protons that would be coming from the Tevatron. Some modifications of the switchyard-beam enclosures (tunnels) were also necessary in order to accommodate the higher-energy beams that were planned.

A major construction job that was necessary to enable higher-energy beams required a major reconfiguration of a section of tunnel. I was able to get an excellent contractor to do the excavation and concrete work that was required. The contractor and I worked very well together. I tended to be hands on. I was often at the construction site with the contractor and his workers. The contractor's name was Jim.

Late one day, Jim and his crew were working on adding a new hatch into the tunnel that would be large enough to drop Energy Doubler magnets into the switchyard. The plan was to test the magnets in the switchyard beam to determine the amount of energy it would take to quench them. A quench happens when a part of the superconducting coil warms up enough to make it go normal or non-superconducting. Quenches tend to spread quickly, and magnet coils can be damaged or destroyed if the current is not removed from the coil quickly.

I was present at the site, watching the progress on the excavation. A backhoe was digging down to the beam line tunnel where the hatch, or opening, would be created. The bucket accidentally hit a discharge line from one of the sump pumps in the beam tunnel and broke it. Water pumped out the tunnel by the sump pumps and was pouring right back into the tunnel. To complicate matters, the excavation itself was quickly filling with groundwater, which was also draining into the beam enclosure. Jim's men had to feel around under the water to find the location where the pipe was broken. They could not find it. I got down in the hole with them to help with the search.

At about ten o'clock that night, we were still looking for the broken pipe in knee-deep water when I heard Russ Huson's voice from the top of the excavation. He called out, "Roger, is that you down there?" I confirmed that it was me, and then he said, "Have you got that 1000 GeV Switchyard Design Report done yet?" I told him I was making progress on it, but I was involved in an emergency at the moment.

He seemed somewhat satisfied. Nevertheless, he had subtly suggested that maybe it wasn't my job to be slugging around in the water looking for broken pipes. He didn't understand that I was still a kid from Pot Creek at heart. I had to get dirty anyway I could. Furthermore, I had to be where the action was.

The bureaucracy was almost nonexistent at the Laboratory in my early days at the lab. This is especially true in comparison to the present time. We simply got work done, and we did it well. We had our pride and the desire to succeed. Nevertheless, I admit that we were a little out of control at times, but it was always in a positive direction.

For example, one day on the hatch job, it was necessary for someone to descend into the excavation, which had rather steep sides, in order to connect the helium transfer lines and other plumbing that entered the beam enclosure through the top. The contractor told me that he was concerned that safety would make him dig the hole back much farther to decrease the slope of the walls in order to make working in the hole safer. This would cost me money. He told me that he could connect the pipes quickly before anyone knew what was happening. I asked him how he would do it. He said he would ride a bucket down himself and quickly make the connections. I told him to go ahead. That is certainly the way we would have done it at Pot Creek.

When the job was ready to be done the next day, I went to the site. I felt that Jim would be safe in the bucket. I had a lot of confidence in him and his crew. He did not disappoint me. He got the job done quickly and efficiently. However, a safety person arrived on the scene just as he was riding the bucket back up. The safety person was very junior, and he didn't know what to do. Nevertheless, his eyes got very big and round as Jim emerged from the excavation on the bucket. As soon as Jim jumped off the bucket, he looked at the safety inspector and said, "If I were you, I would get out of here right away. If anyone finds out that you were here, you will be in a lot of trouble." The inspector quickly departed. The job was done. There were no repercussions. Yet I have to admit, I would have done this job much differently at the end of my career when I could not remember the Pot Creek ways nearly so clearly.

CHAPTER 47

The Characters of the Switchyard Group

We are unable to extract the quarks and gluons from the protons with our powerful accelerator beams. The creator used a special glue with very strange properties that prevents the quarks and gluons from being directly observed. More to come...

*****

During my time as head of the Switchyard Group, I benefitted greatly from the cast of talented and most unusual characters that had been assembled by Helen Edwards. The group she had put together could ostensibly do the impossible as long as impossible was a bit of an exaggeration. Nevertheless, I had a team of technicians, engineers, and scientists who thought they could do anything, and they weren't far from the truth in their belief.

Not only were these people extremely competent, they were also memorable. Sharon Lackey was an engineering physicist in the group. She had a degree in physics, and she was most impressive even though she was very soft-spoken. Her husband, Jim, also worked in the accelerator division in a different group.

Sharon and I had a very good relationship. Nevertheless, I got into serious trouble with her on one occasion. There was a problem late in the evening that involved a system she was responsible for. She had just had a baby and was still recovering. Nevertheless, she had started coming back to work part-time. She was the person I should have called for the problem, but I decided to give her a break. I called someone else. When she found out what I had done, she was very upset with me. She came to me with both anger and tears in her eyes. I did not make that mistake again.

Another character was Jim Walton, a scientist who was really a super technician. Having graduated from Dartmouth, he walked from the east coast to Batavia in order to apply for a job during the early days of the Laboratory. Bob Wilson hired him. Jim was very good at building the electrostatic septa that were used to extract beams from the Main Ring and to split it in the beam lines. They consisted of planes of wires that opposed a cathode. The voltage between the cathode and the wires was typically in a range around a hundred kilovolts or about one hundred thousand volts. The wire planes had to be straight to a few thousandth of an inch over about ten feet. Jim's technical skills made him very good at building septa. Jim's weakness was that he liked to spend his recreational time in bars. Furthermore, he made the most of any party he attended.

Robert Oberholtzer, or Obie, was an extraordinary electronics technician. In addition, he was very much into sports even though he did not look like an athlete. Nevertheless, he had played high school football in Ohio. By the time I got to know him, he had rounded out a little. This could have been a disguise to mislead his athletic opponents. He was very good at any game that took skill and coordination. Obie supervised the electronics technicians in the group. He made certain that the group could do whatever magic was necessary to keep the electronic systems operating.

Jack McCarthy was Obie's supervisor and partner. He was also a character and was one of the brightest people I have ever known. Jack had an electrical engineering degree from the University of Illinois, where he had also been a gymnast. He was very fit, in addition to being one of the best engineers I have ever worked with. Well, he was more than an engineer. He understood the science also. He also knew how to party.

The most incredible character that I worked with in the Switchyard Group was Curtis Crawford, who I hired after becoming head of the group. I was looking for a technician, and a young man who had been working for Lyon & Healy making harps applied for the job. I decided to interview him because I noticed that he had been a PhD student of Jim Cronin's, a professor at the University of Chicago. Jim was well-known at the time and would become a Nobel Prize winner. Curtis never completed his graduate studies at the University of Chicago because it bored him and he had more exciting things to do. I had to hire him.

It did not take me long to determine that he was not only an outstanding technician, but he proved to be much more. His roots bore strong similarity to my Pot Creek origins. He soon proved that he could both outhillbilly me on one day and outthink me on another.

Curtis was a hillbilly from Tennessee. His dad was a truck driver. Nevertheless, he managed to get into the University of Chicago well before he was college age. Clearly, he was an outlier on the intelligence scale. He spoke with a southern drawl, and he loved animals, especially chickens. He kept his collection of rare chickens in his house. Fortunately, he was not married. Well, he had been married to a veterinarian who worked at Brookfield Zoo. They were separated, but they still maintained a good relationship. When someone asked Curtis how much he wanted for his rare chicken collection, he answered in his southern drawl, "'Bout seventy-nine cents uh pound."

Curtis did not have or use an indoor bathroom. This was difficult to accommodate at the lab. He complied sometimes, and often, he didn't. Jim Walton also had this problem, but not as a matter of principle. For Curtis, it was a matter of upbringing. His dad had taught him that civilized people don't take care of their bodily waste disposal needs inside of the house.

Curtis was obviously very smart because he did well enough in school to enter the University of Chicago early where he eventually studied with Jim Cronin. It turns out that Curtis did his PhD research right next to my experiment at Argonne National Lab. It was his experiment where I had been able to see the beam lighting up the wire chambers on my first trip to Argonne.

When Curtis' PhD experiment was complete, instead of writing up his research, Curtis began riding the rails, searching out famous Black blues musicians. He was learning to play blues guitar from them. After he did this for a while, he got some jobs and eventually ended up working for Lyon & Healy, a company that made harps. This is where he was when he applied for a job at the Laboratory.

Curtis applied for a technician position at the lab. I hired him. How could a kid from Pot Creek not hire such a person? It was clear before and after I hired him that he was a genius who was difficult to classify. I soon came to understand that he was a super technician/scientist/artist.

Even though Curtis spent much time playing blues guitar, he was well worth having at the Laboratory. He seldom played at the lab, but he did play in Chicago fairly often. At one point, he went on tour with Honeyboy Edwards. I learned early on that if one wants to have access to a genius, one has to be willing to cut the genius a break because they tend to do what they want.

When Curtis arrived at the lab, I did not have enough office space to give him his own office, so I made room for him in my office. This worked well at first. He would sometimes play the guitar for me late in the day. Sometimes, late was not very late. I always enjoyed it.

It did not take Curtis long to prove his worth by solving a very difficult technical problem that Helen, Jim Walton, and I had worked on. The electrostatic septa, the devices that divided or split the beam for slow extraction from the main accelerator, consisted of fine wire planes. The individual wires had to be aligned so that they were straight to a few thousandths of an inch over the length of the septum. If the planes were not perfectly straight, beam losses would create excessive residual radiation. Curtis was able to make the septa much straighter than anyone who had worked on the problem before.

Curtis was very talented; however, there were times when I needed to cut him some slack. For example, he did not show up for work one morning, and he didn't call in. I was expecting him for a job that we had planned the day before. Late in the afternoon, he finally appeared in our office. Before I could say anything, he said, "Sorry, Rog. I couldn't help it. When I was comin' ta work this mornin', I got stopped at a railroad crossing by a long, slow freight train. I couldn't resist the urge. I stashed my car at the side of the road and jumped into a box car. I rode down to the next town, jumped off, and then caught another train coming back this way. I eventually got back to my car." One might ask whether this was just a story or real. As time went on, I came to realize that Curtis was 100 percent real.

Curtis was married when I hired him, but he was separated from his wife, who worked at the Brookfield Zoo. She was a veterinarian. Anyway, he still had a friendly relationship with her. They had both taken note of the European swans that graced the reflecting ponds in front of Wilson Hall. They thought it would be better to have some native North American trumpeter swans at the lab. They worked with the Brookfield Zoo to have some trumpeter swans delivered to the lab. However, they could not be put in the reflecting ponds in front of Wilson Hall because they were incompatible with the European swans that patrolled those ponds. Curtis's plan was to put them in the Main Ring cooling ponds that were well separated from the reflecting ponds by the main accelerator ring berm.

On the day the trumpeters were to be introduced to the Laboratory, Curtis and I were still sharing an office. I don't remember how the swans arrived at the Laboratory.

At about five o'clock in the afternoon, I was working in our office when Curtis rushed in, more excited than I had ever seen him. He exclaimed, "Roger! You have to help me! All the swans are dying!" We rushed out through a service building to a parking lot located inside of the Main Ring beam where we found the seven or eight trumpeter swans flopping around. They could not walk. They seemed to be inebriated.

Curtis asked me to help him wrestle them into the back of his station wagon. I thought this would be easy, but only because I had never had the crap kicked out of me by a swan before. We grabbed and wrestled with the sick birds, struggling to load them into the back of Curtis's car. After we finally succeeded in cramming them all in, I felt like I had just been on the losing side in a brawl.

Curtis told me he was taking the swans back to the zoo. He had already informed his wife that there was a problem and he was bringing them back. As I watched him pull out of the parking lot with a bunch of swans flopping around in the back of his station wagon, I tried to imagine what other cars on the I-88 tollway would think as they encountered him. It is not every day one sees a station wagon full of swans driving down the tollway.

I later learned that all the swans died. A chemical in the Main Ring ponds that was used to kill the algae in the cooling water had been fatal to them. Apparently, no one was aware that this would happen.

In spite of his misadventure with the swans, Curtis was a great addition to the Laboratory. Later in his career, he was instrumental in helping Sergei Nagaitsev develop electron cooling at the Laboratory. This was a very risky project that many people did not think would work. The idea was to inject a cold beam of electrons into a beam of antiprotons to cool them, thus reducing the phase space they occupied. This makes the beam of antiprotons smaller and brighter, increasing the number of collisions that occur when they collide with a beam of protons facilitating the study of very rare processes that occur in these collisions. Electron cooling was needed once we had turned the Tevatron into a collider where the collisions between protons and antiprotons were studied. Electron cooling was used to cool the antiprotons.

Another amusement provided by Curtis occurred when we were still sharing an office in his early days at the Laboratory. The office began filling up with electronic equipment from the Laboratory's electronics pool (PREP). One could check out standard electronic modules from PREP to use on an experiment. After the experiment was done, the equipment was returned to the PREP pool.

Once the office filled up with electronics modules to the point that there was no room for me anymore, I asked Curtis what we were going to do with all the electronics modules. He replied in his hillbilly drawl, "Nothin'." So I asked why we had it all in our office. He responded that he had a thing for the young woman, Cheri, who worked in PREP. She checked out the equipment. I wanted to humor him, but there was no longer room in the office for me.

I told him, "Curtis, you can't check out anymore equipment. I no longer fit in the office." He said, "Well, I have to see Cheri every day, and I can't just go up there without a reason. I gotta check somethin' out." I said, "Why don't you start checking in one piece of equipment every day?" He looked skeptical, but he agreed. He was afraid the Cheri would be onto him if he started checking the equipment back in. Nevertheless, the equipment slowly disappeared.

Most of the people in the group partied too hard. Obie drank too much, and Jack was no slouch at putting away liquor. Nevertheless, both could always be counted on to solve whatever electrical or electronics problem that came up in accelerator operations day or night, inebriated or sober. Of course, this concerned me, and I would typically deflect calls to them if I knew there had been too much partying. The Operations Crew Chiefs were also good at not letting incapacitated people work on anything.

Nevertheless, there was one time where this almost didn't work. It was New Year's Eve, and I had been called in to resolve some beam-tuning problems. I quickly determined that there was a problem with one of the power supplies at the Switchyard Service Building. I knew that there was a New Year's Eve party underway at Obie's house. Nevertheless, I needed Obie and/or Jack in order to fix the problem. I called and got both of them on the phone. I hoped that they could tell the Operations crew how to resolve the issue. Instead, they indicated they would come in.

When they arrived in the Main Control Room, I was more than a little concerned about their state of sobriety. Nevertheless, I told them what the problem was again, hoping that they could tell the Operations crew how to resolve it. Instead, they chose to go out to the switchyard service building to have a look at the problematic power supply themselves. They seemed to be fairly coherent. I asked them to call me as soon as they arrived at the service building, which was not far from the MCR. I was still concerned.

After what I thought was more than enough for them to get to the service building, I had not received a call. I called the service building. There was no answer. One of the accelerator operators volunteered to drive to the service building to see if he could find them. It was not long before he reported back that he had found them in Obie's van parked beside the road partway to the service building. They had both passed out. We waited until morning to get the power supply fixed. Meanwhile, the Operations crew brought them back to the MCR where they could look after them.

Jack and Obie were both into sports. They played softball and touch football. Jack had not played football like Obie, but since he had been a gymnast, he would often take a playing field with an impressive gymnastics routine designed to intimidate the other team. I suppose it worked. I was a little concerned at picnics and other switchyard social events when Jack would launch into his routine after number of beers. Nevertheless, he always seemed to land feet first.

I was very fortunate to have both Jack and Obie in the Switchyard Group for the entire three years that I was the group leader. Both would still be in the Accelerator Division when I returned as the division head in 1999. Sometime later, Jack left the lab to work for a power-supply company in New England. Obie stayed. Jack would stop by and see us every year. All was well until Obie's smoking finally caught up with him. I was unaware that he was bringing a breathing machine to work with him until one morning, he joined me for the walk from the parking lot into the cross gallery. He was carrying an object the size of a small suitcase. I asked him what it was. He confessed that it was a breathing machine and that he was in bad shape. He told me that he would not last much longer.

It was not long before I heard that Obie was in the hospital in very serious condition. I went to see him. When I got to his room, his wife was there with him. He seemed to be in great distress when he looked up to see me. Nevertheless, he mustered some humor in the face of his grave situation. He said, "Roger, if I were you, I would sell all my stock in Old Style." Old Style was the beer that Obie drank. He may have been their best customer for all I know. His attempt at humor in his condition did not surprise me. I loved him for it.

Meanwhile, Jack flew in from the east coast. He and I spent quite a bit of time together in the hospital as Obie came to the end of his path through life. He did not linger too long. We were both glad.

After Obie was gone, Jack eventually stopped coming to see me every year. I miss him. I miss Obie.

CHAPTER 48

The Tevatron

When a quark is knocked loose, it immediately pulls another quark or two out of the vacuum (almost nothing) to make a proton, meson, or other particle containing quarks. If the energy is high enough, many quark pairs or triplets may be pulled out of nothing to create many fundamental particles. Someone or something is messing with us.

*****

I was the head of the Switchyard Group for about three years. We not only split and delivered more beam to the experiments than ever before due to all-around improvements in the accelerator complex; we also began making serious preparations to extract and deliver beam from Helen's Tevatron slated to be the first superconducting synchrotron in the world. At the time of construction, it was called the Energy Doubler. Admittedly, calling it Helen's Tevatron demonstrates some prejudice on my part. I feel it is largely justified. There were two other scientists who, along with Helen, were awarded the National Medal of Science for designing and building the Tevatron. They were Alvin Tollestrup and Richard Lundy. Alvin designed the superconducting magnets, and Richard oversaw their fabrication.

Helen was responsible for using the superconducting magnets to create the largest and most powerful synchrotron in the world. It was to be installed underneath the original Main Ring Accelerator. Building the Tevatron was a huge undertaking for the Laboratory.

To produce beam at or near 1000 GeV, the original Fermilab synchrotron, the Main Ring, would inject beam into the new Energy Doubler, or Tevatron, for further acceleration. The beam would then be extracted into the beam switchyard to be divided up and sent to the experimental areas where there were large, elaborate experiments that would make use of the beam. Plans were also underway to turn the Tevatron into a storage ring where protons and antiprotons would travel in opposite directions and collide in the centers of two very large detectors that would surround the collision points or interaction regions.

While the Energy Doubler magnets were being built, the Main Ring continued to deliver beam to the existing experiments. In addition to delivering beam, we tested Energy Doubler magnets in the switchyard beam lines to determine how low the beam losses had to be during extraction from the Tevatron in order to avoid quenching the magnets and losing all the beam.

During my early days at Fermilab, Helen brought a young man about my age to my office and introduced him to me. His name was Nikolai Mokhov. He was from the Soviet Union. She told me that he was going to work with me to determine the amount of energy deposition it would take to quench the superconducting Tevatron magnets. Nikolai had written a computer code that calculated energy depositions by various particles in different materials. He was a relatively young scientist, as was I.

I quickly realized that we had a problem. Nikolai spoke very little English, and I spoke no Russian. In fact, I had a language disability that had prevented me from speaking much Spanish even though I had been exposed to it all my life. My grandfather spoke it to many of his friends, and I had taken three years of Spanish in high school including a course in Spanish literature. I could read it fine and understand spoken Spanish fairly well, but when it came to speaking, the words seemed to twist and tangle in my brain until they burned out a few circuits. I had also taken two years of German in college but could not speak that language either. I spoke it just well enough to offend a hotel clerk in Austria by propositioning her when I had intended to ask if she had a room with two beds. I guess she thought my wife, Gail, and daughter, Kelly, who were with me at check-in were going to stand by and watch from the spare bed? Anyway, Gail was very good at languages, and she quickly rescued me from the predicament.

Helen left Nikolai to discuss energy deposition with me. We held the discussion at my whiteboard. We quickly developed a way to communicate by writing equations. Fortunately, Nikolai had been in the States long enough to develop ways of communicating with the language-impaired. We managed to hit it off, becoming good friends in addition to colleagues.

It was not long before he came to a backyard cookout with the Switchyard Group held at my small house in Aurora. He brought the vodka, which seemed to facilitate our communications. I cooked burgers outside on my grill. It was not long before someone in the group asked if this was the way people in Russia drank vodka. He replied, "Nooooo!" And then he went on to explain that the glasses were much larger and almost full. Furthermore, they had to be downed completely in about three microseconds. I was proud of him for being able to explain this so eloquently after having already put away an impressive quantity of vodka himself. Okay, he was exaggerating…slightly. Nevertheless, it is a wonder the neighborhood survived the cookout.

About ten years later, I visited Nikolai in the Soviet Union and learned that he had told stories of the flames from my grill shooting higher than the treetops. I hoped that no one would ask me to put on such a display in the Soviet Union.

With a little help from me, Nikolai was able to do some useful work for Helen. We tested Tevatron magnets in a beam extracted from Fermilab's original Main Ring Accelerator. Nikolai ran his simulation programs that enabled us to measure the beam loss or energy deposition it would take to quench the magnets in the Tevatron.

We concluded that the Tevatron would probably work and we could extract beams from it. We published a paper with our results.

The real excitement for the test magnets came after our measurements had been completed. I was preparing to install superconducting magnets to upgrade the energy of the largest bend in the beam switchyard. It was called the left bend, and it would have to be upgraded to bend the more energetic beam from the Tevatron toward the Meson Laboratory, where several experiments would use the high-energy particles to peer inside of protons in order to see if there was anything worth knocking out of them. In order to upgrade the left bend, I would replace the conventional magnets in the large bend that guided the beam toward the Meson Laboratory with twenty superconducting magnets. This was the first large-scale use of superconducting magnets.

Helen and others were uncomfortable with the project because they were concerned that the funding agency, and Laboratory management might conclude that the Tevatron was not viable if the left bend did not work. I did nothing to ease their anxiety when I accidentally blew up the two test magnets that Nikolai and I had used to make our beam tests.

This dramatic event occurred well after all the beam tests had been completed. I had intentionally quenched the magnets to show the Switchyard Operations Specialist, Bob Mau, a quench. He had never witnessed a quench, and he felt he should see one since his crews would soon be operating a machine that was likely to have them often during commissioning.

To explain how the event occurred, I need to provide the basics of how a particle accelerator works. Charged particles are accelerated by running them through a strong electric field over and over again. In order to get the particles to pass through the electric field many times, their paths are bent by magnetic dipole fields so that they trace out an approximation to a circle, ellipse, or a relatively smooth closed path. In other words, the charged particles go round and round, passing through the accelerating field on each revolution. Dipole magnets are used to bend the path of the charged particles.

The dipole magnets that I was testing were set up so that one of them bent the beam one way and the other bent the beam in the opposite direction. The combination left the beam almost on the same path that it would be on without the magnets turned on.

For the tests I was conducting, we planned to lose some beam in the magnets to measure how much beam loss it would take to quench them. This is a bit of an oversimplification, but not much.

The problem with superconducting magnets is that they have to be maintained at a temperature around 4 degrees Kelvin or about 450 degrees below zero Fahrenheit in order for them to work. This is so cold that time almost stops, or so I say. Temperature has to do with motion, and the colder something gets, the slower the constituent atoms and molecules move or vibrate. When nothing moves at all, the absolute temperature is zero. Time doesn't really stop. I was just pretending. Nevertheless, if there is no motion or change, doesn't time stop? This is amusing, but it has nothing to do with anything—or does it?

The important detail for the accelerator is that it takes very little to warm up a cold superconducting coil. A small amount of beam halo hitting the superconductor will do the trick. When this happens, the struck part of the coil warms and develops resistance, which causes it to warm up even more, resulting in a runaway situation or a quench. The entire process, or quench, happens very quickly. The coil can be damaged if the energy or current is not quickly removed from the magnet, or alternatively, if heaters are not fired in the magnet to distribute the energy over the entire coil instead of a small part of it. There are various ways to do this. However, for the purpose of this narrative, it is only important to note that the energy was not successfully removed from the two test magnets when they were intentionally quenched.

There are many ways this protection system can fail, and we learned about most of them when we were testing superconducting magnets for the Tevatron. It was a failure of the quench protection circuitry in the two test magnets that Nikolai and I had used to make the measurements for Helen that caused them to explode. *Explode* is a bit of a misnomer. The magnet does not come apart in the explosion, but it is damaged internally. And when the helium vents into the tunnel, it is cold, so it causes the water vapor in the air to condense quickly—forming a dense cloud that rushes down the tunnel. It looks and sounds like an explosion.

Bob Mau felt it was important for him to witness a quench. When we were ready to quench the two magnets for Bob, I invited him out to beam line where we were testing the two superconducting magnets. We did not plan to blow up a magnet for him. Instead, we would quench the two magnets, and the relief valves would blow cold helium into the tunnel. This would be dramatic enough without doing any damage. Quenches are common, and this one was to be intentional.

Bob and I entered the tunnel together, and I positioned him near the far, upstream end of the two test magnets near the turnaround box at the end of the magnet string where the helium turned around and headed back through the magnets to the refrigerator where it was re-cooled. I went back upstream where a phone was located and called Jack McCarthy, who was in our makeshift control room in the service building aboveground. We had current in the magnets, and I asked Jack to initiate a quench. This was something he could do by firing heater circuits that warmed the coils in the magnets.

Almost as soon as I made the request to Jack, I regretted it. I heard a big swoosh, and I simultaneously saw a large cloud of water vapor roaring down the tunnel toward me. (The cold helium created a water-vapor cloud when it blew out of the magnet, rapidly cooling the air and condensing any moisture in it.) I screamed, "STOP the quench!" into the phone. It was only thing I could think of to do. There was nothing anyone could do to stop the quench short of calling for a premature end of the universe. The tunnel was quickly filled with the vapor cloud, making it impossible to see anything.

As the cloud roared past me, I became very concerned about Bob, who was positioned at the far end of the magnets from me. I got down on my hands and knees since the vapor cloud clears from the floor up. Once on the floor, I could see Bob's feet about two hundred feet upstream of the position where I had left him. I knew he had to be fine to get that far. As the cloud dispersed, we got back together.

Bob was impressed and excited. He felt it had been worth his while to know what could happen that his operations crews might have to deal with. Unfortunately, the two test magnets were destroyed. We learned something important about quench protection from this event. This knowledge was important to incorporate into building the Tevatron, which would have to endure many quenches as it was commissioned and operated.

*****

Once the Tevatron construction was finished and the big superconducting machine was commissioned, it began delivering beam to the fixed target experiments; I joined one of them that was located on the proton area. I was fortunate to have inherited a graduate student, Robert Jedicke, from the University of Toronto. He had lost his PhD thesis adviser to an experiment in Europe, and he needed a mentor for his PhD research, which was already underway at Fermilab. I had never had a PhD student to advise and work with before, but it didn't matter. Rob was self-motivated and an outstanding student. I enjoyed working with him when we were installing the experiment, running shifts, analyzing the data for his PhD thesis, writing his PhD thesis, and finally presiding over his final oral examination by his PhD committee at the University of Toronto.

Rob was an unusual student. He had played football as an undergraduate. He was an offensive lineman. As one might expect, he was quite large. Even though he had been invited to training camp for the Detroit Lions and a Canadian team, he did not opt for football. (If I remember correctly, he went to one or both training camps.) He was told that he would have to add to his roughly 250 pounds (I am making this all up from memory) if he were to be a successful offensive lineman in the NFL. He was very intelligent. He opted for graduate school in physics instead of pounds.

Rob eventually ended up on the faculty at the University of Hawaii, but only after he and his wife made a yearlong trip around the world. We stayed in touch for a long of time. I noticed that he was spending a lot of time traveling to Europe and other places. I asked him why he spent so much time away from Hawaii. He told me that he took every opportunity to get away from Hawaii because he felt confined on the small island chain. He needed more space. As Kurt Vonnegut would say, "So it goes."

CHAPTER 49

The Russian Connection

How does a quark pull another quark out of the vacuum? It takes energy. Is the vacuum full of particles that just need energy to be released from their nonexistence? Is creation really this simple?

*****

Several years after Nikolai spent time at Fermilab, I had the opportunity to visit him in the Soviet Union. I was attending an accelerator conference at the Serpukhov Laboratory where Nikolai worked. I gave a talk at the conference in English. The conference was interesting. It lasted several days. Toward the end of my stay, I was invited to a barbecue at Nikolai's dacha (summerhouse) to be held on a Sunday morning. I was eager to attend, hoping to meet some of the families of the Russian scientists I had gotten to know while visiting the Laboratory. I had already been to Nikolai's apartment located in a high-rise building near the Laboratory. He lived near the top of the building, which was ten to fifteen stories tall. There was an elevator, but it was broken. The former mountain kid had to climb the stairs. I made it up without a problem.

I had taken some toy trucks and cars as gifts for his two small boys. After I arrived at the apartment, I took them out of my pocket and put one on the floor. I watched with subdued alarm as the toy rolled into the corner of the room without so much as a gentle nudge from me. I took this to be due creative design by the Soviet architects. The boys seemed excited to receive the toys.

When Sunday morning arrived and it was time for the barbecue at the dacha, I met Nikolai and five to fifteen male scientists in the parking lot of my hotel, which was located on the Laboratory site. Apparently, a barbecue was not an event attended by women or families. We walked out to the dacha from the parking lot carrying ten or eleven bottles of wine and other libations. We also had a chicken to barbecue and probably some other stuff to go with the chicken that would not prove to be important to the events of the day.

We began drinking as soon as we arrived at the dacha. I was communicating well with my companions because they all spoke English, some better than others. I think it took us until about noon and several gallons of alcohol to decide that there were no real men in France. I went along with this, but it was the vodka talking—trust me. I also learned that the American culture they admired most was my own "cowboy" culture. I made the most of this to get my share to drink. Anyway, we had so much fun that the dead chicken managed to escape. I don't remember how this happened. Maybe we ate it, or maybe it got disgusted with us and left of its own volition.

At the end of the day, we staggered back to the lab, each convinced that we had made the world a better place. Well, it was certainly much safer for chickens until the alcohol wore off.

A final note on Nikolai: He presently lives in the US and works at Fermilab. He came to this country after the Soviet Union dissolved and was hired to work on the SSC, a huge accelerator that was to be built in Texas. It was never built due to the very large cost. Nevertheless, Nikolai had the opportunity to live in Texas for a while. Over the years, he continued to develop his code, and it is used around the world to do energy-deposition calculations. It is a significant tool for accelerator development.

I had an amusing experience some years after Nikolai began working at Fermilab. I encountered him and one of his sons in the parking lot. His son was in high school at the time. Nikolai reintroduced me to Dima by asking if I remembered him. The son had been a very small boy when I first met him. His size was no surprise, but when he spoke to me with a Texas accent, I thought, *What have we done? How could we have let such a tragedy occur? How could a good ole New Mexico boy have played a role in creating this outcome?* Well, I was a kid from Pot Creek after all.

CHAPTER 50

Leon Lederman

Even though we cannot knock single quarks out of a proton or neutron for careful examination, we are able to determine the properties of these fundamental constituents of matter from hard scatters off of these ghosts of existence. This most often creates a plethora of particles to examine for clues to the fundamental nature of the quarks. Or perhaps the clues are only the teasings of a playful and sometimes deceitful creator.

*****

Over the years, I worked with many outstanding people at Fermilab. One of the most memorable people I had the pleasure of working with was Leon Lederman, the second director of Fermilab. He won the Nobel Prize in Physics while at Fermilab for work on muons that he had done earlier in his career as a professor at Columbia University. His work at Fermilab included the discovery of the upsilon particle. The upsilon came as a big surprise to most particle physicists and some taxi-cab drivers.

Leon was not only a great man; he also had a personality and sense of humor to match. I was still the head of the Switchyard Group when he became Director. However, I soon moved to the Research

Division where I was head of the Experimental Areas Department. Ken Stanfield, my former professor at Purdue, had taken a staff position at Fermilab just months before I arrived on the scene. He had been the head of the Experimental Areas Department and had just been made the head of the Research Division. About a year later, the Experimental Areas Department was dissolved in a reorganization, and I became the deputy head of the Research Division under Ken. This placed me in close contact with the director. I enjoyed my interactions with Leon. I was able to have even more interactions with Leon when Taiji Yamanouchi, the head of Program Planning, decided he wanted a year off to do research. Since Taiji had done such a great job over the years, Leon granted his request and asked to me replace Taiji as head of Program Planning for a year. This meant that I would work in the Director's Office, reporting directly to Leon. I enthusiastically accepted the assignment.

As head of Program Planning, my main responsibility was to handle all the proposals for experiments and make certain they were put before the Program Advisory Committee with all the supporting documentation. I also had to indicate the impact on the Laboratory for each proposal including the cost and person power that would be required to carry out the proposed experiment. In addition, had to keep the PAC informed of the progress of individual experiments.

All experiments had to be approved by the PAC before they could be set up and run at the Laboratory. As experiments progressed, I had to keep track of the progress toward meeting its goals. Furthermore, I had to keep Leon advised of any problems involving any of the experiments. The job was easier than it sounds.

Working in the Director's Office at that time was incredibly pleasant. Leon always had a smile for me as we began our conversations. Nevertheless, I knew that he could be tough when necessary. He was mainly tough on issues that threatened the lab from outside. Furthermore, he was very good at dealing with the funding agencies. He had a real knack for getting his way.

I have many memorable experiences involving Leon. They range from my experiences during my year as head of Program Planning to hiking and climbing with him in the mountains of Colorado during

Program Advisory Committee meetings that were held in Aspen. However, my favorite personal story about Leon occurred when I was acting head of Program Planning and had an office near his on the second floor of Wilson Hall.

One morning, Leon was in his office meeting with some important Department of Energy officials from Washington. His door was open as it usually was. Meanwhile, I was in my office, which was located very near Leon's office with some open space in between where two administrative assistants sat.

I was aware that Leon was meeting with the DOE officials. I was a little bored because I did not seem to have any problems that needed to be chased down. While I was attempting to think of something useful to do, I was leaning back in my chair, playing catch with myself by bouncing a racket ball off the dry wall behind my desk. I got rather rambunctious with the ball as my frustration built. Suddenly, the ball took a bad hop and got away from me. It bounded out of my office and hit the right-angle corner of a wall that was directly across from my office. The impact with the corner was perfectly placed to send the fugitive ball bouncing directly toward Leon's open door. I hurried out of my office, trying futilely to catch up with the renegade ball. I entered the open space between my office and Leon's just in time to see the ball hop through his office door, disappearing under table where Leon and his guests sat discussing funding issues. I could only see Leon's feet from where I stood, but I could see both DOE officials sitting on the other side of the table. I froze.

After a couple of seconds, Leon's feet disappeared, and then he quickly appeared in his doorway with the ball in his hand and a quizzical look on his face. He threw the ball to me, saying, "I can't come out and play right now. I'm busy." And then he disappeared back into his office where the DOE officials were looking curiously at me.

The fact that Leon had his door open during the important meeting says something important about him. He was a very open and approachable director. As near as I could tell, he was loved by most. I knew he could be tough, but I only experienced one occurrence that resulted in someone getting into serious trouble with him. The problem was a Canadian researcher. He was seen intentionally running over some of the geese that inhabited the Laboratory's cooling ponds. When the incident was reported to Leon, he was incensed and asked me to look into it. I determined that the incident had happened as reported. Leon told me to remove the researcher privileges at the Laboratory and to revoke his privilege to access the Laboratory site. I carried out his instructions.

Another large-impact activity that Leon began at the Laboratory was the Saturday Morning Physics Program (SMP). This program invited local high school students to sign up for a series of ten or eleven lectures. *Local* really meant anyone was welcome, including adults. From time to time, students from Indiana and Wisconsin as well as Chicago attended. The lectures were given by Laboratory staff members, including Leon. For a while, a bus was provided to bring students from disadvantaged areas of Chicago to Saturday Morning Physics.

The topics were determined by Leon initially and later by whoever was running the program. The lectures were not rigorous. Instead, they were largely informational with the goal of interesting young people in science and particularly in physics. Drasko Jovanovic, a senior scientist at the Laboratory, initially organized and ran the program. I began lecturing in it not long after the program began.

When Drasko retired, Erik Ramberg and I took responsibility for the program. We led it for more than ten years. Erik was also a staff scientist. Organizing Saturday Morning Physics was one of the most rewarding activities I have ever given to myself. Many of the young people were incredible. It was uplifting just to see what great kids exist in our schools. Well, we never had anyone from Pot Creek attend.

Erik and I also ran a summer internship program at the Laboratory together for more than ten years. This program was inspired by Leon and was for college students at all levels. It gave them a chance to spend a summer working on interesting research projects at the Laboratory. This was also a very rewarding activity for me.

Before Leon's first day as director, he announced that on his first morning on the job, everyone was invited to join him at 7:00 a.m. for a run around the main accelerator ring, a distance of 3.8 miles. All who completed the run would get a free breakfast in the Laboratory cafeteria, even if they cheated by not running the entire distance. I had begun trying to jog to get back in shape, so I decided that I would join Leon and the other runners. The event was so much fun for everyone who participated that it became a yearly event. It was not long before Leon asked me to organize the run every year. He wanted to get T-shirts made for the participants in addition to continuing the free breakfasts.

It did not take much effort to organize the runs. The Laboratory had an artist, Angela Gonzales, who had come from Cornell with Bob Wilson. She served as the Laboratory artist until the end of her career. Bob was very astute to add her to the Laboratory staff. She was an incredible resource. She volunteered to design a T-shirt for the "Director's Run" each year. She came up with some very creative designs over the years. The run and the T-shirts became a great tradition that lasted through two directors, Leon and John Peoples. The latter followed Leon as Director. The tradition ended when directors who were not joggers or runners were selected. This may have been my fault. I forgot to tell the search committee that running was an important requirement for the Laboratory's director. Oh well, nothing lasts forever.

CHAPTER 51

Life in Batavia

Was creation simply a burst of energy that raised a virtual ocean of particles to a higher energy that allowed some of them to become "real"? Let's say yes even though I came upon this notion while playing with my scientist friends in the kitty litter box.

*****

Kelly started to school when we lived in Aurora. Our existence there was very modest, but we did not plan to keep our Aurora house long. It was very affordable for us because it was rundown when we bought it. This gave us the opportunity to fix it up and make a profit on it. This worked better than expected, and we soon had it on the market. It sold relative quickly, and we found a very comfortable house in Batavia on a wooded lot in a small wooded subdivision. Life was moving in the right direction.

Our water at the Batavia house came from a well on the property. Not long after we moved in, the pump in the well failed. I found and hired a local well-and-pump company to come out and replace the pump. The task was not as complicated as I had feared. As the job was finishing up, the man who had replaced the pump said, "This is a nice place, but you don't have a dog." Kelly was standing nearby.

The well repairman went on to tell me that he had one puppy left from a litter of puppies. Kelly overheard the conversation, and she was all over it, looking at me with pleading eyes. I agreed that we would go and look at the leftover puppy.

We followed the well repairman to his house and business location in Batavia where he introduced us to the leftover puppy. The puppy and Kelly took about at five milliseconds to bond. Kelly was so excited that I knew I had no choice. We took the puppy home with us. By the time we arrived at the house, Dusty had a name. Kelly was ecstatic. Dusty looked to be a mixture of collie and shepherd. Kelly didn't care what he was; she had a puppy! Furthermore, Dusty was ecstatic with Kelly.

It took less than a day for Kelly to teach Dusty to jump through a hula hoop. I thought this was unusual. Kelly knew nothing about training a dog. I was astounded. I began paying more attention to the new arrival. He seemed to quickly understand what was expected of him. I had been around many dogs before but had never seen one that was so easy to communicate with and train.

Dusty soon proved to be an incredible addition to the family. Even though he had no indoor experience, I only had to tell him one time where he could take care his business (outside) and where he couldn't (inside). He also quickly learned where he was allowed go in the house and where he couldn't go. He was not allowed on the carpet in the living room or upstairs in the bedrooms. He was given full access to the family room and laundry room.

If this weren't enough, it seemed that he attempted to talk, but he got disgusted with us when we couldn't understand him. He had no trouble expressing his frustration.

When it was appropriate for Dusty to break the rules, he broke them. We were all in bed one morning. Dusty slept in the laundry room, but we never had to close the door to keep him there. However, one morning, he burst up the stairs to the bedrooms where he had never been. He was barking excitedly, trying to get me to follow him. I did. He took me downstairs to the family room, which had a door to the basement. He stopped at the door where he stood very still, pointing at it with his nose. I opened the door, and the two of us went down the steps into the basement. I smelled an odd odor. The basement smelled of gas and smoke. I quickly found a piece of PVC pipe leaning against the wall about ten feet from the furnace. It was somewhat hot and melted. I traced the gas smell to the furnace.

I got a furnace repairman on the scene as quickly as I could. He determined that there was a gas leak in the furnace, and when it had come on, it had flashed over and heated enough PVC pipe and melt some of it. Dusty had apparently heard the boom when the flashover occurred and decided that I better know that something had happened in the basement. Fortunately, there was nothing flammable around the furnace.

Unfortunately, Dusty only lasted eleven years. He succumbed to cancer. I have never had another dog because I knew that Dusty had spoiled me. It was not likely that I would find a dog that I wouldn't be disappointed in. Of course, I get plenty of dog time with the grandchildren's dogs.

*****

Early in my career, I began writing minutes for meetings at the Laboratory and memos as part of my Laboratory business. In doing so, I discovered that I had a difficult time writing a completely serious memo. I almost always injected some humor. I couldn't seem to avoid this tactic even when conducting serious business in the memo. I soon learned that that it was often a good idea to inject some humor. People read my memos. People that had no business reading my memos read them. In fact, I began noticing them posted in places around the lab where I had not even sent them. I concluded that adding some humor was a good way to get people to read minutes and memos.

My writing notoriety was enhanced even further when my friend, Mark Schmitz, got me interested in cycling. At first, we just went out for rides, mostly on Sunday mornings. Soon, more riders were joining us for our rides over the mostly flat Illinois countryside. We typically rode twenty to thirty miles on a Sunday morning. I found the cycling to be a pleasant way to get in shape and stay there.

Only one woman joined us for the rides at first. It was Nancy Grossman. Besides being a graduate student at the University of Minnesota, she was an excellent cyclist who could go toe to toe with the best of the males. I had first encountered her when she was a graduate student, and I was the head of the Experimental Areas Department (EAD). I would sometimes get involved in beam turning in the EAD control room when I was working on an experiment. Nancy would sometimes come into the Experimental Areas control room to tune or to get some assistance from the beam-line operators for her experiment. She was working on her PhD thesis experiment at the time. I could not help but notice that there was some serious competition between the male members of the operations crew to take care of her requests.

Nancy and I later became good friends. She came to me for advice on her PhD thesis. Meanwhile, my cycling friend Mark began a serious relationship with her that is still going on. Well, they are married now. Is that serious? It would seem so. Both are still very good friends.

Anyway, it was not long before I began to write minutes of the Sunday rides with the moniker, The Road Hun. However, I could not stick to the facts. The minutes quickly evolved until they were more than a little ridiculous, containing huge exaggerations and making fun of all of us in a very macho voice. Someone started spreading the minutes around, and more people joined the Sunday rides. Some of them were competitive, and some weren't. It didn't matter. Everyone was welcome. The rides usually broke up into groups as appropriate.

I continued the minutes, making fun of everyone. The minutes were sent out via e-mail, and anyone could get on the list simply by making a request to me. It was not long before I noticed that there were, at most, fifteen cyclists who went on the rides, but my distribution list was close to a hundred and stretched from coast to coast. This widespread distribution occurred because Fermilab had visiting scientists, graduate students, engineers, and technicians from across the country and the world; it was not surprising that I had such a wide distribution of subscribers. Okay, it was a little surprising.

I concluded that the popularity of my minutes indicated that I should turn them into a book. I did this. The title of the book was *And We All Died Laughing*. However, the book was not a laughing matter. First of all, it was not appropriate for all audiences. Okay, it was not appropriate for any audiences. Nevertheless, the book made one prediction that came true. In the book, a particular experiment goes up on the space shuttle. How did this get into a novel that sprang from my cycling adventures? The simple answer is that the entire book was totally out of bounds. It seemed the prediction was based on an experiment proposed by some University of Chicago professors that I had considered joining for the experiment. They were not cyclists. I had briefly been associated with them on the proposal. Unfortunately, when the experiment eventually went up, it was built by a completely different group of scientists. Nevertheless, the book seemed to predict the correct space shuttle for the flight that delivered it into orbit. I counted this as a successful prediction. Big deal! The odds were substantial that I would get the right shuttle. Thank goodness that none of the other predictions came to pass!

The book was outrageous. I had trouble getting agents or publishers interested in the book but finally made contact with a Canadian publisher who agreed very quickly to publish it, or so I thought. I probably was dealing with a Canadian scammer. After I submitted the manuscript, the publisher sent me galley proofs to check. They were more like galley cartoons. Nevertheless, I looked them over and sent them back. It was only a week or two before I got a letter from an attorney, notifying me that "my publisher" had gone belly up. He indicated that for 150 dollars, he would go into the warehouse to see if any copies of my book had been printed. He would send them to me if they had. I did not fall for it. I thought it was probably just a scam to get 150 dollars from me.

The book was never published, and I am thankful for this outcome. If anyone had read it, I would have been in real trouble. Well, there is a small chance that I am being too dramatic. Okay, I will fix this by being way too dramatic. The book was right out of lower bowels of Pot Creek, not suitable for public consumption.

*****

Some of the guys in our Sunday morning group were competitive, and we did a little bicycle racing. I was not very serious about racing, but I rode in a few races. We had an outstanding sprinter who won almost every race he entered. I was in a couple of races he was in. The members of our team felt it was our job to get in the way of everyone but him as we approached the finish of a race, but it didn't matter what the rest of us did. He won.

Even though I was only moderately competitive, I have a plaque somewhere in my basement that indicates a second or third place finish in the four-man-team time trial at the Illinois State Championships. We had entered a young team and an old team. You can guess which one I was on. Our younger team did not do as well. They raced in a younger-age category. This demonstrated that it pays to survive, get old, if one wants to win trophies. Well, we didn't get a trophy. We got a fancy wall plaque. I kept it on the wall in my basement for a long time, but it seems that it evaporated with time.

CHAPTER 52

Dzero

Does the virtual sea of particles exist where there is no space-time? For fun, let's say yes. The virtual sea just is. Didn't it have to come from somewhere? Not if time doesn't exist in our virtual sea. Nevertheless, we need to be able to pull parts of it into space-time or reality. Whoa! I am in way over my head. I am amazed that I am still breathing and not feeling dizzy.

*****

When my year was up in Program Planning, Leon called me into his office to propose a new assignment for me. The Laboratory was well on the way to converting the Tevatron into a collider where high-energy protons would be collided with high-energy antiprotons—antimatter, if you will. Two large detectors to view these collisions were planned and being worked on. Initially, only one detector, the Collider Detector at Fermilab (CDF), had been planned, and its construction in the Research Division was well along. Many, including Leon, thought that a second detector should be built to go into the D0 straight section. The funding agencies agreed. Planning for the Dzero Detector began.

Laboratory management concluded that the only place where the necessary person power was available to build a second detector was in the Accelerator Division. The reasoning was that as the division completed building the antiproton source for the Tevatron Collider, it could begin supporting the construction of the second detector.

Helen was the head of the Accelerator Division when the work on the Dzero Detector began. It was not long before Leon felt that not enough progress was being made on Dzero. He called me into his office and asked me to go back to the Accelerator Division and to become the head of the Dzero Construction Department under Helen. I did not really want this assignment because I was not into large collider detectors. However, I could not tell Leon no. I somewhat reluctantly accepted the challenge. Helen was once again my boss.

My first task was to find out what was delaying detector construction and to get it back on track. It did not take me long to determine that the problem with Dzero Detector construction was that it was being worked on as a fill-in job in the Accelerator Division. The antiproton source still needed much work as it was being finished commissioned. It had priority. I felt that the antiproton source was certainly the appropriate priority for the Accelerator Division. Nevertheless, something had to be done to get the Dzero Detector on track.

To further complicate matters, there was not much expertise for detector building in the Accelerator Division. I felt that I had no choice. I advocated moving Dzero back into the Research Division along with enough technical support to get the job done. Helen was not happy with me. Nevertheless, she continued to tolerate me. Finally, when I had convinced everyone including Leon that moving Dzero into the Research Division had to be done, I began selecting people. I quickly found out how upset Helen was with this solution.

One morning, I was talking with Ken Stanfield outside of his office on the second floor of Wilson Hall when Helen happened by. When she saw Ken, she tore into him verbally and very nearly physically. I tried to work my way in between them, trying to tell Helen that she was blaming Ken for something that was my fault. This was the case after all. She paid no attention to me. She kept screaming at Ken in a very public display. People were trying to get past the conflagration by scooting along against the walls. It was bad. The raging conflict made its way across the second floor to the Director's Office before it finally broke up. Helen was upset at my plan to move Dzero out of the Accelerator Division. However, she used Ken as a screaming dummy to demonstrate to me how upset she was.

Afterward, Ken told me that he didn't think he could ever work with Helen again. Since they were both division heads, it was necessary for them to get along. I told him I would try to work things out with Helen. That afternoon, I went to her office in the cross gallery. As soon as I walked in, she said, "I'm sorry. I owe you an apology." Before I left, we had a short but pleasant chat. Later in the day, I told Ken that Helen had apologized to me, and I thought things were going to work out. He told me that he had to get his own apology. He went to Helen's office by himself. Bad mistake! He got the same thrashing all over again. However, he recently told me that she had apologized. Sometimes, history changes. Is it a memory issue, and not necessarily Ken's? Wait! It couldn't be my problem, could it? Oh well, it happened one of the ways described here.

The transition to the Research Division went smoothly, and the Dzero Detector became a reality. I became the head of the Dzero Department in the Research Division. It was interesting to work on Dzero, but I never felt it was what I wanted to be doing.

Meanwhile, Leon stepped down as Director before Dzero became a reality. Dzero was coming along well, so Ken moved me to the Research Division office as an associate division head mostly responsible for Dzero. Meanwhile, John Peoples became the new Laboratory director, and he asked Ken Stanfield to be his deputy. Ken would be the deputy director of the Laboratory for the rest of his career. Peter Garbincius, a scientist about my age, became the head of the Research Division when Ken moved to the Director's Office.

CHAPTER 53

Research Division

Let's humor the guys and gals playing in the kitty litter. Does nothing separate universes? Could we turn this into a definition of nothing? Not yet even though it would seem that something less than empty space must separate universes. If so, it is a profound nothing, something that may not even exist and that we don't understand at all. Yes! That is it! Now we can put away our pencils, or maybe not.

*****

I thought that all was going well with the Dzero installation when I got a call from John Peoples one Sunday morning. This did not surprise me because John had the habit of showing up at experiments during the owl shift and calling people at all times of the night and day. On this particular Sunday morning, he told me that he needed a head for the Research Division. I was curious about why he needed a head. Since I was in the Research Division, I knew the current head, well, and I expected him to be the head for a while longer. He had not been at the job very long. John explained to me that he had a problem with my current boss, and he wanted me to take the job. I was not excited about doing this, but I accepted the job. I didn't think I had a choice.

During construction of Dzero, I had done quite a lot of shift work testing calorimeter modules. Since I was the head of Dzero during the day, I did this work in the evenings. I have to admit that I was rather tired. I had also spent a lot of time in the test beam where we were testing calorimeter modules with beam. Anyway, the shift work and all my other Dzero work ended when I became Head of the Research Division. The division had three or four hundred people in it at the time. Being the head was not a trivial matter. It was several times larger than Dzero, which was one of the departments in the Research Division.

Going in, I knew that I had a good staff in the division office and excellent people in the field. I knew many of them well. I had not studied any management books to prepare me for all the management jobs I seemed to be getting one after another. After all, my best management experience stemmed from the Robin Hood Gang at Pot Creek, or maybe not. For some reason, I thought I knew what I was doing. It mostly worked out fine.

The most difficult part for me was laying off people or firing them. The firing was necessary from time to time. It was not a frequent occurrence. However, the layoffs were more difficult. I only had to lead the division through one layoff while I was the head. The rules were simple. We laid off the people with the least seniority, but I decided how many each department would have to lose depending on the jobs that were before us.

My simple rules infuriated one of the group leaders. He had to lay off a young person that he believed had a lot of promise. However, I insisted that we stick to the rules I had laid out. The group leader avoided me for the rest of his career at Fermilab. It became somewhat amusing after it went through a ridiculous stage.

CHAPTER 54

Aspen Meetings

Is the electron made of smaller components? No! It is one of those idealistic, infinitely small points that you learned about in geometry or perhaps in shop class. If you believe in the infinitely small, your brain is in danger of retreating to this region of nonexistence. Watch out!

*****

B ob Wilson felt that it was necessary for Laboratory management to get away from the Laboratory once a year for one of the Program Advisory Committee (PAC) meetings. The location he chose for the meeting was Aspen, Colorado. High-level Laboratory staff attended the meeting to give status reports of experiments and review project status. The PAC would discuss the Laboratory's physics program and advise the director concerning changes that would improve the physics program. The PAC also examined the experimental proposals that the Laboratory had received and advised the Laboratory which should be approved. The Aspen meeting was usually held in June and typically went on for a week. Other meetings of the PAC occurred at the Laboratory. The committee met three or four times a year.

I don't remember when I first got invited to attend the Aspen meeting. It was probably when I became the head of the Research Division. Of course, it was a treat for me to get to go back to Colorado for a week. I usually took an extra few days of vacation for some hiking followed by a visit to my family in New Mexico.

My role at the meeting was to answer the PAC's questions about what the Laboratory could and could not do with respect to what a physics proposal required. In addition, I had to evaluate the impact each proposal would have on the division if the committee approved it. Cost and division manpower required to install and run the experiment are examples of the impacts that were typically discussed. The Aspen meeting lasted about one week including a weekend.

Sunday morning at the PAC meeting was free time for the committee. Many attendees to the meeting used the morning to go on an organized hike in the mountains. There were also other more relaxing activities if one was not inclined to go uphill at elevation. In addition, there was a morning in the middle of the week given to a shorter group hike. Both of the hikes could be quite strenuous. They were geared for people who were relatively fit and who had either been above twelve or thirteen thousand feet or wanted to get above this mark.

Dave Schramm, BJ Bjorken, John Peoples, and I were the best climbers although some of the others, such as Director Mike Witherell, did quite well on the hikes. Dave was an astrophysics professor at the University of Chicago. He was not usually involved with the meeting, but he had a house in Aspen; so when he was in Aspen, he was invited on the hikes.

Hiking was the highlight of the meeting for me. No one could ever beat me up a mountain including Dave, who had been on many big mountains. I had the elevation gene. The higher I got, the faster I went. Apparently, Dave also had the elevation gene; but he had been a wrestler in college, and he had much more mass to carry than I had. He was built more like a linebacker than a track star. Of course, this should have given him an advantage on the way down. It didn't. He had no desire to tuck and roll.

We had many great adventures on the hikes. It was fun to lead people higher than they had ever been. We also had a few tense moments, but none of them were very serious.

During one of the hikes, I had a life-changing experience. John Peoples was leading us up a mountain we called Electric Peak. It was really more of a shoulder of Cathedral Peak. Nevertheless, there is a slight dip in the ridgeline between the two summits. Electric Peak exists, but it is not the peak we called Electric Peak. Apparently, we were fast and loose with names.

There were about a dozen people in the group. As we climbed toward the summit of the peak, John was feeling his age. Continuing along the summit ridge, we encountered snow that had to be crossed in order to reach the top of the mountain. John called a halt. He was exhausted as were most of the members of the climbing party. As we rested, John told us that one day, we would follow our old director up the mountain and come down with a new director. This wasn't like John.

After resting a few minutes, John suggested that we call our attempt on the peak good enough. He did not want to navigate the short distance on the snow ridge in order to reach the summit. I looked ruefully at the ridge and the very close summit. It looked very passable to me. The drop-offs on each side of the ridge were significant, but they were far from sheer. I was revved to go. I suggested that I could go to the summit and sign us in on a list that knew existed in a can buried in the summit cairn. John agreed that this was a fine idea.

As I got up to start up the ridge, a fit-looking woman who worked in the Director's Office jumped up and said, "I'll go with you." I knew her fairly well, but she had never been on a climb with us before. She had not worked at the Laboratory long, but I had learned that she was very friendly and always had a smile for everyone who passed by her desk in the Director's Office. Her name was Marilyn Rice.

We borrowed an ice ax for her, and I made certain she knew how to do an ice-ax arrest before we set off across the ridge for the summit. We made it easily. Marilyn proved to be very sure-footed, and she was not intimidated by the ridge at all. I pulled the sign-in can out of the summit cairn and showed her how to sign in. We signed in for ourselves, but not the entire group. I usually signed in with a ridiculous name. I had never signed in on a mountain using my real name. Maybe it was because I never felt that I had a real name. I signed in with my name this time.

After our visit to the summit, we came back down to the climbing party. They were waiting patiently for us. I was impressed by Marilyn's spirit and her ability to easily navigate the snow ridge. When we got back to the group, everyone got up, and we began our long descent to the valley below. I stayed next to Marilyn for much of the descent. On the next hike at the same meeting, we climbed together the entire way. We had become better friends in between the two hikes. Something was going on between us that we could not stop in spite of our best effort. Well, Marilyn was trying harder than I was. Nevertheless, it has not stopped to this day.

CHAPTER 55

Switching Partners

Why do scientists believe that they are the real truth seekers? Don't they make stuff up like everyone else? Heavens yes! The best are good at making stuff up. The real test comes when they try to get their colleagues to believe the stuff they make up. Repeatable experiments reduce the amount of fiction.

*****

The few minutes I spent on the summit of Electric Peak with Marilyn changed four lives for better or worse. I am clearly to blame for changes. There is no excuse I can make for what happened to my relationship with Gail after my encounter with Marilyn. There was nothing wrong with Gail. She was an incredible woman. We had become a couple when we were both very young, but it worked out very well. We had created a wonderful and talented daughter, Kelly, who was just about to graduate from high school and head off to college. Our relationship had seemed fine to Gail. Yet I was not completely satisfied with it. I did not discuss this with Gail. Maybe I should have. I thought it was probably just a normal male problem.

If there was anything unfair in my relationship with Gail, it was the compromises she had to make in her own professional career to accommodate my career. She was an incredibly talented writer who spoke three languages and had a degree in journalism. The two jobs she held after we arrived in Illinois were in public relations: first for Copley Hospital in Aurora and then at Aurora University.

The sparks that flew between Marilyn and me after our encounter on Electric Peak made me think there was something better. Maybe it was just my mother's genes at work in me. Nevertheless, I was not willing to let it go.

Both Marilyn and Gail resisted the change. I knew that I could not leave Gail without supporting her and, of course, Kelly, who was very upset. Gail was starting her own public-relations business, and Kelly was about to head off to college at the Fashion Institute of Technology in New York City. She was very relieved to hear that her plans would not have to change. I was still on the hook to pay for her education. I was also on the hook to continue providing support for Gail.

Meanwhile, I managed to convince Marilyn that we could make it work. We succeeded, and it has worked very well for almost thirty years. It still feels right to me. I wish I could say the same for Gail.

CHAPTER 56

Dark Matter

Question: What if a scientist's results or observations cannot be replicated by other scientists? Answer: Well, he or she can probably get a job driving a taxi.

*****

My time as Research Division Head went smoothly. I did not feel that I did a particularly good job, but it wasn't a bad job either. The Collider came online, and the two big detectors that were operated by my division began taking data.

After approximately four years as head of the Research Division, John Peoples suggested to me that the Laboratory should get into the dark matter business. He knew that I was interested in astrophysics, and he asked if I would like to join a dark matter experiment, the Cryogenic Dark Matter Search (CDMS) being led by Bernard Sadoulet of the University of California at Berkeley and Blas Cabrera at Stanford. They had come to the Laboratory looking for technical support and additional collaborators. They also needed a deep underground site where they could locate the experiment. Fermilab was already sending a neutrino beam to the Soudan Laboratory in northern Minnesota, a site that was about 2,300 feet deep. A neutrino detector already existed in the Soudan mine that was viewing the neutrinos from Fermilab, and a larger detector would soon be built in a new cavern. The old cavern was available for small experiments. CDMS was a good candidate for the old cavern.

The neutrino experiments required a near detector on the Fermilab site to view the neutrinos as they headed off to northern Minnesota where a second detector existed. An improved detector in Minnesota was being added in a new cavern, leaving the old cavern available for other experiments. The idea was to compare neutrinos leaving the Fermilab site with the neutrinos arriving at the Soudan Mine in Minnesota. The goal of the experiment was to measure how neutrinos oscillate from one kind of neutrino to another, a mysterious process that was not fully understood.

The neutrinos from Fermilab cut a cord through the earth to arrive in the Soudan Laboratory. The earth appears to be a very clear window to a neutrino. Very few of them are scattered out of the beam as they pass through the earth on the way to Minnesota. Neutrinos would seem to be almost nothing, and almost everything looks like nothing to a neutrino. The ghostly particles seem to be barely part of this universe.

Since Fermilab was already very involved with the neutrino experiments at Soudan, it was natural for the Laboratory to also become involved in CDMS and support its installation in the Soudan Laboratory, which had ample room for the small experiment.

The neutrino beam from Fermilab was not needed for CDMS. In fact, the neutrino beam was a nuisance due to all the construction going on at the site to make ready for a new, large neutrino detector. CDMS only required a deep site to shield it from the incident cosmic rays and other backgrounds.

The notion of dark matter came about due to astronomical observations of the rotation curves of the galaxies. These curves indicate that there is much more mass present in the galaxies than can be accounted for by the visible stars. The speculation was that the additional gravitational force was provided by undetected matter or dark matter. Dark matter particles would provide the missing mass that would make sense of the rotation curves of the galaxies, preventing them from flying apart as they rotate far too rapidly for the gravitational force generated by the visible matter alone to keep them together. However, no direct observations of the mysterious dark matter had ever been made.

If the dark matter only interacted through the weak force and gravity, it would explain the rotation curves if the dark matter particles had significant mass. Neutrinos only interact through the weak force and gravity, but they don't have enough mass to explain the rotation curves. Nothing had been observed that would explain the rotation curves.

Construction of the new neutrino detector at the Soudan Laboratory would be a minor inconvenience to the dark matter experiment, mainly by creating dust and a trembling earth as a new deep cavern was carved out of the rock to next to the old cavern in order to accommodate the improved neutrino detector. This was not a big issue for the CDMS experiment. It was more of a nuisance.

I was very enthusiastic about getting involved with the highly respected groups at Berkeley and Stanford. The goal was to install some of their very clever little detectors in the Soudan Underground Laboratory where backgrounds, or false events, would be reduced to almost zero, making any dark matter signal more apparent.

Initially, the CDMS activity was all on the west coast where two versions of the dark matter detectors were being prototyped and tested. Each version was about the size of a hockey puck, and six of the detectors would be stacked together to create a small "tower" of detectors that would be less than a foot tall. One version had been developed at Berkeley, and the other at Stanford. Both versions of the detector had to operate at a temperature that very near absolute zero or about minus 460 degrees Fahrenheit.

The experiment was named the Cryogenic Dark Matter Search (CDMS). I knew that getting involved with the dark matter experiment would result in a lot of travel to the west coast and eventually to Minnesota.

When I joined the collaboration, some of the detectors were in operation at a shallow site under the Stanford campus. The detectors were very clever. It was easy for me to imagine that dark matter might be detected before we even moved to Soudan.

Expansion of the Soudan Laboratory for an upgraded neutrino experiment proved to be somewhat of a problem for the dark matter effort. Blasting was occurring to construct a new cavern next to the existing cavern where CDMS was setting up. The dark matter experiment managed to survive the blasting and began taking data.

As CDMS was becoming a reality, I travelled back and forth to the west coast often for group meetings and strategy sessions. It was not long before I became the official project manager for CDMS. This meant I had to deal with the funding agencies. It was somewhat complicated because we had funding from both the National Science Foundation and the Department of Energy. I was never very adept at fulfilling my responsibilities negotiating with the agencies. It didn't matter. Most of the dealing with the agencies was done by Bernard and Blas. It all worked.

Most of the early activity on the experiment was at Stanford and Berkeley. I got a lot of air miles going back and forth to the west coast, mostly for collaboration meetings. At the same time, we began organizing preparations at the mine for the eventual arrival of the detectors. The detectors were initially tested at a shallow underground site on the Stanford campus.

I was very optimistic during this time. I did not see how the clever experiment could fail. Besides, I was having great fun.

I remember getting up at a collaboration meeting at Berkeley to show my collaborators how preparations were going at the mine. My very first slide showed a photograph of the head frame of the mine draped with ice and snow. It didn't look very inviting to my California collaborators who were used to sunshine and warmth. Just for fun, I told them the photo had been taken in early June, adding, "I can hardly wait to get you California sissies working in the North Woods."

I would live to regret this remark. There was nothing humorous about the North Woods when the first detectors arrived at the mine with graduate students, postdocs, and technicians from the west coast. As chance would have it, this event occurred in the darkest month of the year, December. It was bitterly cold. Furthermore, it was dark in the morning when the detector specialists went underground, and it was dark in the evening when they came back to the surface. One could not go up and down during the day except in special circumstances. Lunch was eaten in some porta-a-kamps located in the older cavern at the bottom of the mine.

Accommodations for the night were in cheap and somewhat rundown apartments in the tiny town of Tower, Minnesota. There was one bar in town. It was located beneath the apartments along with the town laundromat, which was frequently used early in the morning. The thumping of the poorly balanced washing machines provided a wake-up call to get the crew up for another day underground.

As CDMS was evolving, I ended up being the mentor and adviser for my second PhD student. His name was Steve Eichblatt, and he was a student at Rice University. Steve was a joy to work with. He had a completely different personality than my first student, Rob Jedicke. He was not as serious, and he had many interests. Even so, he was a good student who was fun to be around. This was an important quality to have when working as a team underground all day and coming up to the dismal Minnesota winter.

The only saving grace of our early Minnesota existence was that Earl Peterson, a professor at the University of Minnesota who worked on the neutrino experiment, was a wine connoisseur. He had an excellent collection of wines in his apartment in Tower, which he sometimes shared in the evenings.

The Soudan Laboratory was operated by the University of Minnesota, which was heavily involved in the neutrino experiments. Professor Marvin Marshak of the University of Minnesota quickly figured out a way to improve the quality of life underground. He commissioned an artist to paint a mural on the wall of one of the two caverns. The artist brought his daughter along to help with the mural. She was the only woman working underground at the time. Everyone ate lunch together in one of the underground Porta-Kamps. It was like magic having two artists, one a woman, present every day. Everyone's spirits were lifted.

As amusing as all of this sounds, it was really a serious situation. We were lucky that no murders were committed during the time we were getting setup for the arrival of the dark matter detectors. Instead of killings or beatings, people slowly adapted.

Well, there was one incident that could be described as a "killing." My student, Steve, loved animals and was very softhearted. He helped me at the mine doing the installation that was necessary before the detectors arrived. When he began working underground, he noticed that the walls of the cavern were covered with bats that had found their way to the bottom of the mine. They were destined to starve to death, clinging to the walls, because they could not find their way out. Being kindhearted, he decided that he was going to rescue them—one at a time. There were hundreds, if not thousands, of them. His short-lived plan was to carry one bat out each evening as we rode the hoist cage to the surface along with the other technicians and workers who were involved in operating the Laboratory.

The first problem with his plan was that the other passengers in the cage with him did not appreciate anyone carrying a bat that could get away and make a nuisance of itself on the long, dark ride to the surface. On Steve's first and last attempt to save a bat, he managed to maintain control of the flying rat on the way to the surface, but his scheme ended dramatically upon the arrival of the cage at its destination. As Steve stepped out of the cage, bat in hand, he tossed the flying rat into the air. It flew only a short distance before a merlin swooped down from a nearby tree and made a light snack of the disoriented bat. This dramatic event ended the bat-rescue mission.

Dark matter did not reveal itself in the amazing little detectors that we installed at the bottom of the Soudan Mine. Nor has it made an appearance in any of other dark matter experiments in the world where it was sought except for one. An Italian group first saw a signal quite some time before we published our first paper indicating we saw no signal. They claimed to see an annual modulation as the Earth moved around the sun half of the year into a dark matter wind and the other half of the year with it. However, the group did not convince anyone else that what they were seeing was a dark matter signal. There were explanations for their signal that did not involve dark matter. Also it did not help that no one could reproduce their signal.

Dark matter remains elusive. We may need a different explanation for the rotation curves. One possibility is that all the detectors assume that dark matter interacts through the weak interaction in addition to gravity. If it only interacts gravitationally, we are up the creek with an excellent hammer but no nails in our pocket. If this is the case, dark matter has already been observed as best it can be observed in the rotation curves of the galaxies. If this conclusion stands, it is a very unsatisfactory. Once again, the Creator is getting a good laugh at us.

Meanwhile, CDMS has continued to evolve without me for many years. They presently have their very clever detectors buried even deeper in a mine in Canada and are about to reach the highest-possible sensitivity for this type of underground experiment. Meanwhile, dark matter remains elusive.

CHAPTER 57

Wisconsin

You might ask, "Are scientists more trustworthy and intelligent than ordinary people?" Heavens no! Scientists are often not very clever, yet their results are trustworthy because each scientist relishes checking the results of his or her idiot colleagues, hoping to show that their results are wrong.

*****

While I was working on dark matter, I made a connection to Frances Halzen at the University of Wisconsin. He was leading an effort to install an experiment at the South Pole to look at neutrinos that passed through the earth and into a very large detector embedded in the ice near the South Pole. I was fascinated by the notion of doing an experiment at the South Pole even though I had never been a big fan of neutrinos. These ghostly particles seemed to be about as close to nothing as one could get and still call it something. Of course, that is what makes them so interesting to many scientists. In fact, the notion of "nothing" could be the most profound concept that humanity has ever come up with, or it may just be nothing. We certainly cannot observe nothing anywhere in the universe because space exists everywhere and it needs verbs to explain its behavior. Remember, space is expanding and has been since the Big Bang. Therefore, it is not nothing. Is it?

Back to something: As my dark matter efforts wound down, I entered a discussion with Francis Halzen at the University of Wisconsin. We talked about a position for me at Wisconsin, where I would join the ICECUBE, a collaboration to study neutrinos from the cosmos that pass through the earth to reach the South Pole. The negotiation had reached the stage where Marilyn and I were about to begin looking for a house in Madison. I had already given a colloquium on dark matter at the university as part of the interview process. I was quite certain we were on our way to Madison. Francis did not discourage me from this notion.

It was not long after I gave my talk at Wisconsin when I called Francis to make certain of some of the details. For some reason, he was evasive, and he was uncomfortable. He clearly did not want to talk to me. He was elusive when I asked him questions about my impending appointment. It made me wonder what was going on. Why had Wisconsin suddenly turned on me? I knew that my colloquium had gone very well, and I was led to believe that an official offer would be made quickly. So why had Francis suddenly lost interest in me?

The puzzle began to resolve itself very quickly. Only minutes after my curt discussion with Francis, one of my boisterous Fermilab colleagues, Peter Limon, burst into my office and said, "I have to talk to you about what you have to do when you take over the Accelerator Division." I must have looked surprised and said something to the effect, "What do you mean when I take over the Accelerator Division?"

Peter looked surprised and embarrassed as he suddenly turned around and left my office. Within minutes, I received a call asking me to come to the Director's Office. Mike Witherell was the director at the time. I went downstairs and found both Mike and Steve Holmes in Mike's office. Steve was the associate director for accelerators. I had known Steve since we had worked together at Cornell. He had been one of the Harvard graduate students on the Cornell experiment. I had a great deal of respect for both Mike and Steve. When I arrived in the Director's Office, they both looked a little embarrassed, but not as embarrassed as Peter had looked when he left my office.

At the time, Run II of the Tevatron collider was starting up, and the luminosity was not going up as quickly as people expected. Mike asked me to become the head of the Accelerator Division. He and Steve thought I could get things on track. Of course, there had been a lot of flak from the Department of Energy about the poor performance on the luminosity to that point. I was hesitant to say that I would do it because I was negotiating with the University of Wisconsin. I don't really know how I handled that initial meeting with Mike and Steve. I do know that I attempted to contact Francis Halzen again. When I finally reached him, he was still very elusive. Something was going on that I did not completely understand, but I could guess what it was.

Several years later, my friend and colleague from Cornell, Don Hartill, confessed to me that he had put the nix on my Wisconsin Job. He was on a high-level DOE committee that was concerned about the performance of the Tevatron. Somehow, he, and maybe some others, had convinced DOE that I was the person who could get the Tevatron back on track. That is how I inadvertently became the head of the Accelerator Division instead of heading off to the South Pole. Fortunately, I had not yet put out a lot of money for a heavy parka.

CHAPTER 58

Final Dance with the Tevatron

What is the most profound question that can be asked? Here are a couple of attempts at an answer: "What are we doing here?" Followed by "What will happen to the universe once all the stars are so far away from one another that it is near impossible for them to detect or influence one another?" Answers: Nothing and nothing...

*****

I felt confident going back to the Accelerator Division. I knew the division well, and I understood the capabilities of the outstanding staff. I was totally relaxed going in even though the pressure was considerable. As usual, I made no big changes. I wanted to get a feel for what was happening and why. This didn't take long. I knew the division personnel well, and they knew me. I recognized that the division was on a good path and would succeed if the pressure from outside of the division could be reduced. I encouraged people to relax and do their jobs. There were many very talented people in the division, and they had a lot of pride. All I had to do was to filter the noise from above at my desk and demonstrate my confidence in the outstanding division I had inherited.

My first job was to establish an atmosphere of calm and reason. I wanted people to know that I was not someone to fear but someone who could reason and help them get more resources. The slope of the luminosity curve began to increase rapidly shortly after I arrived. All I had done was to establish a calmer atmosphere. The division did the rest. Guiding the Accelerator Division during this time was easy and most rewarding. The path was simple and clear.

One of the reasons I could be so cool and calm was that I had history with many of the key people in the division. One was my old friend from the Research Division, Paul Czarapata. He was both an excellent engineer and manager. It was not long before he became my deputy division head. He would stay in this position beyond the end of my rather long tenure as Division Head.

Another person I had much experience with was the head of Operations, Bob Mau. Bob was an outstanding operations head. We knew one another so well that many times, we did not have to say things out loud. Bob knew how to put a crack operations crew together and keep it working smoothly.

Of course, I did make some moves as Division Head. Some optimization was necessary. Department heads need to change from time to time. To complicate matters, two layoffs were necessary because the Laboratory had to survive constant budget cuts.

I did not enjoy doing the layoffs, but I think I did them inflicting as little pain as possible. Department heads were not asked to deliver the notifications. I would do that job. Everyone in the Laboratory knew the day the layoffs were to happen. When a person's department head showed up, they surely knew what was about to happen. The department head escorted the person to my office where I had a private meeting with the person, notifying them that they no longer had a job. A security person was stationed outside of my office just in case. This was one of the most unpleasant tasks I had to undertake at the Laboratory. I had to do it twice as head of the Accelerator Division.

The second time, I changed the procedure. The discussion with me did not occur in my office. Instead, the person was led to the end of the linac gallery where my deputy and I were set up in a small meeting room. It was not a high-traffic area. The person was led past a minimum number of curious onlookers. I also asked that the security guard not be in uniform and requested that he just be in the vicinity instead of stationed at the door.

During this second round, I had to lay off a good friend who was a person I had worked in my early days in Switchyard. Helen had hired him, and he was an incredible resource. He was past retirement age, and what he was doing was not a central part of the division program. I made the decision. He had to be laid off. This was not as difficult as it sounds.

When Jim Walton came into to my improvised layoff office, he was a little upset. I knew he did not need the money. He just needed something to do. I told him he could keep doing what he was doing as an unpaid guest. He was so happy that he invited me to his "retirement" party that very night. Jim did simple parties. He just invited his friends down to his favorite tavern where everyone bought drinks for everyone. I showed up. It made my day a little happier.

Perhaps the most difficult task I had to do as Accelerator Division Head was to shut down Helen's Tevatron. The decision had been made at high levels in the Department of Energy. CERN, our sister Laboratory in Europe, had built and commissioned the Large Hadron Collider (LHC), which was more powerful than the Tevatron. Fermilab would continue to operate the Main Injector to study neutrinos. This activity continues to this day even though I am skeptical, still wondering whether neutrinos are a just figment of our imaginations. At least I like to tease the neutrino specialists with this taunt.

We organized a big party to shut down the Tevatron. Many guests, including many past employees who had worked on the pioneering machine, were invited. The problem for me was how to ceremoniously shut it off. Deciding who would throw the switch was easy. Helen had to do it. A more difficult problem for me was to determine who would be allowed in the Main Control Room with Helen when she performed the deed. I did not want the room packed with so many so dignitaries that Helen could not get to the switch especially conceived for this event.

I made my list and checked it twice. There would be a very finite number of people approved by me to be present in the Main Control Room (MCR). This included the operations crew on shift and a special operations specialist, Todd Johnson, who had rigged up the switch for Helen to throw that would turn the pioneering machine off…forever. I also allowed a few other special guests.

I would not be present in the MCR, and neither would the director of the Laboratory, Pierre Oddone. This did not sit well with Pierre, but he accepted it. My deputy, Paul, would be in the MCR to represent me. Meanwhile, I would station myself in a large tent erected in a parking lot in back of the MCR where I would be master of ceremonies for a large number of Accelerator Division employees, former employees, and special guests. We would have access to the MCR via the Laboratory television system.

Many of the division headquarters staff wore Western hats for the occasion. This was because the Laboratory director had taken to calling Paul, me, and our division a bunch of cowboys. Many of us, most especially me, took this as a compliment. I am certain it would have also been a compliment for the Laboratory's first director, Bob Wilson.

When it was time for Helen, cowboy hat on her head, to throw the switch, Todd was somewhat concerned. He had thought of a reason that his switch could fail, but it was too late to make proper fix. Consequently, he stationed himself behind the relay racks, ready to spring into action if necessary. He would make certain the Tevatron was turned off one way or another. It was fortunate that he planned for failure. His switch did not work, but only a few of us were aware of the problem because Todd worked quickly behind the relay racks to get the mighty beast to expire quietly and sadly. The beam current trace on the oscilloscopes plunged to zero. The Tevatron was done… forever. It was a very poignant moment.

I remained the head of the Accelerator Division until I retired after forty years at the Laboratory in 2017. Marilyn retired a few days before me. Now I am back to the career loaded into my genes by my ancestors. It is good that I don't have to earn a living doing this because getting paid to write is not included in the genes.

CHAPTER 59

Mom's Tragic End

Why is science so complicated? Because human beings are so simple. Even so, we have figured out many complicated ways to be defective. This makes Life, the Universe, and Nothing most interesting.

*****

Mom continued to live with Doc at the house they had built on the property they bought from Grandmother and Grandfather. Their life was rather wild with many parties and social activities. They both drank too much but seemed to be happy most of the time. There was also much inebriated hunting and fishing. For example, they frequently pulled their trailer out to one of the local lakes. When they arrived, they would put some fishing lines into the water and drink for most of the rest of the time they were there. Gail and I stayed with them overnight at a lake at least once. The main excitement on one of those nights that I remember occurred when Mom thought she heard some raccoons getting into the fishing gear. She woke us up and told us that she was going to turn the light on them. She did. Oh no! She had surprised several skunks who were getting into things. Needless to say, this trip ended early even though Mom and I were veterans of a skunk war.

I knew the drinking and the parties were too much for Mom, but I did not have a clue as to what to do about it. Apparently, Mom was also worried, but she didn't know what to do either. The problem was partly resolved one afternoon when Doc was returning home from town. He was apparently three sheets to the wind. A mile or so from the house, he ran off the road in his pickup and hit a tree in the front yard of a little house that was near the road. He was seriously injured, but he lived. The pickup was totaled.

I was visiting some time afterward as Doc was recovering. Mom made me a proposition that I did not really want to take her up on. She was afraid that Doc would not be so lucky next time. If Doc had another accident, he could seriously injure or kill someone. Mom worried that they could lose everything. She proposed that I buy their house and they would rent it from me, making it easy for me to make the payments on a mortgage. I was not crazy about her plan, but I did not feel I could say no. I bought the house. It was a big hassle to get a mortgage, but it all worked out.

When Doc's son, Dale, heard about Mom's house arrangement with me, he was miffed. He wondered why he was not asked to buy the house. Nevertheless, things settled down for a while. However, the drinking went on as intensely as ever for both Mom and Doc. I surely knew that a happy ending was not possible. Dale and Sally, Doc's son and daughter, were both upset with Mom for selling the house to me. They accused her of stealing their father's money. Dale began screaming these accusations at Mother. She recorded him doing it. He was able to easily convince his dad that Mom had stolen all his money. All Mom could think of to do was to make the recordings of Dale's screaming.

Finally, she came up with another plan. She decided to quit drinking cold turkey. Sam, Diana, and I were not forewarned that she was going to attempt this. One afternoon, she asked Sam to come and get her. She wanted to go home with him. He noticed that she was not drinking. Was she quitting? He did not know. None of us understood how dangerous it is for an alcoholic to simply quit drinking cold turkey.

Sam took her to his house in the mountains. She seemed very coherent to him. They spent a wonderful evening on Sam's deck, looking at Comet Hale-Bopp, a brilliant visitor in the night sky. All of the stars were brilliant as usual at the high elevation. Finally, they went inside to go to bed. In the morning, Mom did not get out of bed. Sam went in to check on her. She had passed away during the night.

My very special little brother had given Mom a beautiful last evening alive. Nevertheless, he feels guilty about it to this day. We all should have known that Mom could not just quit drinking cold turkey like she did. We were ignorant, and it cost Mom her life. I have a different perspective than Sammy. He and Kathy gave her a beautiful ending. I love them both for it.

I flew to New Mexico without Marilyn as soon as I got the word. It was a mistake not to ask Marilyn to go with me. I don't know why I did it this way. I guess it was because our relationship was not very old at the time. Nevertheless, there was no doubt in my mind that she was my life partner for the duration. She should have gone.

When I arrived, I went straight to my brother's house in the mountains. Doc and his family had arranged for a memorial service at one of the churches in town. Since Diana, Sam, and I knew what they had subjected Mom to during her last few months, we declined to attend. We had Mom's ashes at Sam's house, and we had our own ceremony. It ended with us scattering her ashes on Sam's property in the mountains that she loved.

It was not long after Mom's death before Doc ended up in the hospital in Las Vegas. He had apparently been very upset since she passed away. He managed to hang himself in the hospital. It was a horrific ending for both families.

I don't remember how it happened, but an attorney got involved to settle the estate. Mother may have set it up. Dale and Sally had both accused Mom of stealing Doc's money. I am not certain how a wife steals a husband's money. Fortunately, Mom kept excellent records, and the attorney was able to sort it all out. The only funds that were missing were 3,000 dollars that Sally took out of their bank account. She was required to pay it back.

I owned the house since I had purchased it. I didn't really want it. Sam advised me that I would have no trouble selling it. I put it up for sale.

Sometime after both Mom and Doc had passed away, Dale began sending me conciliatory emails. I answered them, but I don't think I gave him what he wanted. He was smart enough to know that what he had done was very wrong. He wanted forgiveness. I was not big enough to give it to him. My excuse is that my brother would have never forgiven me if I had let Dale off the hook. Well, that is just an excuse. I really could not forgive Dale. Not long afterward, he passed away.

The house didn't sell after being on the market for a long time. I wanted to lower the price, but Sam assured me that it would sell. I needed to get rid of it. Finally, I got an offer for the asking price. I told the real-estate agent I would take it. The agent would not tell me who the buyer was. As it turned out, it was my brother. He still owns the property. He rented the house out until it burned down. Now he owns some land.

CHAPTER 60

Family History Destroyed

Question: If time doesn't pass, how do we get out of our lives? Answer: You don't, but you will never notice it because your brain tricks you into believing that time passes…unless you read this book. Whoops, too late…

*****

E ven though Mom spent much of the time during her last years drinking, fishing, and partying; she also managed to do something that was potentially very valuable to the family. She had inherited many family-history documents, letters, and photographs from Grandmother and Grandfather. She also spent a considerable amount of time interviewing her sisters. In particular, she interviewed her older sister, Audrey. My cousin Dorothy Simpson used much of the history that Mom recorded from Audrey for her book, *Audrey of the Mountains*. Her book turns out to be a most useful resource for me or anyone interested in our family history.

Mother had organized the history documents she gathered into binders that filled several shelves in her home office. Whenever I visited, I would be fascinated by what she had. I could not thank her enough to putting so much effort into keeping the family records and organizing them so well. As one can tell from the early chapters in this work, I benefitted greatly from what she did. However, I could have benefitted more.

During the time between Mother's death and Doc's passing, Doc wanted to get rid of all of Mom's stuff. He had been worked into a frenzied rage by his son and daughter who had convinced him that Mom had stolen all his money. He invited Mom's sisters and brothers to come to the house and take what they wanted before he threw the rest away. He did not invite Sam, Diana, or me. What her siblings didn't want, he threw out. I don't know what happened to all the work Mom had done on family history. I don't know where it ended up. I can only hope someone has it.

By the time Sam and I got access to the house after Doc passed away, all we found was trash. All of Mom's history binders were gone. Items, such as my brother's Marine Corp boot-camp book, were found in the trash. Almost nothing of value was left. Another example of a lost item is the dagger and the handle that little Sammy had miraculously found at Pot Creek. Many other artifacts from our lives were also missing. The bottom line is that there was almost nothing left.

Consequently, Sam severed ties to most of the rest of the family. Exceptions were made were for Diana and me, in addition to our cousins Dorothy, Crystal, and Crystal's husband, Wesley, who live across the mountain from Sam. I was very glad he severed the ties, and it was enough. Had he let his violent tendencies take control, the outcome could have been much worse. Meanwhile, I communicated with Aunt Jessie for a while. I was never comfortable doing this, and she never offered to let me have any of the family history that she might have taken. Maybe she didn't take any of it. Nevertheless, I could tell that she felt guilty. I have a feeling that Doc or his son may have trashed much or all it. The bottom line is that it was gone.

Sam and Crystal's husband, Wesley, hunted elk together for years. They are my favorite hunters. I love them both. They have stopped now, and there is a tear in the corner of my eye. It all has to do with the passage of time, which doesn't really happen. At this point in time in Sam's and Wesley's lives, they are a little old to be traipsing across hill and dale looking for elk.

Wesley is an incredible story himself. He is a Native American who spent his early life living in a cave with his grandmother. Against all odds, he became an electrical engineer. He is a real character. His life is an incredible story.

I have also been in e-mail contact with my uncle Frank, but our communications stopped. He has passed away.

My family is smaller now, but the quality is better. Plus I have added Marilyn's salt-of-the-earth, central Illinois relatives that includes, among many others, her identical twin sister, Carolyn, and her husband, Mike. In addition, Marilyn has an older sister, Barbara, and a brother, Mike.

Meanwhile, I retired from the Laboratory in 2017 after forty years on the job. Marilyn retired a short time before I did. I still have an office at the lab, but I have not used it much recently. We are good to go.

CHAPTER 61

The Illusion of Passing Time

I f you have been paying attention to these pseudoscience notes, you are very likely brain-damaged. Should this chapter make sense to you, call 911 or, at least, make an appointment with a doctor, a member of the clergy, an astrologer, or Mommy—your choice. Regrettably, there is no treatment for your malady, but making the call could make you feel better. Maybe I can help; I will try.

Recall that Einstein's Theory of Relativity indicates that we live in spacetime, a four-dimensional space that includes time as one of the four dimensions. Relativity theory has been tested and verified in many physics experiments. One conclusion drawn from the theory is that time, like space, does not pass. The passage of time is nothing more than an illusion created by the mind. Practically, what does this mean?

The first questions that comes to mind are, "What does death mean in an existence where the passage of time is nothing more than an illusion? Don't we need the passage of time to get out of the predicament of life?" After all, birth and death mark the boundaries in time of an individual's existence much as zero and twelve mark the boundaries of a ruler. However, these boundaries do not create or destroy the ruler. Similarly, the boundaries in time do not create or destroy an individual's existence. No creation or destruction is necessary. Existence simply is. Our existence lies between the two boundaries in time—forever. We never exist outside of the time boundaries of our lives, but we "always" exist within these boundaries marked by our birth and our death. Nonexistence is nothing more than a comforting illusion.

Without the passage of time, how do we explain the perception that events appear to arrive from the future and then slip into the past? The illusion of passing time results from the nature of our awareness. Our active awareness is limited to one moment of time at a time. From any moment that we are aware, we only have access to information from the past direction in time, and we seem to be moving to an adjacent, future moment of time. How can this be if time does not pass?

This apparent asymmetric motion of time is caused by an important reality of existence. From any location that we view existence, we only have access to information originating in the past direction in time. Information does not flow in the reverse direction from future to past. Consequently, when our conscious awareness takes up any position in time, we are only aware of moments previous to that time. We cannot remember, or carry, information from the future to past times as our awareness moves back and forth in time.

It appears that we flow through time from birth to death. This is just an illusion. Our lives are bounded by our birth and our death. Yet an individual's death does not mean that that the individual ceases to exist between the boundaries marked by his or her birth and death. After all, the interval of time defined by these boundaries simply exists "forever" if time does not pass.

One might ask why we are not aware of our motion in both directions of time? After all, we are aware of all of our motions in space. We can blame physics again. Physical law only allows us to carry information in one direction in time—toward the future. We cannot carry information backwards in time. No matter where we are in time, we cannot remember future events that we witness when our awareness is in the future.

One might ask whether information might occasionally leak from a future time to a past in time. Could an information leak cause the sensation that one has experienced a particular event before? I don't know. Maybe?

The interval between our life's two boundaries defines where our lives always exist. They do not make our lives go away just like the boundaries of a ruler at zero, and twelve inches do not make a ruler go away. Space and time are just alike except for the way we perceive them. The total of existence includes the space and time where we always exist and the space and time where we do not exist.

One might be concerned that if time doesn't pass, there is no way for us to get out of the predicament of life. Don't we need death? Nonexistence? The good news is that nonexistence is real. The bad news is that we can't get there from here. We exist. We are alive. We cannot arrive at nonexistence. We can only imagine the peace and quiet of nonexistence. This has to be enough.

The illusion of passing time makes an interminable existence tolerable and maybe even comfortable. If this reasoning is not satisfying, the reader can simply pretend that I don't exist and that I did not write this book. Or, if I did write the book, find comfort in the possibility that I could be completely wrong—just like you.

Well, I am certainly having fun. I realize that these notions concerning time can be rather confounding and depressing. If you are not comfortable with my conclusion on the passage of time, there is a way out—escape to heaven! Religion! Or perhaps, assume you understand the nature of time better than I do. There's a good chance that you are correct. It might help to remember that I began my education at Pot Creek Elementary School under the tutelage of Mrs. Torres. She was a great teacher, but she had not quite mastered the English language and neither had I. Maybe this seemingly wonderful situation caused my education to go horribly wrong very quickly. For a blissful existence, simply pretend I don't exist and never did and never will. You could be right. And please know that Mrs. Torres did the best she could for me given the circumstances. I was quite a challenge!

Epilogue

You might ask, "Is there anything I can do to erase this book from my memory?" The answer is "Yes! Clean your glasses and your ears thoroughly, use mouthwash every day for two weeks, and pretend you didn't read the book by starting to read it from the beginning a second time."

THE END

Author's Note

Please note that paper copies of this book are very combustible. Please be careful! Find a safe, moist place for your book-burning event. Burning doesn't really accomplish much other than making you feel good and warming you on a cold winter evening. This book should burn very hot!

About the Author

Roger L. Dixon was born to a "country girl" mother who sang for the USO during WWII and subsequently married into a wealthy, high-society family in New York. She proved to be too adventurous for a staid husband. The resulting divorce made front-page news in the New York papers as she retreated to New Mexico, pregnant with an illegitimate child. Not long after she arrived back in New Mexico, she married a much older man who was an automobile mechanic and sometimes a race-car driver. A little brother, Sammy, and sister, Diana, arrived via stork mail on the front porch sometime later. Roger, his mother's oldest son and outcome of his mother's New York adventures, quickly began creating his own excitement by breaking an arm a few days before beginning his education at Pot Creek elementary school just outside of Taos, New Mexico. In the middle of the eighth grade, his family, broken by divorce, moved to Breckenridge, Colorado, where his mother had taken a job with the company that would transform the old mining town into a major ski resort. Breckenridge provided the opportunity for the author to upgrade to his broken-bone experiences to include lying in a body cast for three months. His college experience began at New Mexico Highlands University and finished with a PhD in physics from Purdue University. He continued his tour of universities with a postdoctoral stint at Cornell University before accepting an appointment as a scientist at Fermi National Accelerator Laboratory, where he downgraded his bone-breaking experiences to a broken shoulder (skiing) and a few broken ribs (daredevil feats in the shower) in addition to multiple scabs (cycling).

The author was born into a family of writers that included his grandfather, his mother, a cousin, and an aunt. It was inevitable that he would attempt to be a writer even though only the aunt made a living writing. She wrote for a small local newspaper. This is the author's second attempt to write a book. The first attempt was a total disaster. Fortunately, the book was never published! Had it been, the author would be required to take all his meals while hiding underneath his bed.